Frogpond

A FARMBOY'S
UPPER PENINSULA MEMOIRS

Clifton B. Nixon

Davisual Media Publishing

Livingston, Texas

Copyright © 2021 by Rebecca Nixon Davis

All rights reserved. No part of this publication may be reproduced, distributed or transmitted in any form or by any means, including photocopying, recording, or other electronic or mechanical methods, without the prior written permission of the publisher, except in the case of brief quotations embodied in critical reviews and certain other noncommercial uses permitted by copyright law. For permission requests, write to the publisher at the address below.

Scripture quotations are taken from the King James Version. Public domain.

Rebecca Nixon Davis/Davisual Publishing

249 Rainbow Drive #14924

Livingston, TX 77399

Book Layout ©2017 BookDesignTemplates.com

Cover Design Kirby Davis

Ordering Information:

Quantity sales. Special discounts are available on quantity purchases by corporations, associations, and others. For details, contact the address above.

Frogpond/ Clifton B. Nixon. —1st ed.

Paperback ISBN 978-1-7368726-0-4

Contents

The Little Red Coat 1
Haul Backs 9
Sure and Begorrah I'm Irish 17
Hiawatha Land 21
Pickford "The Little, Holy Town" 27
Revivals & Bootleggers 41
Our Farm Home 45
Home on the Range 53
Frogpond Schoolhouse 63
A Great Plenty of "Characters" 79
High School Days 87
JANUARY Better Than Black-Eyed Peas 99
FEBRUARY Our Winter Wonderland 117
MARCH Kite Tails & Remedies 139
APRIL Brought Hints of Springtime 151
MAY Spring Mischief 161
JUNE Pick'ns 169
JULY Hay Days 177
AUGUST While the Sun Shines 189
SEPTEMBER Competition and Jamborees 203
OCTOBER Rubber Boots and Barn Dances 213

NOVEMBER Thanksgiving and Hunting Season..........227
DECEMBER Greatest Month in the Whole Year! 235
ABOUT THE AUTHOR 245

Dedicated to my little sister, Vivian Nalley, who helped me remember stories and events of our childhood and ramblings from our mother.

In memory of Rev. Clifton B. Nixon
1918–2003

INTRODUCTION

Our son Bob handwrote this note on my birthday card one year and it became the spark and ignition for these memoirs.

Dad, we really enjoyed our Thanksgiving visit. Most memorable were the stories you told about Christmas at your house and other boyhood yarns. I request that you write down or tape these and other experiences. It would be a great legacy to leave your grandchildren.

I Love you, Bob

CHAPTER ONE

The Little Red Coat

DAD AND MOTHER AND A CREW of volunteer neighboring farm couples were in the midst of fall "Threshing Day" when somehow the news came through that Germany's Kaiser Wilhelm had surrendered. World War I was over. When the message got from our house to the barn, Mr. Romeo, owner of the huge threshing outfit, leaped onto the big Titan 10-20 steam engine, blew the whistle, cut the throttle, threw the belt clutch lever, and rushed onto the threshing floor yelling, "The war's over! The war's over!"

As the roaring engine slackened, the fifty-foot drive belt, the pulleys, the straw blower and all the shaking cradles inside the mammoth separator slowed to a halt. Dusty men jumped from the separator feeding table to the floor. Men scrambled down the long ladder from the grain mow above. Masked men came down out of the straw stack, and the grain carriers dropped their metal buckets in place. Those blackened men hit the threshing floor yelling, jumping, shouting, spilling out into the barnyard, throwing their hats in the air, whooping and dancing.

Someone yanked the whistle rope on the steam engine. Blast after blast rang out. The women and children came bursting out of the house into the barnyard. All were weeping and shouting for joy. Hats were flying. Ike MacDonald's mighty sawmill whistle in Pickford joined the bedlam, sounding out for miles in every direction. The long, bloody war was over! "Old Kaiser Bill" was licked. His dreams of empire smashed. "Our Boys are coming home!" That was Armistice Day, November 11, 1918.

I missed the celebration by thirty days. On December 11, Mother gave birth to her brand-new baby boy right there in our country home, with Dr. T. Greeley Fox of Pickford attending. The good doctor signed and filed my birth certificate with the name Willard Nixon, born to Bert and Selena Nixon, December 11, 1918, Pickford, Michigan, Chippewa County, USA. Dr. Fox signed his name at the bottom, and it was recorded by him at the county courthouse in Sault Ste. Marie, Michigan.

A good friend, Minetta Kerr, came from Stirlingville to help Mother for a couple of weeks. It so happened that her grandparents, the Gabriel Kerrs, who came from Grenville, Canada, had siblings named Shirley and Clifton, who died as children. They probably came up the Munuscong River on the *Northern Belle* riverboat. Mother and Minetta got their heads together on the name subject. Minetta thought Clifton sounded like a really good name, and it had just the right ring for Mother. On December 14, 1918, a corrected birth certificate was filed, reading Clifton Bertram Nixon. Uncle Ern Nixon's signature is on that one. He must have delivered it to the courthouse in the Soo (Sault Ste. Marie). I now have a copy of both certificates. I have always been thrilled that my dad's name is part of my name too.

Dr. Fox was a hero to us. Oftentimes, we overheard our parents talking about his faithfulness and caring attitude; he would come at any hour of the day or night, no lame excuses. They told us how, during the awful World War I flu epidemic, Doctor Fox traveled by fast cutter in winter no matter what the weather or condition of the roads. He kept two lively young driving teams stabled nearby during those tragic days. When one team got worn out, the fresh team was hitched to his cutter or buggy. They said he dozed while bumping over those rough roads and snow tracts, and that he sometimes went two or three days without ever getting into bed. Whole families were wiped out. It was indeed a tragic time in Northern Michigan.

We kids could not help but develop a high respect for this good man. He never failed to come when we needed him. I can still hear that knock at the kitchen door and see him enter the front room downstairs where I lay sick. I think my temperature began to mend as soon as I saw his relaxed, warm smile. It seemed like he always had some magic cure to pull out of that little black bag he carried. You could count on a bitter pill out of that bag every time, bitter as gall. Likely, you would also be given a dose of castor oil. Still, if Doctor Fox said so, it was okay. With a wee trace of humor and a twinkle, he would add, "This will drive the cuss out of you." Yes, he was our hero, and we have never forgotten him.

One day in my high school years, I was standing in the Hamilton & Watson Grocery store and saw the now elderly Doctor Fox walking down the opposite side of main street. A car was parked at the curb. When he came alongside that car, the man ducked way down so that Doctor Fox would not see him. I thought, *Now there's a genuine ingrate and a coward*. I was glad that Mother and Dad, though they often could not pay in the hard depression years, had by and by happily paid Dr. Fox in full.

When I arrived on the scene, I already had a four-and-a-half-year-old brother, Forrest, a three-year-old sister, Marie, and another younger brother, Clarence, a year-and-a-half old. Eighteen months after my birth, little brother Merlin was born. Mother and Dad were to know great sadness. They talked about the children they lost, and the memorable little things those children used to do. Merlin died on August 23, 1921. He was just fourteen months old. Barely nine months later, Clarence contracted meningitis and died. Those were terrible blows.

When Clarence died, I was almost three and a half years old, and Mother was pregnant with Vivian. Aunt Jeanice Portice was still living at home with Grandma and Grandpa (Portice) when Grandma asked her to go over to be with my mother (Selena) to help her for a week or so. Aunt Jeanice said that I carried Clarence's little red coat around with me wherever I went. I clung to it as a remembrance of my brother who had passed away.

She recalled that one day while she was there, I had disappeared. They began a frantic search for me through the house, the barnyard, and the barn. Aunt Jeanice ran out to the road and looked down toward the bridge over Uncle George's creek. There I lay fast asleep on the very edge of the bridge with Clarence's red coat under me. I had fallen asleep watching the swift waters fifteen feet below. Oh, how I would like to remember my thoughts that day. Even as I write this today, I weep for the loss of my two brothers and little Eva, and for the suffering of Mother and Dad.

Nixon Family
Left to right: Marie, Selena holding Merlin, Clifton in high chair,
Bert behind Clarence, Forest

At the time Clarence and Merlin died, we lived on the "Old Gady Place" on the east side of Sunshine School Road, just across the road from Uncle George and Aunt Martha Portice. The creek formed our north property boundary. We called it the Armstrong Creek on our side of the road and Uncle George's Creek where it flowed through his farm. The bridge was "Uncle George's Bridge." We never knew the official name of that bridge, if it ever had one. Dad farmed there several years before he bought Uncle Ern's eighty-acre farm a half-mile north on the same side of the road. That is where we did most of our growing up. The farm we left was ever after referred to as "the Old Place" or "the Old Gady Place." Our new home, a half mile from

Frogpond School, was a new community for us. The one and only recollection I have of the Old Place was of skating with my brothers, Forrest and Clarence, on dried field peas on the granary floor. We were having a great time pretending we were skating on ice. Marie might have been there too. We had good times together. We must have loved each other very much. That is why I clung to his little red coat.

Less than a year later our second sister, Vivian, was born on May 30, 1922. Our third sister, Eva, was born on March 14, 1924. Our sweet little baby sister, Eva Elizabeth, developed what they called the "summer complaint." The doctors tried everything they knew to save her, but she lived just over sixteen months. Recently, my sister Marie wrote me about that heartbreaking time. Here are her words: "Eva got so sick with the summer flu. Dr. Fox told Mom to boil rice and feed her the gruel of it. She seemed to be doing better when, on Sunday morning, she took convulsions. Dr. Fox was out on a call somewhere, so we called Dr. Cameron. He got to the Frogpond School corner and had a flat tire. Instead of walking on to our house, he took time to patch and change the tire. By the time he got to our house, Eva had passed away. I can remember the sadness I felt when Eva died. She was so beautiful. Mother and Dad tried so hard to save her. On the day of her funeral, Mom had me in the washroom, doing my hair, but I was crying and did not want to go into the front room where she lay in her little cloth-covered casket."

Mother's last baby was Douglas, born June 30, 1927. We called him Dougie. What a delight we had in our little brother. I toted him around most everywhere I went, and we enjoyed playing together. I became like a shepherd to Dougie through all the rest of our growing up years until Uncle Sam drafted me into the military service.

In their elderly years, Dad and Mother bought burial plots in Oak Lawn Memorial Gardens. They had Clarence, Merlin, and Eva's graves moved to the new plot. Mother and Dad and their three dear young children lie there together now. I made careful notes of the bronze plaques: Bert H. Nixon 1888–1967, Selena B. Nixon 1892–1986, Clarence A. Nixon 1917–1922, Merlin M. Nixon 1920–1921, and Eva E. Nixon 1924–1925.

Mother lived with my sister, Vivian Nalley, and her husband, Francis, in her very last years. In her ninety-second year, she fell and broke her hip. They took her to the hospital in Morristown, Tennessee, where Vivian faithfully visited her. When under heavy sedation, Mother would begin to tell Vivian about the early days of her life. Much of it, Viv had never heard before. So, she got a pen and paper to carefully write down Mother's words. I am so glad she did, for much of this was unknown to any of us. It is my pleasure to share Vivian's notes:

> *"Just a few notes I took while Mom was in the hospital in 1985, while she was on a few of her talking jags. I never knew a lot of things she told me, but it's unreal to be able to remember all this from back so many years. I just sat and kept writing as she talked. What a life she and Dad must have had back there. When she refers to the boys or girls, she means her brothers and sisters, our aunts and uncles."*

I am going to quote my mother's memories in appropriate places throughout these memoirs. They will be indented and italicized.

> *Vivian: "How did you and Dad meet?" [I'm thinking this will be super!]*

> *Mother: "I worked at the old Taylor Hotel. I met Dad one Sunday night at the old Methodist church. Some time, walking down the street, Dad asked if he could walk me home. He took me by the arm and walked me home. He was kind of shy, but I thought it was love at first sight pretty much. I think Dad went to church, as did a lot of other young men, to meet the girls. When Dad and Uncle Ern were young, they would play their violins at house parties. Aunt Mary worked in town too. I think Dad and I went steady for a while, then broke up for about a year.*

> *"Then we went back dating. I was twenty-one years old. Dad was in his twenties. Dad was buying and working this farm over from Uncle George's. Uncle Ern had bought it from Archie Clark. Dad owned a horse and buggy and he had two cows. I was working at George Wilson's boarding house when Dad and I got married. I saved money for a new suit and coat for the wedding. Margaret was going with Gordon Beacom then.*

> *"We considered ourselves pretty well set when we got married. Dad had bought his farm and was making payments once a year, owned his horse and buggy and a nice new cutter for winter. We were both*

saving our money when we decided to get married. They didn't have any big wedding dinners then and didn't need any witnesses either when getting married. Those old house parties were just a place to meet people.

"We were married in August by T. R. Easter, minister and principal of schools. No big weddings then. The main thing was to get a good, ambitious husband and no drinker. We spent our honeymoon night at Aunt Selena Watson's.

"It stormed the next day on the way home to Dad's farm from our wedding. We had to go into the old Green's place where Clarence Green used to live and wait till the storm was over. We built a little shanty until we got the house built. Uncle Tom Portice and the rest helped Dad and cleared land. Dad bought a stove, table, and chair. I had been collecting dishes and pots and pans. Uncle Ern Nixon and an aunt from Canada came to visit us the first day after our wedding."

CHAPTER TWO

Haul Backs

MY MATERNAL GRANDFATHER came from Ireland after the worst of the devastating potato famine was over, but poverty reigned. The exodus continued because there was little or no opportunity for young people. His parents were tenant farmers and for all practical purposes were bound to the large landholder. Their little thirteen-acre farm could barely keep body and soul together. They were allowed three pigs each year, for example, and one of those pigs must go to the landholder. Merchant ships brought cargoes of lumber from Canada and would sign on a load of immigrants for the return voyage. They were dubbed "haul backs." Many ships came into Ballyshannon, Ireland. We were told that some simply stood offshore from Rossnowlaugh, Ireland, and sent in rowboats for their passengers. They became indentured servants until they worked off the cost of their passage.

Ballyshannon surrounds and overlooks the mouth of the River Erne. Sailing ships came right into town. Most likely, it was there young George Portice (my mother's father) boarded the ship that carried him to far-away Canada. He was only seventeen. I can see and hear the sobs of his mother (Mary) and Dad (George), as well as his brothers and sisters, as he rubs the tears from his own eyes. They are waving goodbye to each other. The anchor is lifted; the wind catches the sails; the ship moves westward. They stand close together, watching until the last speck of sail disappears over the horizon with both sadness and hope.

No one has written down or orally transmitted anything about young George's voyage to the New World. Did he never talk about it? What was the name of the ship? Surely, Mother would have told us something about it if she had known. To my knowledge, none of his twelve children ever mentioned his crossing voyage. Was it so painful that he cast it out of his mind completely? Perhaps it was common for young immigrants to be silent about the painful departure from their native country, much as soldiers seldom talk about their battlefield experiences. Grandpa Portice's ship probably dropped anchor in Halifax, Nova Scotia, where he worked off his passage debt. We know he went down to the Owen Sound area of Ontario, a settled immigrant farming community. However, the land of opportunity for husky young men was in the lumber camps across Lake Huron in the new State of Michigan.

George soon found work in the Muskegon area and followed those camps up into the Upper Peninsula of Michigan. He became a naturalized American citizen and filed for a homestead from the United States government. He cleared the required acreage and built a log cabin, winning the homestead. After making sure the area was safe from the threat of Indian attacks, he went by ship to retrieve his fiancé, Esther Barber. They sailed back to Sault Ste. Marie where they were married on June 9, 1887.

Grandma Esther Portice had the sweetest smile. She was born in Tara, Ontario, Canada, on September 25, 1866. Her father and mother were William Barber and Agnes Morrow. We have no further genealogical data. The cabin George built for Esther was two and a half miles southeast of Pickford on the banks of the Little Munuscong River. The town of Pickford itself was on the Big Munuscong River, twenty-four miles south of the Soo and founded by Billy Pickford. The solid virgin forest was being punctured by lumber camps and brand-new, land-cleared farms. Grandpa Portice became a successful farmer and harvester of timber from their homestead. They raised a family of six boys and six girls and lost not a one. My mother, Selena, was born in their log cabin. Today, a log from it forms the mantle over the fireplace in our Smoky Mountain home.

There was soon a little red schoolhouse on every two-mile corner. Each was proud of its name. Mother grew up in the Sunshine school community. The "lads," as Grandma affectionately called her sturdy boys, helped Grandpa milk cows, farm eighty acres of rich clay loam soil, and saw cut logs from their adjoining timber holdings. Harvesting timber each winter was an important task for valuable lumber, as well as home heating. When they were grown men, Grandma still called them her lads. They were crack Irish storytellers to the core. Each had his own sense of humor and way of talking: George, Tom, Jim, Andrew, Ervin, and Webster. My wife met Uncle Ervin when he was in his eighties. She was so captivated by his manner of speech and facial expressions. She should have heard Uncle Tom back in the day! Those two would top "Lum and Abner" or anyone on television today. They were local, nonconforming "characters," yet all six were honest, hard-working men—good lads.

Grandma and Grandpa had six "garls," as Grandma called them. Where she got that pronunciation, I do not know. Canada, I suppose, but with her it never changed. The girls were each pleasingly and interestingly unique as were their six brothers. It is unexplainable—except that it could be the Irish in them. Each would arrest your attention as they talked, whether in laughter, argument, or storytelling. The sparkle in their eyes and their body language formed a mixture of earnestness and humor. They were premium young ladies. I am glad my dad won and married Selena Portice. Mother's sisters were named Mary, Margaret, Jeanice, Esther, and Frances.

Mother and Aunt Mary were the two oldest girls. They worked hard helping Grandma in the early pioneering days of the family: housecleaning, dishwashing, scrubbing wood floors, laundering clothes on washboards in tin tubs, making lye soap, carrying water, cooking over wood stoves, berry picking, canning, wool combing, knitting, sewing, darning socks, and ironing.

Clifton Nixon

Portice Family: (back row) Esther, Tom, George, Margaret, Jim, Andrew, Jeanice
(front row) Selena, Webster, Ervin, Frances, Mary

Portice Family: (back row) Web, Tom, Mary, Margaret, Esther, Frances, Jim
(front row) George, Ervin, Andrew, Jeanice, Selena

Their daily chores included cleaning the smoked-up lamp and lantern chimneys, wick trimming, plus reloading them all with coal oil. There were a dozen milk pails and cream separator parts that had to be washed twice a day. Top all that off with bringing in wood when the boys let the wood box get empty.

When the Portice girls grew up, they were readily qualified for many awaiting job opportunities. Mother told Marie about the times she worked for Dr. Fox's wife, for Mrs. Ed Taylor, and other affluent matrons of Pickford, Michigan. Sometimes she worked at Uncle John and Aunt Selena Watson's dairy and truck farm in the Soo. Marie was impressed that Mother was a hardworking person, and she would tell you with a set and sober countenance, "What she did, she did right." There is a lot of Irish that comes out in Marie when she tells you something. For sure, we kids can remember growing up on the adage, "If it's worth doing, it's worth doing right." Her earnest eyes and face strongly supported those pronouncements.

The Portice garls were well-trained and honorable young ladies. Six of them! All married and had happy families. The older children, like my mother Selena, had little opportunity for education, only making it through the third or fourth grades at the primitive log schoolhouse on the bank of the Little Munuscong River. In winter, they walked the river ice to school. Grandpa Portice was a prosperous farmer and timber man with six fine sons to help him. Work had a higher priority than schooling.

The log cabin house soon became too small for the growing Portice family. Grandpa hired Mr. Quackenbush, a professional carpenter from Detroit, to build him a large two-story house. It was indeed a fine home for those times. We loved to go to Grandma and Grandpa's house. It was so big and had so many rooms. It must have cost a lot of money. Grandma would let us go into the kitchen and watch while she found us cookies. Other times, she cut us a large, thick slice of homemade bread with butter and wild berry jam on top. Yummy!

Clifton Nixon

Portice Family Home

Here is a quote on Mother's growing-up days:

"Mother would put eggs in trays of salt so they would have eggs when the chickens were molting. She bleached flour sacks with homemade bleach for sheets, pillowcases, and dish towels. Soap was made with ashes and pork fat after they butchered pigs in the fall. They always had a surplus of soap made ahead.

"Shirts were made for the lads for winter with wool material from the Soo Woolen Mill. Each spring when Dad (Grandpa Portice) sheared his sheep, he would make the once-a-year trip to the Soo to sell the wool and trade it for woolen goods and cash. It took two days each way, with overnight stops at the 'Half-Way House.' Mother (Grandma Portice) always knit the socks with homespun yarn. She did most of the knitting. Aunt Mary and I liked to do it too. The girls wore home knits, too, only they were a little fancier. Mother made most of the girls' clothes. Sunday dresses were bought sometimes, and Mother made some also. Mrs. Crawford used to do some of Mother's sewing. She lived in the old Izzard place.

"Dad (Grandpa Portice) used to take wheat and feed grain to the Old Grist Mill to have ground for flour, midlins, bran and 'chop' for the livestock. The winter's supply of flour was ground fine for bread, cakes, etc. Bob Crawford owned the mill. The flour was packed into seamless bags and held about a bushel and a half. Dad used to store the ground stuff up in the barn.

"Dad always got lots of stove wood out of the woods. All was cut with crosscut saws. If anyone got sick, the neighbors were always

there to help. We had bells on the cows in the summer, so we knew where to find them."

Mother rambled while she talked.

—*from Mother's hospital talks, November 23, 1985*

Grandma Portice had brothers and sisters. I remember Mother talking about her Uncle Bob Barber and her Aunt Maggie Bagnel in Western Canada. She had a sister, Selena, of whom Mother always spoke with affection. Mother was named after her Aunt Selena Watson, who lived in the Soo. Grandpa Portice died in 1925, and Grandma passed away in 1944. I have fond memories of Grandma Portice. I used to go over and "work" for her in my teen years. I was only seven years old when Grandpa died; I can scarcely remember him. At his passing, several of their children were still at home; Webster and Frances were still in high school. Uncle Tom never married and always lived with Grandma. She suffered the loss of her wonderful, big home by fire during the Great Depression and could not collect a dime of insurance. The company had folded, but Grandma was one heroic little lady and managed through it all. I admired her greatly, as did all our family.

My sister, Vivian, recalled something beautiful about Grandma Portice: "She went home to Heaven in 1944 during World War II. It has always remained in my mind that in the evening after her funeral, Uncle Andrew Portice was the one to have all his brothers and sisters gather around in the living room as he read Grandma's will and presented a wrapped package from her to each of her twelve children. Each package contained one new quilt and one used quilt, both made by her. None knew which they were getting. Those old quilts undoubtedly conveyed Grandma's very own sweet memories. Across the years she had made them and kept her dear children warm through many a cold winter night. The new quilts spoke of her provision for the future of her growing family."

There was another small package with Vivian's name on it. It contained a little scarf that Vivian had given to her. Grandma remembered and knew that it would be treasured by the giver. Vivian also recalled that on the day she and Francis were married, January 1,

1946, they received a package from Aunt Jeanice and Uncle Art Davis. "Low and behold, when we opened it, we found this beautiful starburst quilt that she had gotten from Grandma. In a lovely card she wrote: 'Some wonderful advice from a dear friend of mine when we were married: *Never pillow your heads one night without a kiss and an I Love You.*' It remained in our home fifty-two years! What a wonderful aunt and uncle."

CHAPTER THREE

Sure and Begorrah I'm Irish

MY GREAT-GRANDFATHER, MICHAEL NIXON, was born presumably between 1811–1813 in Ireland, possibly in Donegal. When in Ireland, I went to Letterkenny, the county seat of County Donegal, but discovered that they had no records prior to 1846. That is as far back as we can trace Michael Nixon.

He emigrated to Canada and then married my great-grandmother, Hannah Tomkins, on July 1, 1844, in the Chatham Presbyterian Church in Grenville. She was born in Quebec, Canada. My grandfather, William Elgin Nixon, was the youngest of their four children, all born in Grenville, Argenteuil, Quebec.

Grandpa William Elgin Nixon married Elizabeth Steele in Grenville. Both were born there in 1854. Their children, Ella, Ernest, and Herb were born in Grenville before they emigrated to Pickford, Michigan, in the United States, where my father, Bertram Hoyt Nixon, was born as was Edger, Clara, John Gilbert, Laura, and Dewey.

I remember Grandpa Nixon's death. He was staying at our house, and it was a cold, dark, wet December night. While Dad was finishing currying the horses, Grandpa and I went on ahead from the barn to the house. I was right behind him, only five years old, carrying the kerosene lantern. Just as we drew near the kitchen door, Grandpa fell right at my feet. I cried out, "Open door!" Mother or Marie heard, and we got him inside, but he was gone. His heart had stopped; he was not breathing anymore.

Dad and Mother had gotten his body onto a single bed in the front room, though it seemed to be higher than a bed. I saw Mother put coins on Grandpa's eyelids to hold them shut. My "open door" cry was the one we used when bringing a huge armful of wood from the woodpile. That dark night is engraved in my memory. The only other recollections I have are of the wake. It seemed like the house was full of people, and they stayed all night talking with one another. It felt so good to have them close. Like our grief and loss were being eased up and spread out over all these good neighbors. I cherish the little paperback revival song book from God's Bible School with William Nixon written on the front. It is his real signature. The book is well worn. It stirs hope in me of seeing Grandpa Nixon again in Heaven.

I remember my dad often telling how a "big Philadelphia lawyer" once came to our house and talked him into signing off on some "insignificant" papers pertaining to a very distant relative in faraway Scotland. The name was Scott. They later learned it had to do with the estate of the famous Scottish author, Sir Walter Scott (1771–1832) of Edinburgh, Scotland. Who knows? We might have become suddenly rich! Seems like I read that Sir Walter died poor, but his estate subsequently became unbelievably valuable from royalties. Perhaps Grandpa, Dad, or both signed off too soon. Oh well, it may have been a blessing.

I have but one faint memory of my Grandma Nixon, Elizabeth Steele Nixon. I was a small boy. Grandma was sitting near the kitchen range in her rocking chair while I was sweeping the floor with the long-handled broom and hit her on the head. My height was only about halfway up the broom handle, so I had simply fumbled the large stick and didn't mean to hit her. Marie remembers that when Grandma Nixon came to stay at our house, she would bring little wooden boxes of salted herring.

I knew vaguely that I was related to Cyril McKenzie, who died early in life at age twenty-two. I cannot remember him at all. Alex

McKenzie, his wife, and daughter, Stella, lived only a half-mile from us. Their farm was across the road from our Frogpond schoolhouse. Alex was not too outgoing a fellow, and we boys at school always snowballed him when he passed with his team. He always gave us an angry reaction! Great fun.

For whatever reason, I had totally submerged the fact that Alex's first wife was my Aunt Clara, my dad's younger sister, and Cyril was their son. Clara died giving birth to their second child, and Cyril died too early for me to know him. Dad often spoke of Aunt Clara, but somehow I never took note of the connection. In tribute to Aunt Clara, my sister, Vivian Clara, was named after her. Cyril was my cousin. Here I was, heaving snowballs at my one-time uncle.

Art Stewart, a close neighbor and schoolmate at the red Frogpond schoolhouse, told me this about my cousin, Cyril McKenzie: "Cyril McKenzie was older than us, and he always carried a bucket of water to school for drinking because there was not a well there. Cyril got kicked in the leg by a horse, got gangrene, and died." This was all new to me. I do not know why—perhaps this may shed some light on the "wall" between us.

Art told me that Alex put up a line fence that was over on Jim Stewart's property. This rankled Jim for several years until finally, his dad had it surveyed. The encroachment proved true. So, Art Stewart's dad and my dad moved the fence over where it belonged. Alex promptly hauled them into court before Judge Hart, Justice of the Peace. Trial was held at Judge Hart's country house. Jim and his household, and probably my dad, were torn up because the judge ruled against them, citing a "grandfather law," declaring that seven years of unprotested occupancy created permanency. Alex tore down the fence and threw it over on Jim's field. They never did replace it. I knew nothing of this. Perhaps the reason was, an "Iron Curtain" hung across those fields.

CHAPTER FOUR

Hiawatha Land

NOT MANY YEARS BEFORE I WAS BORN, this area was a forest of white pine, birch, maple, spruce, balsam, cedar, hemlock, tamarack, poplar, and balm. Chippewa and Algonquin Indians roamed the dense forests and camped along the Big and Little Munuscong Rivers. Tall virgin timber awaited the coming of the white man. Wildlife and fish were abundant. The soil underneath all was a rich clay loam.

Long before Michigan became a state, the canoes of French Catholic missionaries and fur traders plied the St. Lawrence River and the Great Lakes. In 1772, Father Marquette and Nicolet planted the village of Sault Ste. Marie just twenty-seven miles north of our home where the overflowing rapids from Lake Superior formed the St. Mary's River. This was Henry Wadsworth Longfellow's "Hiawatha Land." Lake Superior to the west by northwest was "the Shining Big Sea Water" where nearby stood "the wigwam of Nokomis." The famous Soo Locks would be built amid those rapids. Monuments to Father Marquette and Father Nicolet are tourist attractions today. Our county is named Chippewa and Sault Ste. Marie, the county seat. The boundary of Marquette Township of Mackinac county goes right through Pickford.

In 1877, James Clegg, John Crawford, and William Gough came to the wilderness of the Upper Peninsula of Michigan in search of pioneer home sites. Twenty-five miles straight south of Sault Ste. Marie, they found the ideal spot on the banks of the Big Munuscong River and picked good building areas where they would clear the land and build. The next summer when they returned with their families, they discovered that Charlie Pickford had settled on the same location. In a few years, a cluster of wood-frame houses became a little town with muddy streets. They named the town Pickford after their first settler. John Mullet had surveyed the whole Upper Peninsula of Michigan in 1845. He marked out section lines and corner posts in preparation for the homesteading to come. Mr. Samuel Roe was another settler in the area and was a "land looker" for the state for several years.

If we stood at the Pickford settlement for a full-circle panoramic sweep of our Upper Peninsula, we would see Lake Superior to the northwest. Swinging our eyes to the right, we would see Sault Ste. Marie twenty-five miles straight north where the rapids splash down over rocks to the St. Mary's River twenty-two feet below. Circling to the east and south, the St. Mary's River runs through Lake Nicolet, then Munuscong Lake, whose shore is only four miles from our farm home. The waters then flow south through the Detour Passage into the upper end of Lake Huron. Our panoramic sweep continues westward past Cedarville, eleven miles south of Pickford. Going through the Straits of Mackinac south of Pickford, the upper end of Lake Michigan is visible to our west. Passing through the expansive Hiawatha National Forest, we complete the panoramic view of our Upper Peninsula to the largest of all the Great Lakes: Superior, "the Shining Big Sea Water."

On damp, foggy days, you could hear the deep bass foghorns of the huge lake steamers. The St. Mary's River carries the overflow of Lake Superior around the tip of our Upper Peninsula and into Lake Huron toward Detroit where it connects via the St. Clair River with Lake Erie, which connects with Lake Ontario at Niagara Falls. Thence, the St. Lawrence River runs eastward to the Atlantic Ocean from whence came our grandparents. Looking eastward, nearly all the land north of that trail of water is Canada. Most of our grandparents came to Pickford via Canada. Grandma Portice always called it Canadee.

A Farm Boy's Memoirs

When he was an old man, Pickford pioneer William H. Gough wrote an article for the *Soo Evening News* on January 5, 1938, under the headline: "W. H. GOUGH RECALLS EARLY DAYS OF PICK-FORD." Here he gives us fine-tuned descriptions of the first settlers. He wrote: "I came to Pickford June 21, 1877. I arrived on Sunday and started to work for Mr. Charles Pickford the next day and continued work through the summer. My first job was helping to raise a log building on the farm now owned by Harry Best. At that time, the Pickford family was living in a board shanty, but Mr. Pickford built a good farmhouse that summer which is now owned by Mr. F. H. Taylor." My sister Vivian and her husband bought this house from Mr. Taylor in 1947. It still stands in a neighborhood in the small town of Pickford today.

"During the summer of 1877, a number of people came here, took up land, built log shanties, and then in the fall brought their families. In total there were six families: the Pickford, Crawford, Clegg, Cook, George Raynard and William Gough families. It was the summer of 1878 that things seemed to move ahead, and development was made in many directions. More people settled here. Pretty soon we had a store, blacksmith shop, boarding house, grist mill, sawmill, and Mr. Charlie Pickford built a frame barn. Our first meeting place for worship was held in the Pickford home. Weldon and Henry Pickford had our first store. In the summer, they got their supplies from the Soo by boat. The name of the boat was the *John Auger* and landed at Jolly's Landing which is now called Stirlingville. Then everyone would rush to the store with a cotton bag to carry home some flour."

William Gough had an exciting experience when he was young that he reminisced about: "In those days there were plenty of wild animals in the woods. Charlie Pickford and I were going to Donaldson and on the trail, we were faced by a big bear. We drove the bear west and stood talking about how easy it was to chase a bear. But turning around, we saw two large bears coming toward us. I shouted, 'Climb a tree!' We started climbing a nearby tree, but Charlie shouted that he couldn't climb. We climbed the tree... looked down... at the trunk sat two bears and a second later they were making their way to climb the tree after us...we slid down some then jumped... landing on the ground a few feet from the bears standing on their hind feet. One bear started at Charlie and backed him up toward the trail... he ran hollering 'Will!' The other bear came at me backing me up... I turned and ran with leaps and bounds to the trail thinking every moment the bear would have me. When I reached Charlie, he was trying to build a fire on the riverbank to keep the bears away. The joke of it all was we had climbed the tree that the bear's cubs were in, and this of course made the old bears angry. In the escape, I lost my hat and suggested to Charlie that we go back and get it, but Charlie answered sharply, 'I wouldn't take the United States to go back for that hat.' I started for my hat, and when I came to it, I could see the bears again sitting at the trunk of the tree with the two cubs up it. They watched me as I grabbed my hat and ran."

Pickford is right in the middle of the narrowing eastern end of the Upper Peninsula of Michigan. Lake Superior, Lake Huron, the Straits of Mackinac, and Lake Michigan are at our elbows. We had harsh winter snowstorms and blizzards with below-zero temperatures. Many times, it reached forty and sometimes fifty or more below. But we loved it; we had the glory of the Northern Lights. In summer, the surrounding lakes spawned terrific thunder and lightning storms, creating spectacular fireworks with prolonged and deadly strikes. Lightning rods were a must. Many cattle and horses were killed. When dense fog fell over the peninsula, you could hear the deep-throated foghorns of the lake steamers going through "Mud Lake" like they were right up at our line fence. We called Lake Munuscong Mud Lake because it was a muddy red most of the time. Storms stirred it up, yet walleyes thrived in those waters.

Indian trails from the Soo to the Straits of Mackinac became wagon roads that we called "The Meridian"—M-129 today. John Daley came in 1881, and he remembers: "Pussy Day carried the mail with dogs from the Soo to St. Ignace through the woods before the trail was cut through for stages. There was a stopping place at the huckleberry patch, one at Pine River and one at the Carp River." Uncle Ern Nixon told us about a man named John White who carried a stove on his back from the Soo to his log house north of Pickford.

There was a second gateway into the Pickford settlement and the whole Munuscong valley. The good ship *Northern Belle* paddle-wheeled up the muddy Munuscong River from Mud Lake. John Everleigh was there and tells the story: "It was the year 1884 when me and two boyhood friends were sitting on the loading dock at Mr. Stirling's store, located just below the hill in Stirlingville. Suddenly the stillness was broken by loud swishes mixed with sharp blasts from a boat whistle. We leapt to our feet, fishing forgotten, for around the bend in the river came the *Northern Belle*. She was an enormous craft in our eyes with her paddle wheels churning the smooth surface of the river as she made her way to the dock." John Everleigh came here from Canada at the age of two years with his father, Joseph, and family to settle on a piece of land at Stirlingville. The deed for his property was signed by Grover Cleveland. Hazel and Effie Everleigh were our classmates. The Richard McConkey children also came to our Frogpond school. Richard came from Canada by boat with his parents when he was eight years old. They came up the Munuscong and settled along its banks for about a year until they took 160-acre homestead three miles east of Pickford.

John Daley wrote down even more: "The first preacher was Mr. Donaldson, who walked four miles north of Pickford, then to Blair's settlement and then to Stirlingville. I walked through the ox trail through the swamp with Sandy Hill. There were no bridges then; there was no Pickford then, only his barn and house. He came from Bayfield, Canada. Lots of people followed to Pickford and took up homesteads. Hank Pickford had a little boat with which he brought things to his store (up from Jolly's Landing)."

The *St. Ignace News* of October 8, 1998, carried a story by Berniece Waybrant that adds beautiful color to those early days of Munuscong glory: "Many of the first settlers of Pickford came up the Munuscong River from the St. Mary's River as far as Stirlingville on the John Auger or the Northern Belle. A sloop owned by Charles Pickford brought supplies from Sault Ste. Marie to the mouth of the Munuscong. On the appointed day, Mr. Pickford, Tom Morrison, and William Best rowed down the river to meet the sloop for supplies. Mr. Pickford bought the

John Auger, a large boat, from some Indians that would meet the sloop and bring the cargo and passengers the rest of the way to Stirlingville."

Here are a few lumber camp nuggets from John Daley. They are of keen interest to me because around the supper table as a young lad, I hung upon every word of the logging camp tales. The best tales included my dad and Mr. Jim Gough, or Dad and Uncle Ern. Dad had a young team of horses, and he "decked" logs with his team in a Gogomain lumber camp. Mr. Daley reported: "The Miles brothers came from Saginaw and started to lumber at Kinross. They paid thirty dollars a month. They also built a mill at Detour. I was there with a team at two dollars a day. They cut 100,000 board-feet a day. I helped to take out their drive. Also, Robert Crawford of Stalwart cooked for McKniff's drive. Will Brown, Charlie Wilson, and Barney Tillen were rafting the logs to the mill across Mud Lake to the Island."

From "Memories of Pickford" by Otto Storey:

Now some folks long for mountains,
Some for the ocean or forest glades;
But to live and to have lived in Pickford,
For no other life would I trade.

CHAPTER FIVE

Pickford
"The Little, Holy Town"

WHEN I WAS A BOY, THE STREETS in Pickford were still muddy, but we had boardwalks. A daily horse stagecoach brought in the mail. A road came in town from the farms west of Pickford that became Main Street, crossed a bridge over the Big Munuscong River at the end of Main Street, and continued east to more farms. At the one-mile crossroad, it passed over the Little Munuscong River. At the two-mile corner, the road passed our country school. Three more miles passed by farms and down a steep hill until the road ended at the five-mile corner at the banks of the Gogomain Swamp. We always called it the "Townline Road." Numbered dirt roads were laid out from Pickford on the mile in all four directions to reach the many eighty-acre homesteads. Most farm families could make a living on a fully cleared eighty acres with a herd of milk cows, horses, hogs, chickens, and other animals.

    The face of Main Street Pickford changed during my growing-up years. This busy block and a half still glows beautifully in my mind. Hugh Carr's blacksmith shop was on the southeast corner of Main Street and the Meridian. I think he was a favorite blacksmith of the farmers west of town. We did not go there often. "Wobbly Geared"

Smith worked there. No making fun of Mr. Smith was intended; that is just the way folks were given descriptive names. Mr. Smith had a short leg from an early injury. No, it was not a put-down. We had two Harvey Campbells. One was called "Red Harvey" because he had red hair. We were taught to say "Mr." and "Mrs.," not "Yes sir" and "Yes ma'am." When inducted into the military services, the mandatory *sir* was quite a jolt. We learned fast! Nevertheless, our parents thoroughly taught us to respect adults and the elderly, and pretty much to speak only when spoken to.

Jack Thompson's Ford Garage was a block south from this corner. Jack was a very talkative fellow, much loved for his bravado and stories. He once was boasting publicly of shooting a deer out of season, not knowing that an unknown game warden was in his audience. When the warden asked, "Do you know who I am?" and revealed his identity, Jack fired back, "And do you know who I am? The biggest liar in Chippewa County." Sons Morrell and Pete later took over the garage. His daughter Shirley was a high school classmate of mine. In our freshman year, Shirley and I were recruited to play parts in the senior class play of that year.

V. L. Lipsett's Chevrolet Garage was built in 1912, on the very spot where the original William Hannah boarding house had burned down. VL, as we called him, was a big man, always well dressed and a rather taciturn fellow. I still picture his frequent catty-corner walks across the street to his Lipsett Hardware store, a little farther down. Never straight across and down, always a mid-street beeline, relaxed, erect, almost military-like. We kids allowed; he must be pretty well fixed since he never crossed in work clothes. They drove a new car most every year and would be gone to Florida every winter. He had our respect, and his son, Ford attended high school with us. Ford must have been named after his father's first car agency selling Henry Ford's Tin Lizzies.

The most important building that stands out in my boyhood memories was Oak Roe's Blacksmith Shop. Mr. Roe was the "real McCoy", right out of Oliver Goldsmith's *The Village Blacksmith*: "The smith a mighty man was he, with large and sinewy hands." I can see him now;

his face blackened with smoke and soot, turning the bellows with his right hand until the coke glowed red hot, then white hot. His left hand held a clamped horseshoe in that orange-to-white hot pile until the shoe came out glowing and pliable. Quickly, he seized a big hammer and began pounding and molding it to the right shape and thickness. His calculating eye must be satisfied. An iron shoe must fit the horse perfectly. Often, it went back into the fire, and the heat was cranked up again. It was exciting to behold. When completely satisfied, he plunged the masterpiece into a tub of water. It sizzled and came out cold, ready for fitting on the horse's foot. I was spellbound.

Doc Cameron's theatre had ornate furnishings inside, cushioned folding seats, an elegant stage, and an orchestra pit down front. Beautiful curtains could be opened and closed with ropes. It was fancy, for our little town. Movies were shown regularly in my high school years, and the annual senior high school play was put on there. We knew truly little about theater activities, except for the school plays in that theater. Our high school's WLS Barn Dance Program was a grand success there with three repeat performances.

There was a vacant lot between Lipsett's Garage and a store building that housed the short-lived Jenks pool hall and beer garden, followed by a successful but brief stay of the A & P Grocery Store. After that, it became the Sam Roe Grocery. When the Great Atlantic & Pacific Tea Co. came to town, it was great news. Business was great, and Pickford was going modern with our first big chain grocery store, but it did not last long. The Prohibition Amendment had been repealed, so the A&P applied for a license to sell beer. Not in Pickford! The whole township voted a resounding no. That is when the "Little Holy City" tag was pinned on us. The big city press stuck it on us as a badge of scorn, but we wore it as a badge of honor. Old John Barleycorn was not going to get his nose in the door.

Fred Taylor's Hardware was a two-story building owned and operated by Mr. Fred Taylor and later by his son, Aldren. In the earlier days when the Pickford school burned down, classes were temporarily held above Taylor's hardware. Somehow, I had it in my mind that Mr. Fred Taylor was the undertaker. I know he had coffins stored upstairs over the hardware store. I recently read somewhere that a lady in town had a ministry of helping prepare bodies for burial. There was no funeral director as we know them today.

Aldren and his Dad seemed a little more flexible in their prices than the competition across the street; they had connected with a chain hardware supply outfit called, True Hardware. We shopped both sides of the street, of course. Taylor's often had a little better price. Lipsett's hardware seemed more unbending; they stuck strictly to big brand names and manufacturer's price tags. We knew the quality might be a shave better on some things, but we had to stretch our dollars.

Next to the theatre was Bob Harrison's drug store. Powders and bottled medicine were stacked high on the walls. There was a soda fountain in the drugstore with artistic iron tables and all kinds of goodies. I only remember one time sitting at one of those fancy tables. Sometimes, we went in for the big double-decker ten-cent ice cream cones on a Saturday night. Mrs. Harrison was especially nice. I think she took a delight in stacking those nickel or dime cones high for the country kids. Mr. Harrison would be busy pouring tonics and powders, counting out bitter pills, and pulling all kinds of liniments, salves, cathartics, poultice agents, and sundry patent medicines from those shelves, jars, and wooden drawers.

A long stairway went up from the street to living quarters above. Their son, Haley went out of his way to be friendly to this farm boy. When I graduated from Cleary Business College in Ypsilanti and came back for my first job in Pickford, I needed a car. Haley was working for a finance company in the Soo. He got me a loan for $120 to buy my first car, a 1935 Ford four-door sedan. Snazzy. It had a radio too. I was twenty years old and had not learned to drive yet.

I recall having a big laugh about a fellow who always talked about going to the "Calf" to eat. It was Libby's Cafe where Jack Thompson outwitted the game warden about the buck he killed out of season. It was good yarn-telling territory. Jack Foster and later Glenn Gough took over the delightful eating place and made it a center of good food and fellowship for many years. My brother-in-law, Francis Nalley, was given a big birthday cake there. Amid the festivities, he took up the knife to cut the cake and struck tough going. The beautifully decorated cake was a big metal dishpan; however, it covered a mountain of homemade doughnuts. It was there the old- timers came to harangue one another and continue their storytelling heritage.

The V. Lipsett Hardware store was next door. Harvey Blair, the long-time manager, was a very capable and accommodating man. When the Grist Mill, post office, telephone office, and Best's Grocery all burned down in the big 1932 fire, a temporary post office was set up in Lipsett's hardware. The Soo Stage pulled up in front each afternoon and departed from there each morning. Every time we went to town, we did a lot of looking. Lipsett's was always a must, even if only for Harvey Blair's friendly greeting.

Our Bank of Pickford, sometimes called Beacom's Bank, was on the corner of Main and Pleasant. Dad and Mother often spoke highly of the senior Mr. Beacom, the founder of the bank, saying he was a good man who could be trusted. It was kind of scary to go in there, what with everybody behind cages and speaking so softly. Like you would do damage if you spoke out loud. I went in a few times with my dad when I was small, but I never said anything. It was always full of people on Saturday nights. Mr. Beacom's son, Ford Beacom, was the President of the bank when I had a bank account there. He drove a big, long automobile. When the bank closed during the Depression, I lost my entire savings account money—thirteen dollars and some change. It was my rat-tail bounty money, and I never did get it back.

Across the street was Harry Best's grocery. He moved in there after losing his store in the big fire of 1932 and operated it a few years until it became the Bud Watson Grocery. Next to Best's Grocery store was the large corner plot with the Central Hotel. Frank (F.H.) Taylor built this hotel on the corner of Main Street and Pleasant in 1889. Mr. Frank Taylor was a man with great community vision. With amazing energy, he got more commercial buildings up and more prime services going than any man in the territory. In 1886, he rebuilt the original Charles Pickford store. Just a year after the hotel was built, he built both the three-story "Red Block" facing Main Street and the Creamery in 1890.

In 1883, Frank went to the Chicago World's Fair and observed the telephone in use. He purchased the new machines, then came home and strung a wire from his store in Pickford to his store in Rudyard and started the Pickford Telephone Company in his own home. In 1893, he was the chief instigator with Washington, D.C., in getting the daily mail service started between the Soo and Pickford.

Young Frank Taylor started out as bookkeeper in Charlie Pickford's store. He owned the store in just a few years. They raised three fine sons: Percy "Pat" Taylor took over the Pickford Telephone Company, and Harold "Putsy" Taylor oversaw the Land and Lumbering Company. I was a bookkeeper for both. Herb, the eldest son, became president of Club Aluminum in Chicago during the Depression. He was a nationally recognized leader in Christian youth sponsorship.

I know that when the Church of the Nazarene was started in Pickford in 1939, Mr. F. H. Taylor was an elderly man and a friend to our cause. He deeded the building site to the church. I was appointed to the church board as treasurer. In 1941, Mr. Taylor gave our church another adjoining lot. That was an inspiring time in my life, knowing my life calling was to be a minister. Uncle Sam was calling Charlie Ames and me into the Army, the first two inductees from the Pickford area. The popular song that year was "I'll Be Back in a Year, Little Darlin' " by Texas Jim Robertson.

Clifton and Charles Ames

The Grand Hotel served as a community center and a place to hold going-away parties for local citizens. A row of captain's chairs lined the front entrance where local citizens used to sit and watch the people go by. The Grand Hotel in the horse and buggy days was a halfway stop between Cedarville or Detour and the Soo. When the lumber camps broke up in the spring and all the men were headed back home, they would come to Pickford to catch the Stage. Many nights, they would not be able to make room for them all.

The Grand Hotel was divided up in 1928 and moved to make room for a smaller two-story telephone office. I was bookkeeper for Pat Taylor in 1941 when drafted into the service. During the war, my sister Vivian was a switchboard operator upstairs for Pickford Telephone. She and Cora Hughes had a great time working together. Harold Taylor's Land Management office was also on the ground floor, and his father had a desk there. He was an unashamed Christian gentleman. It was just outside a window of that telephone building that I preached my very first sermon on a Saturday night. The town was filled with people. My pastor, Rev. Leroy Harris, had asked me to preach, and a tiny platform with a lectern had been set up. I had no training, but faith and zeal prevailed. My boss, "Putsy" Taylor, teased me a bit about being ready. I think he listened out the window. I remember that Uncle Ern was in the encircling crowd that night along with my family.

There were other buildings of note on the same side of Pleasant Street near our church: Adam Roe's Blacksmith Shop, Sam Brown's house, and the old Orange Lodge Hall. Across the street stood Pickford High School, Harvey Campbell's log home, the vacant jailhouse, Ken Smith's Radio Shop, Bert Smith's Barber Shop, and Hamilton & Watson's. Pleasant Street continued north across Main down a steep hill to the old Woolen Mill and the Creamery. Both buildings backed up against the Big Munuscong River. Many a ten-gallon can of cream did we take to Jack Gough's Creamery. That was a lifesaving source of cash for the farmers during the depression. We were desperately frightened one time when Jack had to tell us that his market was drying up, and he might not be able to buy our cream. Mercifully, it did not happen. Jack made the cream into butter or ice cream and found the buyers. Each Christmas, he gave us a quart of ice cream.

Jack's sister, Helen, was his full-time secretary. She helped during the building of our Nazarene church. I would go by on my noon hour break to collect the latest bi-weekly pledges we all made to the building program. It was part of my job as church treasurer. Helen always came forth faithfully with her check. Mr. Will Talbot not only helped with a bi-weekly pledge; his construction skills built the church. One serious pledge moment was turned into laughter when Charlie Ames turned his pockets inside out, proclaiming bankruptcy. Looking back, it was a genuinely happy adventure for every one of us.

The Red Block, F.H. Taylor Building, Taylor's Emporium, and Hamilton & Watson's are all the same place. The building burned to the ground in 1928 and was rebuilt immediately. The first floor was a general merchandise store selling groceries, meat, dry goods, and shoes. The back portion was the *Pickford Clarion* newspaper, which was gone before my time. The second floor consisted of Dr. Fox's office and apartments. The third floor was used as a town hall and auditorium where many school plays were given in the beginning days of Pickford Township. A traveling show that included a ventriloquist performed in the auditorium every year for years. The east end of the third floor was used as a lodge room for the Modern Woodmen of the World. One of the first Boy Scout troops in America also met there, organized by the local Presbyterian minister in 1912. When Ed Taylor bought the place, he called it the Emporium. There was a livery barn just south of the Emporium on the riverbank with a narrow horse track for getting out to Main Street between the back end of the Emporium and the Munuscong River.

The Fred Smith Grist mill was a fascinating place. Dad would pull up beside the long, front-loading deck with wheat, oats, flax, or whatever and unload to the weighing scales. I would get to go inside the mill office—at least I guess it was the office. All was a great whirring sound with puffs of grain dust or flour coming from a wonderful network of wooden shoots going up and down through the floors above.

A mighty power was vibrating all its timbers, creating an all-surrounding awareness.

Men buzzed around, carrying big bags of grain or pushing loaded dollies. One man opened a little slide in a shoot to fill the bags with things like golden grain or peas. A general dust filled the whole place, and it smelled so good. So wholesome and inviting, like nothing I'd ever smelled before. I was never in a hurry to leave that grist mill. Everything was alive and shaking. Big pulleys and belts turned overhead. I figured it must take a lot of power to make all that go. Dad said they even made the flour right there. That took a lot of grinding, sifting, and separating to produce. By-products like midlins, shorts, and bran went into cow chop and scratch feed for chickens.

Dad and I would talk about all this on the way home on the wagon or sleighs behind Bess and Colonel, our big draft horses. We took our whole crop of wheat there to bring back flour and sometimes a bag or so of the other stuff. Mother cooked those midlins or shorts for breakfast sometimes—a prototype of Cream of Wheat. But it did not measure up to good old Quaker Rolled Oats. Sometimes in the winter, Mother would get bran from the big fifty-pound bag and sprinkle a little on top of our oatmeal. We ate oatmeal every morning.

A huge bag of bran did not weigh much, but it went a long way. Dad gave it to the horses for medicine in the winter because they were mostly just standing in their stalls. Bran kept them from getting stove up. Mother probably sprinkled it on our porridge for the same reason, maybe at Doctor Fox's suggestion. The bran sure beat that senna tea Mother would get at Harrison's Drug Store. I am sorry that old grist mill is gone. If I could go back, I would go back tomorrow just to feel, hear, and smell that grinding, rumbling, vibrating place. Delicious dust. I know Dad would too; like I said, he was never in a hurry to leave.

My dad had only been able to complete three grades at the country school—and likely with interruptions. Sadly, his mother and dad, my Grandpa and Grandma Nixon, divorced, leaving Uncle Ern head of the home to his almost-grown siblings. It was never discussed, and we never asked Dad to give us any details. He always spoke kindly of his parents and loved his brothers and sisters. The older children were able to get more education; somehow, Dad did not get the opportunity. He never told us why or complained. But he and Mother were both zealous that we children get a good education. It was my joy to almost unwittingly help my dad learn to read. He would ask me to identify words, sounds, and spellings.

As I moved along in arithmetic, Dad would invite me to calculate the number of bushels. I marveled how he could check out the final weight tally on the load we took to the mill. We were paid by the bushel, so he could check the conversion of total scale weight into bushels. Not an easy job because each grain has a different weight per bushel—wheat, peas, oats, barley, and flaxseed are all different. As I remember, oats were thirty-two pounds per bushel. Dad had a system that went something like this: Twice ten is twenty, and twice twenty is forty. Half of eighty is forty. Half of forty is twenty, and half of twenty is ten—until he got the right answer and made it check out! I am still not sure how he did it. As I grew older, he would have me work out the answers to see if we agreed. It was fun. We nearly always got the same answer. If our load of peas weighed in at 965 pounds, you could count on it, Dad and I always double-checked Mr. Smith's tally on the number of bushels. It was a matter of dollars and cents. We did not have many dollars, but Dad sure had good sense. Believe it or not, even when I was in high school, he could get the answer just about as soon as I could. I would look at him with that *How did you do that?* eyebrow. He would just grin. He had a very sharp mind. Looking back, I can see that he was a most excellent father, a natural psychologist, and he demonstrated wonderful judgment. He was real. The tears run freely as I write about him.

Right next to the grist mill was the post office. Besides running the mill, Mr. Smith was also the Pickford postmaster. There were a lot of cubby holes for town folk's mail. There was also a busy counter where you bought three-cent stamps and sent packages. It was there we often inquired about packages: "Has the Soo Stage come yet?" If not, we lived on a rural route and hoped that our mail carrier, Earl Miller, would bring it the next day.

A Farm Boy's Memoirs

Among the buildings clustered near the grist mill was Harry Best's Grocery. Mr. Best was a kindly gentleman, and we young children would get a grandfatherly smile from him. A person could feast the eyes, even though you did not have a penny in your pocket. If you had a penny or two, you got first-rate attention and could march right up to the candy boxes and order a couple of lollipops or whatever. Some candy was sold two or three for a penny, and you could come away with a surprisingly good handful. Mr. Best appreciated everyone's business. It paid off to shop around though. Best's Grocery was good for two or three stops on a Saturday night.

Wee snatches of history stick in my mind. The years could not erase this one. It was the winter of the double-whammy blizzards that resulted in a two-week "snowbound." Dad let me come to town with him where he joined an army of volunteers to dig snow trenches along each side of the road leaving town. The men hoped the snowplows would then be able to take a running start to pitch the packed snow up and out. All morning long and way into the afternoon, they shoveled.

The lunch Dad and I brought was all gone, and I was desperately hungry. We had no money, and Dad hated to drop out of the road crew. I was roaming around and happened into Mr. Best's Grocery; there sat a rack of three-foot, square empty boxes that had contained little round blocks of sugar maple. A few crumbs and broken pieces remained in the corners— what a waste. That good man, Mr. Best, read my face. He came up beside me and asked, "Would you like to have those crumbs and pieces of sugar maple?" I gave him a big "um-huh" and the best smile I could muster. I explained that my dad was shoveling snow, and we had eaten up all our lunch. He shook every crumb and chunk out of all three boxes and sent me off with a bag of pure maple candy. I wonder if he ever stopped to think what it meant to that little country boy that day about seventy-five years ago.

Early one November morning in 1932, Ike Macdonald's sawmill whistle awakened us. A great, fiery cloud was going up in Pickford with streams of mingled smoke and flames. We knew immediately that it was beyond control. *Is it Hamilton & Watson's again? Or is it the grist mill? It could be the Presbyterian church or the Methodist church*, I thought. It was my beloved grist mill. Everything on that block was burned to the ground.

Saturday nights in Pickford were memorable times in my childhood, right up there with the county fairs. Nearly all the farmers came to town on Saturday night. All the stores were open until eleven o'clock. Most of the townsfolk also came out to join in the fellowship. Talk about community spirit. We had it. We kids could cruise around with our friends and hop in and out of our favorite stores again and again. We ranged the full length of Main Street, the side shops on Pleasant Street, Bert's Barber Shop, the two livery barns and Ken Smith's Radio and Film Store. Horses were sheltered in the livery barns in the winter. Sleighs, cutters, wagons, and buggies were parked mostly behind Hamilton & Watson's.

I would have to say that Hamilton & Watson's was the hub of it all with great candy displays and the smell of freshly ground coffee. It was a regular mall. You walked from the large grocery and meat market division into Otto Watson's Shoe Store division and on into the clothing store. All under one roof with doors opening out to Main Street from each.

Groceries were stacked clear up to the ceiling with rolling ladders that were pushed back and forth as the busy clerks climbed up and down filling orders. People stood in short lines before counters where several clerks skillfully gathered and packaged the groceries. You did not go around picking up your own stuff. Oh boy, could those clerks move. Art Rich was my favorite. His hands moved like lightning. Above each clerk's workstation hung a large cone of wrapping string. Art Rich could close a bag of sugar, reach up for that string, wrap the package, and tie a knot in the blink of an eye. Before you knew it, he had your groceries wrapped, tied, bagged, and ready to go. He was in his glory going four hours straight at full speed on Saturday nights. It was worth coming around several times just to watch Art Rich in action.

A close second was Leonard Rye at the meat counter. He could cut a piece of meat to order and practically wrap it in midair, whip the string down around the butcher paper, and shove it over the counter with a smile, calling out, "Next!" Lennie flitted from meat block to freezer to customer with the greatest of ease. He was lightning fast with that overhead string.

When you moved through the open space into the shoe store, a whiff of leather greeted your nostrils like a tonic. Otto Watson was the son of Mr. James Watson in the Hamilton & Watson's name. He was mild in temperament while busy giving his undivided attention to each customer. He exuded reliability and never rushed you. It was easy to have confidence in Otto. He called you by your first name and knew whose children you were.

He always carefully measured your foot and brought out two or three pairs from his floor-to-ceiling stock. If he said the shoe fit, you could count on it. We all liked Otto, and he gave us gentle credit in the Depression years. He never once turned Dad and Mother down when, in the cold, wet fall and approaching winter, we did not have enough money for all the needed footwear. Every one of those credit bills were paid off faithfully.

After business college, Otto asked me to come over after hours and set up a bookkeeping system for him, which I was happy to do. It was one evening while working at Otto's that a knock came to the storefront door. It was Charlie Ames, who came to ask me if I would go with him to the revival in the old skating rink the next night. I went and before the week was out, we both gave our hearts to Jesus. At least a dozen teens and young adults became Christians in that revival.

From the shoe store, you went through a large opening into the clothing store jammed with outfitting for the whole family. Undoubtedly, we had to ask for credit there also. I think all our credit went into one single charge pad. When Dad would inquire as to how we stood, it was always Mr. Jim Watson who brought out a thick Bert Nixon pad to show Dad the exact balance. They never charged any interest.

At eleven o'clock, the lights started blinking. Folks headed for their tethered horses in the livery barns. Mother always had a prearranged meeting place for us when it was time to head for home. What a wonderful evening it was for all: kids, teenagers, parents, grandparents.

We had mingled and talked with neighbors and friends for three or four hours. A little bit of everybody rubbed off on us. It was a two-and-a-half-mile ride home with Bess and Colonel at four miles per hour, but we had lots to talk about on the way. Ole Buster always came to meet us, wagging his tail. Our straw tick beds felt so good, and we were soon fast asleep.

I must tell you about our Pickford Oil Well. They drilled for black gold in Pickford at the turn of the century. I do not know whether F.H. Taylor had anything to do with it or not. He never mentioned it. Men came to town and sold stock, which would finance the first well. Sales were successful and drilling soon got underway. Interest was running high with spectators from morn to dusk. Week after week, they drilled: 100, 400, 800, 1000, 1400 feet! They hit it! Oil? No! Water? Yes! Thousands of gallons of crystal-clear water.

That oil well always thrilled me. Just to see that eight-inch steel pipe gushing forth night and day, year after year. It was scary too. *What if all that water down there in the earth should suddenly burst out? It could flood the whole town. And how would they get it stopped?* my mind always wondered. At that very location, the Pickford Fairgrounds was built and is now The Glenn Gough Memorial Park. Years later, I used to go back just to see the oil well as a reminder of the wonderful Pickford Fair days. The last time I went there, I could not find it. I wondered, *What in the world have they done with the oil well?* Bill and Verna Watson came to see us in Florida recently. Bill explained that the EPA made them plug it up because the water was corrosive. It cost them $300,000 to stop the flow, fill up the pipe. and kill the Ole Oil Well I loved so much. But who knows, there may still be oil down there another five thousand feet or so. Pickford might still become an oil town and be famous again like it was in the Pickford Fair days of my childhood.

CHAPTER SIX

Revivals & Bootleggers

THE TINY FOURTEEN BY TWENTY-FOOT wooden jail had been closed long before I walked past it for four years going to Pickford High School. The door was boarded up, but a high window with steel bars was visible. The Methodist and Presbyterian churches held such glorious old-time revivals. I think God "cleaned up" a high percentage of the people and the jail was put out of business.

I never heard of anyone ever shoplifting. Hamilton & Watson's had a line of large open cookie boxes in an aisle of barreled goods. We kids were never allowed to touch those cookies. Somehow it was known, accepted, and expected by all that certain persons could reach in for a cookie of their choice when they were passing through. Deputy Sheriff Nixon, our Uncle Ern, was one of those special persons, and maybe Judge William Batho or the ministers. We knew they had been given that privilege out of appreciation from the management. Uncle Ern cruised the town on Saturday nights ready to enforce the law.

Uncle Ern called me "Stubby." When I would run into him on Saturday nights, he often slipped me a nickel for candy or ice cream with a gentle lifter on the seat of my pants with the side of his big foot. I knew what it meant. He loved me and would lay down his life for me. Uncle Ern was always on foot moving about the town, chatting with people. He carried a billy club and a gun holstered under his coat. The only time I ever saw him get tough was at a street dance following the Pickford Fair one year. A drunk fellow showed up and got to smarting off with his mouth. Uncle Ern was soon on hand and moved right in on him, gave him a tap on the head with that billy club and some firm instructions—or else! The drunk was almost as big as Uncle Ern, but he sobered immediately and behaved himself. I never saw a fight on a Saturday night in Pickford. One time, Uncle Ern showed me his big pistol. I think he always carried an automatic rifle in his car.

"Ole Judge Batho" lived just across the street from Uncle Ern and Aunt Nellie. The judge held court in his own living room. Uncle Ern and Joe Hill hauled the villains in, and Judge Batho dealt out swift justice on the spot. Joe Hill was the game warden. There were no lawyers. We kids always thought Uncle Ern and Judge Batho were tough. They probably gave people what they had coming. Uncle Ern admired Judge Batho and often quoted him in our hearing. I figured he designed this for our ears to help keep us out of trouble. The judge sent the bad criminals up to the jail in the Soo. It seemed strange that a gentle giant like Joe Hill could be the game warden. He had a warm, friendly smile we all liked. Must be we were born good environmentalists and animal lovers at heart.

Uncle Ern used to tell this story with great delight. He had collared a drunk and brought him in before Judge Batho, who delivered the sobering sentence. "That will cost you ten dollars," the judge stated. The jollied-up, inebriate fellow laughed sarcastically as he reached for his pocketbook, replying, "Your Honor, I've got that ten-spot right here in my pocket!" Quick as a wink, Judge Batho shot back: "And thirty days in jail! Have you got that in your pocket?"

I cannot remember ever hearing of a murder in the whole township while I was growing up. Dad did tell us about a big racial fight in the Italian settlement over in Mackinac county. A man was killed in the fracas. One man had barely escaped death by hiding in the big water tank of an icing sleigh used to ice logging roads. Fifty years later, we met a lady selling butter churns in the Italian settlement area and asked her if she remembered that event. She replied, "Yes, that was my grandfather who was killed. He is buried in the Italian cemetery just up to the corner and down on Black Mike's Hill." We drove down to see the old cemetery once more. The famous hill had been cut down into a long grade.

We used to go down that naturally steep hill into the cedar swamps below to pick wild raspberries and huckleberries near an old lake where they had taken out timber. Our Model-T could not make it back up. The gas flow failed, and the motor quit just short of the top. We all had to pile out and walk back down that hill while Dad cautiously backed the car all the way to the bottom again. Now, the gravity-fed gas flowed to the engine okay and started right up with one turn of the crank. Dad steered the flivver around backward, then we all climbed aboard for traction. Up Black Mike's Hill we went in reverse gear with gravel and dirt flying, yet plenty of power to make it. The gas tank on that famous Model-T was just under the hood in front of the windshield. Handy and all of that, but on a sharp slant upward the gas could not get to the cylinders. Nevertheless, she was a great machine. We made it home by milking time, safe and sound—kids, raspberries, and all.

The prohibition years brought bootleggers from Chicago running whiskey from Canada across the St. Mary's River into the Upper Peninsula. Uncle Ern would deputize Jim Watson and Joe Hill. Wild chases occurred trying to shoot the tires out from under the bootleggers. The big, high-powered Essex was too fast for those bootleggers. They were badly handicapped firing their rifles out the half-windshield opening with a cloud of dust and dirt in their eyes as they hung out the side doors. Hard to aim while bouncing over rough gravel roads at high speed.

They once tangled with the John Dillinger gang. The Sault Ste. Marie *Evening News* reported that one of his gangsters, a guy named Hamilton, was a distant relative of someone at Joe Kelly's Corner five miles east of Pickford. The G-men closed in on a carload of them there, and a shooting battle took place, but the gangsters escaped. "Pretty Boy Floyd" was captured and jailed in the Soo. A day or two later, he broke out of jail and got away. But their days were numbered. Not long after that, J. Edgar Hoover's FBI men shot and killed John Dillinger as he came out of a theatre in Detroit. That was high drama. Uncle Ern, Judge Batho, and Joe Hill kept our whole territory wonderfully civilized.

CHAPTER SEVEN

Our Farm Home

IN THE FONDEST PATHS OF MY MEMORY, only one "old farm home" stands out: the cedar-shingled house with a fenced-in yard, a huge barn with horse and cattle stables, a chicken house, a milk house, a well house, and privy. It lay just a half-mile south of Frogpond School on the road toward the Sunshine community. I want to tell you about this "complete" farm.

My dad grew up on a farm west of Pickford. Uncle Ern, the eldest son, became the titular head of the family. He was a big fellow and had undoubtedly made good money in the lumber camps. He purchased two farms on our two-mile road east of Pickford. He sold my dad the first one: forty acres of cleared land near the Sunshine School.

Dad must have been dreaming about a bigger farm someday. He may have kept his two cows at their home place west of Pickford. He had a new horse and buggy to commute to the small farm he was buying from Uncle Ern—the Old Gady Place. Mother said he had bought pots and pans and a stove before they married.

Marie tells about an interesting event: "When we were very young and lived on the Old Gady Place, I don't know where Dad was; most likely out in the fields working. Mom decided she would go back in the woods and get the cows. It must have been Grandma Nixon that was at our place; she was getting supper ready and Forrest took the pepper shaker and sprinkled pepper all over the hot stove. There sure was a lot of coughing going on there. That Forrest probably got a good talking to! He was plumb full of mischief."

Dad and Mother moved up the road to the bigger farm when I was two or three years old. Dad and Uncle Ern must have simply adjusted the purchase deed. Both farms were Uncle Ern's. Now Dad was buying his dream farm, the fully cleared one with all the necessary farm buildings. Forrest, Marie, Clarence, and I were all born on the Old Gady Place. Our new, well-equipped farm became our old farm home.

This move made us part of another distinct community called Frogpond. Our weathered, cedar-shingled home stood in a seventy-five by one-hundred-foot yard with a woven wire fence separating it from the larger fenced-in barnyard area. Each had a road gate. The fields on the north, east, and south sides were rotated from pastures to grain fields, to hay fields and back to pastures again. Each field was woven-wire fenced. Nothing but homemade fertilizer was used. We had lots of it manufactured on site by our herd of cattle and horses.

The whole eighty acres was rich and level farmland, probably ancient lake bottom. The soil was a clay loam that consistently yielded bumper crops of hay and grain under Dad's skillful management. It produced two tons of clover hay per acre and equally good crops of winter wheat, sixty-day oats, barley, speltz, flax, and field peas. Our gardens produced potatoes, rutabagas, beets, and carrots. Our greatest limitation was the short growing season of sixty to seventy days. Corn could not mature, and tomatoes never ripened. The hayfields were loaded with wild strawberries, and the woods with raspberries. We still farmed forty acres on Uncle Ern's Old Gady Place nearby.

We thought of our fenced-in yard as a very special compound. It contained our home, the milk house, the clothes stand, the privy, a garden patch, a play area, a rhubarb bed, and a giant maple tree. "The Big Tree" was just off the porch on the south side toward the barnyard gate. The kitchen door was on the tree side, too, and was the main door to our house. In fact, the front door toward the road was more like a decoration; it was never used. Lilacs and balsam trees lined the path to the road gate. Wild strawberries grew in our lawn of clover.

We had no mower, but the clover was short. An unbelievably valuable hops bush grew just inside the swing gate.

The main entrance (or kitchen door) of our house opened out onto a five-foot-wide porch on the south side. Directly opposite the kitchen door, fifteen feet away, stood the little milk house where the hoop churn was set up for making butter and curds. Many an hour I logged on the hoop of that big churn. It was a remarkable piece of machinery, right up there with the cream separator and the force pump at the well in terms of muscle consumption. A closed wooden barrel was mounted between the uprights of a wooden frame with a fastened axle unit on each side of the barrel. The huge molded U-shaped wooden handle hooked onto a metal offset on the end of each axle. Thus, the operator could make that barrel whirl end over end at high speed. One end of the barrel had a removable lid.

Five to seven gallons of sour cream were poured in, then the lid screws tightened and a half hour or more of churning got underway. Once you got it rotating at top speed, it was not so bad, you just kept it whirling. Mother was always on hand to supervise. There was a glass peephole engineered into that barrel. Mother could look in to see how the butter was forming. Periodically during the process, you had to come to a halt and remove the plug from the bung hole to let the gas out. Otherwise, the staves might burst out, or the bung blow out at high speed spewing cream, butter, or whey on the operator, the floor, the walls, and the ceiling!

I think Mother could make about two one-gallon crocks of butter in one batch. Sometimes she spooned the butter into a wooden butter press that formed one-pound prints of butter with flower engraved tops. The Pickford ladies liked those custom-made prints. More importantly, they were a source of something very scarce in those days—cash. By the time you went through two or three churning cycles, you knew you had been somewhere. Your first batch might be fun, but the fun soon wore off. We kids got satisfaction knowing that we were helping.

When Mother peeped in and pronounced the butter ready, the bung was removed, the gas blew out, and the whey drained off into buckets for the pigs. After that, the end lid was unscrewed and the butter removed. I believe Mother made curds or poor man's cottage cheese by simply whirling the whey again. When two boys got into a scrap back then, someone would say they were going to "knock the whey out of each another."

The precious ten-gallon cans of cream were kept there in the milk house. Scrubbed milk pails and cream separator parts hung on the walls, ready for the next milking. Cows must be milked twice a day year-round, with no days off and no vacations. I often heard my dad talking to city folks about farm life and how the chores and milking routine became "a steady round of pleasure."

Thirty feet from the east end of the porch was the well gate to a field path that went another 150 feet to the pump house. Just before you got to the well gate, a short path branched southward to the two-seated privy backed up against the east fence. Up and down, unpainted boards covered the structure. It must have been built with green lumber that shrunk in place. The result was reliable ventilation in summer and winter. That unit was environmentally sound. Away from the house, it confined air pollution. It was energy efficient and effectively recycled the Montgomery Ward catalog.

The north side of our house was five feet from the woven-wire fence that kept the cattle and horses out. Our never-failing rhubarb bed was in one of the house yard corners. We kids used to break off stalks of rhubarb and stick them in the sugar bowl to dip and chew. Mother's rhubarb pie was the best.

Our old farmhouse seemed adequate for us. Every square inch was important. Twelve feet of the end toward the road was two-story and about eighteen feet wide. The downstairs of that was the front room, and upstairs was our family bedroom. The rest of the house to the east was single story, twenty-four feet long and fourteen feet wide, which contained the kitchen, the washroom, and pantry. The entire layout was not much, an eighteen-to-thirty-six-foot rectangle with 768 square feet of living space. It would not measure up today. Of course, we were way below the poverty level of today, but we were not poor. We were making it on our own with a plus mark!

The pump house was built over a two-inch well pipe driven down into the gravel and sand strata below until a vein of water was struck. A four-by-four-foot wooden curbing sixteen feet deep formed a cistern that usually stayed full of water up to within three feet of the trap door in the floor of the pump house. The stream of water from the iron pipe kept flowing night and day. A twenty-foot length of one-inch lead pipe was inserted down into the well pipe, and the iron force pump was attached to that pipe.

If you hung your ten-gallon milk pail on the spout, poured a quart of water into the top for initial priming, and pumped that iron handle up and down, cool water would come gushing out, almost a quart on every stroke. When you got your pails filled, you hung the end of the wooden trough back on the spout. It carried water to the stock tank on the outside. It took a lot of pumping every day to keep that thing full. Another must-be-done job, 365 days per year. All in all, quite a marvel with no engine, no gasoline, no electricity, and no water bills. Just pump that heavy iron handle. Bodybuilding exercise equipment with no monthly fee.

The kitchen door got all the wear and tear. It was a fine door, but it was very plain with no glass and no key. If you were coming in with a maximum armload of stove wood, you just yelled, "Open door!" There would be a quick response from within; the knob turned and the door was flung open. Have you heard the old poem about "barring the door with the wagon tongue"? Well, we did not use a wagon tongue, but we did always prop the back of a wooden chair under the knob and give it a wedging shove. Who needs a key? It had been missing for years.

The stairway up to the family bedroom was not really a stairway at all. The entire well space measured only thirty by sixty inches, and a twenty-inch landing at the bottom came off of that. We called it "The Ladder." The angle was about sixty degrees; you climbed up with the angle of the steep roof using both hands. The steps were narrow to make good handholds. The "old green bag" hung by its drawstring on a nail on the left as you went up. All important papers were kept in that safe deposit bag. It was faded with time. "No meddling with it, ever," we were told. Precious things were kept in the big steamer trunk in the opposite corner just as you got upstairs. Things like the large family Bible, Christmas decorations, and family keepsakes were kept in the trunk. It was treated with special care and not often opened. I remember it as an historic piece of furniture with a lace cover on the top.

The upstairs was a half story with three-foot sidewalls and twelve-by-eighteen feet in total size with a window in each end. On the ladder end a short rail defined the well. The end of the boys' double bed was right up against that rail and against the sidewall. There was a dividing curtain across the entire room at the middle point. Inside that curtain, our sisters' double bed was against the same east wall as ours. Mother and Dad's bed was across from theirs along the west wall, leaving a thirty-inch space between. We had tick mattresses that were frequently refilled with fresh oat straw or hay. It was fun getting up onto those ballooned mountains. Warm homemade quilts kept us cozy on the coldest winter nights, even if it got down to forty below zero or more. If the cold got the best of us, we simply laid on more quilts. Mother had plenty.

The stove pipe from the big heater downstairs came up through the bedroom floor in front of the window between our sisters' bed and Mother and Dad's. A protective stand-off metal plate went around the six-inch stove pipe. Fires in both the kitchen range and the heating stove below were *always* smothered down before we went to bed. All drafts were closed, and the stoves usually went completely out by morning. *Safety* was the word. Years later, we learned that the walls of that old house were filled with sawdust for insulation. What a tinderbox we lived in, with dried cedar shingles on the outside, wood lath and years of wallpaper on the inside, all stuffed with dry sawdust. Good thing we never had a fire because we never had fire insurance.

A dresser and chamber pot occupied the old trunk corner where the ladder came up. When Dougie was small and Forest was still home, we three boys shared that one bed. We always knelt beside our beds and said the Lord's Prayer individually and softly before climbing in. Dad and Mother did the same. Then the noise began with the boys laughing, talking, and pushing one another out of the bed. Our sisters would be gabbing, talking, and giggling in their division. All too soon, Dad would change the order of things with a gentle but firm command: "That's enough now, it's time we're all getting to sleep; tomorrow will come early." Soon we would all be fast asleep, but the time of chatter and rumpus was always enjoyable. I think Dad and Mother enjoyed it right along with us. A sleeping pill was something unknown to us.

CHAPTER EIGHT

Home on the Range

IT BRINGS ME GREAT PLEASURE to tell you about the glories of our old farm kitchen and the wonderful Renown range. Suppertime around our kitchen table with the old Renown "just a poppin' " is an intense focus of my childhood memories. Other warm memories of musical evenings in the front room around our fancy heater with the drafts open come to my mind. Singing along with the Victrola "Wreck of The Old 97," "The Lonesome Cowboy," or "Carry Me Back to Ole Virginny."

Like all good housewives, Mother was proud of her brand of cook stove. She most often referred to it as "The Range." I suppose because it could do so many things. The wide-top surface could easily handle six cooking pots going at once, heat tubs of water on washday, boil the white clothes in the big copper boiler, or heat hand irons for ironing and pressing. Round sections of the surface called lids could be removed with the lid-lifter tool to check the flame path from the fire box to the stove pipe. Both lids and a support section over the fire box on the left end could be lifted out for putting in more wood or to poke the fire.

In that big oven, Mother could make mouth-watering Boston baked beans with pork strips, brown sugar, and lots of molasses. It took two days to brown them just right. Eight loaves of golden, crusty homemade bread were made each Saturday. She could roast beef, pork, venison, a plump goose, or a twenty-five-pound turkey. That Renown oven turned out twelve-inch pies, Johnny cakes, layered cakes, oatmeal cookies, raspberry tarts, date-filled cookies, cinnamon rolls, and sugar cookies. Even years later, those cinnamon rolls and sugar cookies were a must for her children, grandchildren, and great-grandchildren whenever she came for a visit, clear up into her nineties.

From the Renown topside came creamed vegetables from the garden, fried meats, pancakes, corn fritters, homemade doughnuts, puddings, soups, or fresh shelled peas right out of our own field. Mother did a lot of canning to preserve the bounty of our garden, including the wild things we picked, like berries or pig weeds. I remember the wild plum jelly she made and even headcheese! The reservoir on that famous Renown produced hot water for wash basins in the washroom and for the galvanized washtub baths on Saturday night. The flames from the fire box on the other end somehow traveled around the oven to the hot water reservoir on their way to the stove pipe. An amazing invention!

Also, that old stove had a warming oven two feet above the cooking surface. The stove pipe's hot draft went right up there to keep food cozy warm. It was a good clothes dryer, too, for such things as wet gloves, caps, touks, and tams. That warming oven also kept the old yeast "witch" fermenting for bread making. Of course, Mother always made her own bread. Dad always claimed that the store-bought stuff had a bitter taste. After the Grist Mill in Pickford burned down, we bought our flour in hundred-pound patterned bags. Maid of Minneapolis and Pillsbury's Best were Mother's top brands. She and my sisters made many a dress from that material. It was of good quality. Those Duluth millers were thoughtful of the people in those hard times.

Having the hops bush out by the front gate came in handy for making bread. Mother used those hops to brew a yeasty starter solution for leavening her homemade bread. Potato water and hops were combined in a half-gallon sealer and placed in the warming oven. A sealer was a greenish glass canning jar. In a few days, it was frothy, fermented, and ready to make the dough rise. We called it the "Old

Witch." A portion was mixed into each batch of dough and placed in a big twenty-two-inch dish pan. A wary eye must be kept on that bread pan lest the dough mushroom clear over the rim. At that crucial point, Mother used both fists to punch it back down near its original size and let the rising start all over again. When the rising dough once again was about to overflow, she emptied it out on the baking board, punched it down again, and separated it into eight or ten loaf-size pans. The loaf pans were set on the warming oven to rise again. When they rose once again to individual mountains, into the oven of the old Renown they went. We kids were cautioned, "Now, no rough play or jumping around here. The bread's in the oven, so keep quiet or you'll make it fall." Mother had carefully loaded the fire box and set the drafts just so. Her oven was hot and ready for the job at hand.

Before long, from every seam and crack of that ole wood stove oven oozed the most delicious aroma you could imagine. Yum! Yum! I can smell it now. Eight loaves of the puffiest golden bread you ever set your eyes on. They were perfectly crusty, tasty, and beautiful. "You must never eat hot bread until it cools down!" That was a standing medical warning from both Mother and Dad with no exceptions. Dad had once eaten hot bread right out of the oven and swollen up with acute indigestion until they thought he was going to die. There was no 911. We were all thoroughly convinced and obeyed. Could it be the Old Witch still a workin'?

Mother's pantry bin held a 100-pound sack of flour. Next Saturday, eight more loaves came out with a good chance for cinnamon rolls and pies too. When the witch jar was used down on Saturday, she filled it up again with potato water and put it back up in the warming oven. Next bread-making time, a week later, the sealer would be back to full power again. There are two things you must always remember. One, never use it all up; two, always keep it from freezing. If you let the Old Witch die, you are out of business. In wintertime, there are no hops to harvest, so you cannot make more. The only thing you can do is borrow a starter batch from a neighbor across the fields and hope Jack Frost did not get their yeast witch too.

Our beloved Range did indeed have a wide range of usefulness. Mother, Marie, and Vivian heated their curling and crimping irons on the Renown to create stylish hairdos. Sometimes on a thawing day in the winter, when the draft controls on the Renown were nearly closed, we kids would dare one another to run across the stove top barefooted. It was quite a trick. You hardly felt it. Mother was probably knitting or quilting in the front room. Dad may have been taking a snooze.

It took a lot of skill to get the most out of that wood range, for it had to keep us comfortably warm while doing all the other tasks. The large wood box was at an arm's reach from the stove, backed up against the nearby wall. It held at least four big armfuls of wood and had to be heaped up full at night so there would be wood for the front room heater too. Come rain, snow, blizzard, or forty below zero, the ole wood box must be kept full. We boys or Dad had to carry it in from the wood piles in the barnyard a hundred feet from our back door. It took about fifty cords of wood a year to cook our food and keep us warm. A cord is a pile of wood four feet high and eight feet long. Dad thoroughly taught us boys how to handle a sharp axe so that we never once cut our feet while splitting small stove-sized pieces of wood. Come to think of it, that was quite a safety record.

Mother was an expert at controlling temperatures on that Renown. Draft shutters measured the oxygen supply, and the selection of wood made a big difference. A crank could be inserted to shake the grates and make the ashes fall into a carry-out container below the fire box. That had to be emptied most every day onto the garden patch inside the house yard. We had to find Tamarack from the woodpile when Mother needed a super-hot oven for baking cookies. I am quite sure there was a heat gage built into the oven door. Drafts were lowered for slow-baked Boston beans. It took maximum draft for big meals, washdays, Saturday bread baking, and baths. A quilt was hung over the double opening to the front room on extreme below-zero days. Whatever the situation, we always had a warm, cozy kitchen.

If the stove got sluggish and began underperforming, Mother would attack it with fury. Perhaps the air outside was a dead calm, resulting in a poor draft. Maybe the ashes were blocking the draft intakes. The ash container could be backed up, causing the problem. Off came the lids directly over the firebox. She gave the fire a mighty stirring with the iron poker. Then she would put in place the exterior crank and give the grates an awful shaking. I feared she would shake every live coal out with the ashes, but she knew exactly what she was doing. In went some choice pieces of wood, back went the lids, and soon that fire started cracklin' and poppin'. It took off like a scared rabbit. That "Now we'll get something done around here" was written all over her face. I was amused and snickered watching her. We kids liked to tease Mother. She liked it too.

Our house was kept snugly warm in the winter with the kitchen range going at nearly full power and the big, fancy heater in the front room dampened down to medium low. Much of our stove wood was fast-burning poplar. We cut some birch, maple, and tamarack, but not much. Mother liked to operate on a full wood box. If it got cool in the kitchen, the oven door would be opened for immediate comfort. When Uncle Dewey Nixon came to see us, the wood box was his favorite perch. The box top angled up toward the back with a flat board across the very top. Uncle Dewey sat with his feet on the lower front edge. It was a satisfying roost for our favorite uncle when good stuff would be cooking on the range. If Mother happened to be baking oatmeal cookies, the old Renown would roast him off the wood box. We were always in a high state of joy when Uncle Dewey came.

Mother stuck by her faithful Renown cookstove. A traveling salesman came through and tried to sell her a Home Comfort model. He took a lid off his stove and beat it with a pole axe to prove that it was wrought iron and would not break. No sale. Who pounds a stove lid with a pole axe anyway? Mother knew her range and was not about to part with it. Once a week, our Renown was cleaned from top to bottom, and the whole cooking surface polished with stove black. That was good stuff that would even cover up scuff marks on your best shoes if the Shinola can was empty.

Grooved wainscoting went around our kitchen walls, about three feet up. Every spring they got a new coat of pea green paint. For years, the three-inch pine wood flooring was scrubbed weekly with water and yellow soap laced with lye. The floor came out bleached and smelling clean, long before we ever heard of Clorox. That is the way Grandma Portice did it down on her hands and knees. Any germs in the cracks between those boards took a beating. Thoroughness was Mother's motto. When my sisters got older, they helped.

I used to tell folks about Marie swinging a floor mop at me, but that was after we had graduated up to Congoleum on the kitchen floor. Marie claimed that Mother never had a mop. "That floor was always scrubbed by hand on your knees with a floor cloth," she said. Maybe it was the wet floor cloth she swung at me. Maybe Mother bought the floor mop when we put down the fancy Congoleum but never liked to use it. We all remember that landmark day. Dad must have gotten a good price for his hay at Rudyard that year.

Both the washroom and pantry were small rooms off the kitchen that formed the east end of our house. Mother's baking board faced the porch side with her flour bin on the east wall. On the pantry side of the partition wall, floor-to-ceiling shelves were filled with many different things like canned wild berries, pickles, and venison.

The washroom on the other side was small. A counter across the north wall side contained a water pail, wash basin, towel rack, and a cistern pump to draw water in from the well. That pump worked great in the summer; but in winter, it was frozen up most of the time. Then we had to carry water in all the way from the pump house out in the field. The water pail would be frozen over when we got up in the morning. Hats, caps, and coats hung nearby on that side of the partition wall. There was one more important item in the washroom. The old .38-55 deer rifle hung up there on the wall high above the washstand. It was never to be touched by any of us kids, and it never was. Only Dad took that rifle down for deer hunting season in November, or for some very needed purpose. Dad's brothers were all hunters. Any gun loaded or unloaded was considered *loaded*. That was an instilled discipline in hunting season or out of hunting season. That old .38-55 brought home a lot of venison, but it was untouchable up on that wall.

The clothes stand was about thirty feet south of the porch at its privy end, far enough away to clear the branches of the big maple tree. It was made by three twelve-foot cedar poles sunk in the ground to support an elevated platform. Two poles for the clothes lines were at the steps end, four feet apart. The platform tapered back to a single cedar pole at the other end. The steps went up about five feet off the ground to clear the snow. Clothes lines were anchored to a short cross bar on the single pole end and strung back to the two poles at the steps. Mother climbed up there to pin out her winter washing. The sheets, dresses, and long-handles hung clear of the snowbanks below. It worked great unless a subzero front moved in during the night. Many times, the cold spell persisted. Long-handles had to come down and be stood up in the corners of the front room to thaw. Inside, clothes drying racks were set up. Lower summertime clothes lines were over by the rhubarb bed.

That clothes stand put quite a scare into me one time. It was a great place to play. One day when I was about five years old, I decided to take a shortcut through a narrow space between the boards at the pointed end of that platform. *Nothing to it. I can slip down through there easy*, I thought. I got through alright, all but my head! Somehow my chin got caught, and there I hung. No way could I get back up, so I dangled in midair, screaming. Marie, Forrest, or Mother heard me and rushed to my rescue just in the nick of time. I am sure I did not forget to say The Lord's Prayer that night, and I am sure I was in my dad and mother's prayers too. I expect I added some to The Lord's Prayer. On the farm, we had our share of near misses. By the mercy of God, we all survived. For example, there was the time the runaway team and hay wagon ran clear over my dad. We thought for sure he was killed, but he did not have a scratch. Or the time old Colonel kicked Forrest in the chest and knocked the wind out of him for a few minutes. One summer night in a thunderstorm, Mother had gotten us all out of bed and on the floor downstairs for safety. Forrest fell asleep too close to the iron heater. A lightning bolt struck nearby that stunned him, but he soon recovered. It was a close call. Then there was the day Vivian and I got buried in the huge new straw stack and might have suffocated.

The famous old maple tree was our playhouse and stood right in the middle of our house yard between the porch, the milk house, and the clothes stand. We made all kinds of contraptions in that tree. It was our recreation center, bird capital, and umbrella of shade. Well suited for climbing adventures, water fights, swings, games, and daring. Many a happy hour we spent under and up in that old tree. When company came, all of us kids had a riot up there.

The path to the barn jogged around the milk house before it straightened out going south through the henhouse gate. East of that stretch of path was another good play area. West of it was garden space. The whole house yard would be a fenced-in rectangle, approximately seventy-five by one-hundred feet. We always kept the mailbox gate, well gate, and barnyard gates shut in our "compound." We took pride in that house yard. It helped us feel secure from any stock that might get loose, day or night. It protected our garden from invasion by the cattle. Only our dog and cat had free passage. It was important to keep all gate fasteners in good shape. There was something more about it that I cannot explain. Something felt special about this place. It was our place, our very own.

Our old farm home included a much bigger fenced-in barnyard surrounding the huge forty by one-hundred-foot barn. Two manure piles were outside the barn near the horse stable door and the cow stable door. There was room for a giant straw stack on the south side of the barn. There was also space for an overflow haystack on the north side just outside the double roller doors to the threshing floor. The team of horses and a two-ton load of hay could go in that side and drive out the double doorway on the other side. The single horse working the "hay rope" had to have room to pull out eighty feet or so from the threshing floor for each lift of hay or grain. Our barnyard had a wagon road leading out from the barn to a big gate at the road.

Other barnyard fixtures were the hen house, a small brooder house for spring chickens, and the old stable building. There were woodpiles out there and a log pile. The barnyard included a second fenced-in garden for us besides the one in the house yard. Still more room was needed at the water trough for the herd coming around milking time. Gates were necessary for cattle control. They loved to invade our grain fields or gardens at night. "The Lane" was a ten-foot-wide fenced path that conducted the cows to their proper pasture field. All the back-field crops were hauled down that lane with plenty of turning room for loads of hay coming out of the lane gate and into the barn. The Big Ditch ran through the middle of our farm. It was great for watering cattle, but it took a strong wooden bridge to carry our loads of hay and grain across it.

It is unbelievable the hours of hard work it took to operate our farm year-round. But we all loved it and cherish our heritage. After all these years of pastoral ministry in large cities, the farmer is still in my heart. Parishioners have often expressed how much they delighted in my wealth of first-person illustrations from growing up on the farm. One is so close to reality, to God, and the breadth of His creation on the farm.

CHAPTER NINE

Frogpond Schoolhouse

ON MY VERY FIRST DAY OF SCHOOL, I walked a half mile north on our mud and gravel road to Frogpond School accompanied by my older brother and sister, Forrest and Marie. The moment we reached "Frogpond Corner" on the Townline Road, this little red schoolhouse became a fixed milestone in my mind, the wheel hub of my young world.

Farms stood shoulder to shoulder in this area of Pickford, and most of them were eighty acres each. In settled places such as this, a schoolhouse was built on every two-mile corner. By 1915, three years before I was born, John Shobrook donated a small portion of his farm for our school. The schoolyard measured about 150 feet by 150 feet with a woven wire fence around it to keep out the cattle. John Shobrook's farm was typical with a wood frame house, huge barn, outhouse, well house, and hen house. The entire summer's crop of hay and grain had to be stored up in the barn lofts because of the severe winters. The heavy weight of this harvest created cozy, warm stables for the cattle and horses underneath.

Our farm was perfectly visible from Frogpond School. Each corner schoolhouse was the center of its own community. Pride and loyalty were strong. When the school locations were laid out, ours had been given the fancy name of Pleasant Park School. However, we called our seat of learning the Frogpond School for good reasons. A mucky swamp area east of our school was drained by a large ditch running south right through the middle of our farm into a creek in the Armstrong forest. Parks should have trees, but there was not a solitary tree on our school grounds. We had frogs! That peat-like swamp was the frog capital of the whole Upper Peninsula of Michigan. This ecosystem automatically spawned them by the millions. It could have been thousands, but they croaked like millions.

When the spring thaw set in, the melting snow soon became a general flood. All the ditches overflowed, making the fields turn into lakes. Toward evening, the frogs began to sing. They were crawling out of the mud that had preserved them through the long-frozen winter. When a solitary frog croaks, it's not profoundly noticeable. But when a million more join the choir, it becomes a vast concert in stereo sound. The "break-up" had come! At sundown, the concert began softly but soon grew into a powerful, grand chorus filling every nook and cranny of the night. The sound was overwhelming, yet beautiful. When the frog chorus "sang," sleep always overtook me. I never did hear a finale. I have lived many other places, but never heard anything like it again. The frogs celebrated with us the exciting arrival of springtime in Frogpond community.

Each homesteader cleared his own land. There were no swamp hogs or bulldozers, only horse and human power. A few shade trees were saved around each farmhouse. Many forty-acre blocks of private "bush" were reserved for stove wood and the harvest of renewable timber. It was nice to have a sheltered pasture for the cattle in summertime and a natural home for wildlife in your own bush. Beyond a one-mile view of the naked eye, varying shapes and shadows of green were showcased. Mostly untouched wilderness surrounded Pickford. In these forests lived deer, coyote, bear, fox, porcupine, partridge, pheasant, beaver, and other fur-bearing animals in abundant supply. On summer evenings, we watched the white-tailed deer come out for pasture at the back of our farm. They tarried till dusk and departed with long, graceful leaps over the fences back into the woods again.

They made it look so easy, as if they had springs on their feet. Often, we heard the drumming of a partridge on a distant log or the howling of coyotes in the night.

Townline Road was our superhighway, graveled, graded, and maintained by Chippewa County. In winter, the snowplows kept it open—most of the time. Traveling east from Pickford at the grist mill, Townline Road went down a steep hill over the old rattling Maltas bridge before it pitched up again to the level plane. Forrest loved to take that dip in our Model-T at top speed, scaring the daylights out of everyone on board! *Rattle. Bang. Clatter.* Frogpond School was two miles from town on that road, the little Sand Hill Church four miles, and "Kelly's Corner" five miles. There, the gravel road took a sharp, banked turn to the right to Fairview School, Fairview Cemetery, the Maltas log church, and the open gravel pit close to where Francis Nalley grew up.

At Kelly's Corner, the Townline Road died. If you kept going, you went straight down a steep hill into the Gogomain swamp. In our imaginations, this swamp was an unknown world of lumber camps and endless forest. It was often impassable when the winter frost had melted. Tree trunks were laid across boggy places, but you could easily get mired. In summer, it was called a corduroy road. It was just a logging trail. But oh, there were scrumptious wild raspberry patches and cranberry marshes down in there. So, if we went berry picking, it was *down* Kelly's Hill, but if we were going to Fairview, it was *around* Kelly's Corner.

I was slightly under six years of age on that first day of school. The wood-sided little red schoolhouse was standard size. I went in and out its door many a time in my happy childhood. It was a twenty-four by forty-foot rectangle with a ten-foot ceiling. The steep roof angle accommodated heavy snows at our forty-sixth latitude.

There were three double-hung windows on each side and a paneled, three-foot wooden entrance door facing the road. That was the only exit. Risky? Perhaps, but the only time we had a crowd was at the annual Christmas program. There were two steps up to the door. The designers must have had the spring floods in mind. A twelve-by-twelve-foot woodshed attached to the schoolhouse also sheltered the door. This was an important addition. *First*, it was a welcome relief upon arrival in rain, wind, or blizzard. You could shake the snow or water from your coat and cap as well as remove heavy footwear before stepping up into the schoolroom. *Second*, at least a week's supply of dry stove wood was kept there for ready access, no matter what the weather. The teacher would have good, dry wood and kindling close at hand to start the stove fire upon arrival each morning. A large woodshed outside the north end of the school was filled up with a year's supply. The *third* usage was of a more long-standing benefit, for it had to do with character-building. If a student became incorrigibly mean, disobedient, or stubborn, a trip to the woodshed was the court of ultimate repair. This was hardly ever used. In fact, I can only remember one time.

I can still hear Billy Shobrook bellowing when our good teacher gave him a touch-up with a branch from the Christmas tree. Billy was a junior-high boy, big for his age. We were practicing for our famous annual Christmas program. Billy kept acting smart and just kept it up. Since Mr. Haywood boarded at the Shobrook home, Billy thought he had an inside track. Alas, the patience of our longsuffering teacher gave out. He called time, took up a trimmed-off lower branch from the Christmas tree, and marched the surprised, "clever" boy to justice. Down the steps into the woodhouse they went; first Billy, then Mr. Haywood—and the door was shut. "Poor Billy," as his mother used to call him, began wailing and bawling out, "You treat me like a beast." *Wham! Wham*, went the Christmas branch. We could hear every stroke clearly. All thirty of us on the inside were rooting for Mr. Haywood. "Lay it on him!" we cried out. Billy had enjoyed using his size and position against many of us. Now his world was turned upside down. Our good teacher was giving him a new outlook on life.

No serious damage was done. Billy was not abused. Mostly Billy's pride was hurt. His self-esteem was intact. All in all, we judged it to be good for him and well-deserved. He may have gotten a second touch-up from his daddy that night. I do not know. Mrs. Shobrook was indeed a dear lady. She was always kind to all of us; we loved her very much. I am sure William Shobrook Jr. grew up to be a better man because of the healthy instruction our teacher gave him that day. We all admired Mr. Forrest Haywood. He was always good to us, even-handed and fair with all. He loved every one of us, including Billy. The Christmas program, by the way, was a smashing success.

On a frosty morning, when you walked through the shed and opened the school door, you were met by the warmth of the big iron woodstove. It had a three-foot metal skirting around three sides. The metal did not go all the way to the wood floor so that a circulating current of air was set up, just a convectional heating system! The black stove pipe went straight up to an elbow and then along the full length of the schoolhouse to an exterior chimney. The radiating expanse of stovepipe was suspended from the ceiling by bailing wire. Nothing fancy, but super performing. We were kept cozy warm even in below-zero weather.

There was a center aisle with two rows of double desks on each side and a narrow side aisle by the windows. Each desk had two ink wells. On the west wall from the last window to the northwest corner, a tall bookcase ran from floor to ceiling. The teacher's desk sat on an angle in that corner, and the blackboard extended from her desk area across the north wall to the "dunce's corner" on the northeast. Nobody wanted to be sentenced to stand there, not ever.

The ten-foot "recitation bench" would seat most any one of our eight grades of classes. It faced the blackboard. Here was the genius of the country schoolhouse: expression, accountability, and opportunity. Many enjoyable events took place there: questions, answers, spelling bees, speeches, songs, and blackboard work.

I must tell you about an unforgettable blackboard incident. One year we had a little teacher from a big city "down below." Down below referred to any place below the Upper Peninsula. The Straits of Mackinac separated us from Lower Michigan. There was no Big Mac bridge to connect us in those days. Miss Gazway was a genuinely nice teacher, but she was not up to handling this one-room school. Those big boys once tied her to a post in the school yard during noon-hour playtime. They thought it was great sport. The rest of us could not see anything funny about it, even though it was only for a minute or two. There was no principle to come to her aid.

One day our little teacher sure did shine with this example of masterly discipline at work in the one-room country school. Big Russell Shobrook, Mervin O'Brien, and probably Harvey Pennington were at the blackboard doing arithmetic. Miss Gazway looked so tiny next to those full-grown boys. Big Russell was Poor Billy's big brother, and Miss Gazway boarded at their house. Well, Big Russell was putting on quite a show. All study had come to a halt. The air was tense. He had gained the attention of all and was enjoying the limelight. Petite Miss Gazway proved equal to the situation. She quietly took a big dictionary from her desk and with the greatest of ease moved over behind the backs of the big lunkers at the board. Russell did not see her approach behind him or see her draw back for a haymaker swing. We all stopped breathing. Big Russell towered a foot above her and was really putting on his act when *Wham!* She connected with that heavy Webster right up beside his head! She really poleaxed him! It was a great show, an unabridged success! Poor Russell slunk back to his desk about two feet tall. Miss Gazway won an Olympic Gold Medal right then and there. The giant was shattered before the whole school. The fourth grade reading class was immediately called to the bench. Order was restored and study renewed at every desk. I could not help wondering once again about what might happen at the Shobrook supper table that night. We kids could not wait to get home to give Mother and Dad a full report. It sure made good conversation around our supper table that night. Miss Gazway got one-hundred percent support.

It is still a miracle to me how we learned so much in that little red schoolhouse. The genius must have been that "recitation bench" and the blackboard work. Our place to learn self-expression, challenge, and responsibility. For each subject you were studying, you had to go up to that bench with your class right on schedule for about ten to fifteen minutes. If it was reading, you had to read aloud; if spelling, you had to spell aloud; if history, you had to answer questions aloud. The same with geography. If it was writing or arithmetic, you went to the blackboard to write, add, subtract, or divide. Whatever was called for, you had to demonstrate under the teacher's watchful eye. If you faltered, our good teacher came right to your aid and explained. It was an excellent learning discipline for all involved and a powerful stimulant to study hard throughout the day while the other classes were up to bat. You might say it was "marketplace" learning. It gave us an excited desire to perform up to standard. Sort of like energetic athletics outdoors with our teacher as our respected coach.

Degrading? No, no, no! It was challenging. Positively building up self-confidence. Shortfalls were immediately discovered, and remedial action got underway. Our parents could bet the farm on our graduating from the eighth grade with the ability to read, write, add, subtract, multiply, and divide, plus have a lot in our heads about world geography and world history. Our minds were expanding. The James Cuzzen circulating library packet came in every month or so. It was packed with select literature. What a brilliant gift to rural youth! Most of us became hungry readers, eagerly devouring the contents and looking forward to the next arrival.

Eight grades in one room? And one teacher? Yes, and we country kids did just fine when we hit the consolidated high school classrooms. Charlie Ames, Art Stewart, and I kept going to school even though we had to walk two and a half miles each way to high school. I had no trouble taking the upper grades in stride and graduated valedictorian of my Pickford High School class of 1936.

Spelling was another required subject and developed into exciting spelling bees. We studied hard and got pretty good. Toward the close of the school year, we would have a match every day. The recitation bench could not hold all the contestants. Age groups would form a line up front facing the teacher's desk. The teacher called out the words coming right down the line. If you misspelled, you stepped out and went to the tail end. When you misspelled three times, you took your seat. The line shrunk. When you got to the head of the line, the challenge was to hang on! The last one standing was the winner.

I remember receiving spelling-bee gifts at the picnics held at the end of the school year on Sandy Hill Church grounds two miles east on Townline Road. One year I got a box of chocolates; another year I got a fancy automatic pencil with a magazine of refill leads. Gold medals! One year I got to enter the Pickford Township Spelling Bee Tournament, where I held out until there were just two of us standing. Quite a battle; you could taste victory before that great gathering. Unfortunately, I misspelled, and it was all over. However, it was a particularly good experience.

Violet McConkey Smith told me that her father was a leader in Sandy Hill Church, and that a Mrs. Ben Dorsey played the organ. They were Methodists. We used to pick wild huckleberries in the woods behind the church in the summertime. Years later, when I was grown and the church was closed, two traveling lady evangelists came through our part of the country and opened it up for a two-week revival. My Aunt Mary Hanna and members of her family were saved under the ministry of those ladies, I believe. The lady evangelists were dubbed the "Black Socks" because they wore black stockings. They were genuine Christian witnesses and won souls into the Kingdom of God. Lives were changed; they were wonderful people.

Each day we had a one-hour noon break and a fifteen-minute recess in midmorning and midafternoon. Those were outstanding moments in every school day. We all finished our lunches in a hurry so we could get out to play. Only a rainstorm or a blizzard could keep us inside. Softball was a favorite game, and the girls got into that with us. We chose captains. They tossed for the first choice, then made alternating choices for their team. A couple of old bats had been scrounged up. We often had to make our own sewed-up soft balls or fashion a substitute. The spirited game was on.

We boys used to go to school early in the morning so we could have a few innings before the bell rang. Those were considerably more competitive—no girls allowed. Our teacher seldom participated but kept a general oversight to see that there was fair play. Everyone was involved in something even if two people were just gabbing and talking. The big bell was up on the roof with a one-inch rope coming down through the ceiling. When that bell rang, we had only five minutes to get our coats off and be back at our desks. Often the teacher was busy with schoolwork inside. If anything went wrong outside or anyone got really contrary, someone would raise the warning: "I'm going to tell teacher." That usually settled things down.

In the winter, we chose sides for country school hockey. We had no ice rink; frozen ground and snowbanks were our playing field. Not a single hockey stick existed. We designed them from young tree trunks with root angles or from crooked tree branches. The school's iron stove poker also made a good hockey club, and often saw action. The puck was usually a battered tomato can. It was a strange assembly of "make-do" with our own "shinny on your own side" rules. That warning was real and well heeded. Each team had to play on its appointed side of the scrimmage. If the competition got over on your side, you yelled, "Shinny on your own side!" If he failed to take the warning, it was "legal" to whack him on the shins. That steel poker was the worst. Of course, we all wore heavy high-top leather boots with two pair of wool socks on the inside. We never whacked that hard, just hard enough to convince.

Seldom did weather ever stop our games. Hockey went forward even when there were snowbanks. We just scratched and pawed, battling for possession of that puck until it was found and driven toward the goal. The battle raged back and forth. Heavy jackets had to come off. A new-fallen snow would be tramped level before the day was over. We all had rosy cheeks and hot steam spewing from our lungs. That was great sport, and we always got along okay. I cannot remember any fights. Below-zero weather was great for hockey.

Winter games were especially creative. We just had to get out of that roasting schoolhouse, both boys and girls. The girls loved to make snowmen and engage in snowball fights with the boys. They would pull their chooks (stocking caps) down over their faces to keep the boys from washing their faces with snow. They liked it as long as we did not get too rough. Those girls could hand it out, too, and heave a snowball right on target. Caves were dug into the sides of mammoth snowbanks using apple box sleds with low runners to do the mining.

Huge opposing snow forts were built for the wars being fought between enemy forces. War games called for volunteers for each side. Some royal battles were fought. It was wise to keep your mouth shut at all times. Snowballs were coming at you from every angle. It was hard to tell who your enemy was sometimes and hard to keep from hollering in the fight. More than once, I got a high-speed snowball right in my mouth. My jaws locked open, and it took my breath away. Until I got it out, I was pretty much choking. Those were rugged wars. When the bell rang, we had five minutes to get into the woodshed, shake off the snow, shed coats and galoshes, and get back to our desks on time.

Of all the games and outdoor activities we had at Frogpond School, the greatest was wrestling with Mr. Forrest Haywood. He was the only male teacher the school ever had. He became our hero. I was a junior boy when he first came. He would always come out and wrestle during the noon hour. He would take on two of the big eighth grade boys and two of us younger kids in a wrestling match. We two young fellows would go for his legs while the big lads would attack from above. Charlie Ames and I were often in the foursome. We would each grab a leg and hang on like wildcats trying to bind them together to get him off balance. Sooner or later, all four of us would come tumbling down in a rolling heap, trying to pin our teacher to the ground. I doubt if we ever succeeded, even though we had two giant boys above us who were big and strong. Mr. Haywood was tall, lean, and wiry; he was tough. He would break loose despite all we could do and wind up back on his feet again, laughing at us. He was such a good-natured man. If one of us small boys got to hurting in the mangled heap and hollered, he would loosen his hold. That did not happen often; we relished the fray.

We all loved Mr. Haywood. This was his first teaching job. He was the twenty-one-year-old son of a Free Methodist preacher. His mom and dad must have been good and wise parents, for he taught us in such a good way. For example, he threw out a challenge to our school: if we got all our required recitation bench and blackboard assignments completed satisfactorily and on time, we would have a "sing time" on the last hour of the school week. His flock rose to the bait. At three o'clock on Friday afternoon, we had our first of many, many sing times at Frogpond School.

A Farm Boy's Memoirs

We had the old *Golden Book of Favorite Songs*, and he taught us nearly every song in the book. We had no piano or guitar, but he taught us anyway. After a few sessions, he would call a student up to lead the singing. I am not aware of anyone declining or being particularly nervous. We just did it for Mr. Haywood; it was something we enjoyed. There were a few hymns in that school song book, and we seemed to gravitate toward them. One I shall never forget was "Jesus, Lover of My Soul." That one really got hold of me; I thought upon the words and often sang them to myself. Other favorites were "Old Black Joe," "Auld Lang Syne," "Columbia the Gem of the Ocean," "Comin' Thro' the Rye," "Long, Long Ago," "My Old Kentucky Home," "Loch Lomond," "Down by the Old Mill Stream," "Darling Nellie Gray" and "Old Uncle Ned"—"He had no wool on de top ob his head. De place whar de wool ought to grow." I still hum and sing portions of the old Frogpond School songs; they are very pleasant recollections. Often, it is only a single line I remember. If I keep at it, more of the song will come to mind.

Miss Mary Allen was my first teacher at Frogpond School. I think it was normal for all school families to have a close and admiring relationship with the schoolteacher. We kids thought of them as special people in our lives and addressed each of them as Teacher with a capital T. Good manners and respect were genuinely reflected in the way we addressed them. We were also taught to respect our elders by calling them Mr. or Mrs. Twice each year, we would have our teacher come to our house for supper. Those were grand occasions.

The names of Mary Allen, Agnes Morrison, Olive Rye, Miss Gazway, Forrest Haywood, and Irene Hughes all stand out in the memories of our family. Miss Gazway was a nice young lady. She was from far away Indiana, and I recall how she used to say "buckets" instead of milk pails. We were sorry she left after only one year. She was a good teacher but could not manage those big, overgrown country boys. Irene Hughes was our teacher in my seventh and eighth grades. She won an honored place in all our lives. She was a teacher par excellence with abilities far beyond the challenge of our country school. Miss Hughes handled our eighth grade year with the greatest of ease, bringing out the finest effort from every student. If ever there is created a Hall of Fame for the One-Room Country School Teachers of America, the names of Forrest Haywood and Irene Hughes will be at the top.

We did have one teacher whose one-year contract was not renewed for good reason. Among other shortcomings, she showed blatant partiality for some and developed outright dislike for those who questioned her actions. My older brother Forrest and two other classmates became special targets. Increasingly mean after-school punishments were dealt out. Those big boys were probably not entirely innocent, but it soon got out of hand. At four o'clock their names would be called out to stay after school for punishment.

Forrest was commanded to lay his hand flat on a desktop, palms down. She brought a heavy, eighteen-inch wooden ruler with an embedded metal edge on one side down on the back of those hands. Sometimes he would jerk his hand away, making her come down on her own knuckles. She lost control completely and kept pounding away on his hand, demanding that he say, "Enough." My brother had red hair and was approaching manhood. He refused to be humiliated one step further, so he must have jumped up and ran. When Forrest showed Dad and Mother the ugly black and blue lump on the back of his hand, that was it. Until this point, our parents had always been one hundred percent supportive of the teacher's point of view with assurances that we might get another paddling when we got home. In the morning, my dad went to the schoolhouse. He never told us what he said to the teacher or what happened. We just knew there were no more punishments afterward; she did not get her job back the next fall.

This incident may have happened when I was in third grade; I am not sure. Anyway, a strange thing happened soon after. The following year, Frogpond School was closed for a one-year experiment to consider the consolidation of schools. We were transported each day into special classrooms in the Pickford High School building. Mr. Art Ames was hired by the school system to haul us to Pickford and back each day. During winter, he created a homemade closed-in "cab" for us, built on heavy double sleighs drawn by his draft horses. It was an odd-looking outfit, but practical.

Mr. Art loved us and was always cheerful. He provided a big supply of blankets for us and possibly a charcoal heater. We were always cozy. He would sometimes make shortcut trails across open fields to get us closer to our homes. He always talked real loud like we were hard of hearing. He and his wife Martha had big voices. They always sang "Star of the East" at our Christmas programs. "Art and Mart," we called them.

I was disappointed to discover that I had not been passed into the fourth grade when I got to the new consolidated classroom. I did have a dear and thoughtful teacher in my new large third grade class in a big room. Within a week or two, she came to my desk and asked, "Clifton, why were you not passed into the fourth grade? Your work shows me that you belong in fourth grade." "I really don't know," I replied. "I had no trouble with my work, except for a problem at the blackboard once with division arithmetic. It was never made clear to me."

She said, "After you've eaten your lunch at the noon hour, I want you to come to my desk." She was so kind and serious about it; I was eager to respond. Within a few minutes, she solved my division problem and assured me that she was placing me in the fourth grade that very minute. I wanted to hug her neck, but we just did not do that in those days. Every time I think of this, I get a warm, huggable feeling of gratitude for Miss Wilkie. In fifth grade, we were back in our Frogpond one-room schoolhouse again. I never did have any more difficulties in grade school or Pickford High School where I graduated at the head of my class.

It was a landmark day in our country school when Miss Corrine Ormiston came to organize the hot lunch program. She was an assistant to County Agricultural Agent, Mr. McMillan, with whom we got well acquainted later. On this day, a wonderful opportunity was opened to us. First, she introduced us to toothpaste and gave each of us a small tube of Pepsodent and a toothbrush! Next, she announced that Chippewa County would furnish a big pressure cooker, which would sit right on our schoolhouse wood stove to make hot soup and other hot food to eat along with our box lunches. In just a few days, that came to pass. It is a mystery to me who furnished the ingredients. I guess it probably was the County Agricultural Department. The hot food was delicious tasting, just like it came from our woodstove at home. Our lunches became luxurious. That was not all she did for us.

Miss Ormiston began telling us about the 4-H Club, also sponsored by the county agricultural agent. There were a variety of clubs within 4-H for both boys and girls to consider joining: calf, horse, sheep, sewing, canning, handicraft, and such. Forrest and I signed up for the calf club right on the spot. Marie went for the canning club and Vivian for the sewing club. Besides trying out Pepsodent toothpaste that night, we got excited thinking about the 4-H Clubs. A new world of adventure was opening for us.

I must tell you about the silent man who could slip into our school unheard and unseen. No one would know he was there until you felt his presence. All became deathly still. Cautiously, I would turn my head to see the unsmiling head of Mr. George Newman, superintendent of our whole Pickford Township school system. Austerely, he stood there with folded arms like a statue, and we all froze. There was a long pause before our teacher could even get out a word of welcome. He was the very first superintendent of schools in our township, serving from 1922 to 1931. They say he was a Pennsylvania Dutchman. He was sober as a judge. He must have finally stepped to the front of the school and spoken to us, but I cannot remember his ever doing so. He departed about as silently as he had arrived. We feared the man and probably our teacher did too.

One spring, when the pike had come up in the rivers and creeks, Jack Ames and my big brother Forrest took off down the road to go fishing. Charlie and I took out after them. Unfortunately, the teacher saw us and called out our names just as we cleared the school grounds. Our courage collapsed; we surrendered and came back crestfallen. Teacher said Mr. Newman would be called about the punishment for runaways. That shook us up. As it turned out, Forrest and Jack did not make it either. Dad saw them running down the road and stopped them at our road gate. He worked out a deal with no fishing and an apology to the teacher. Small comfort to Charlie and me because old iron-face Newman would be coming to give us a whipping. Next morning, I went to school with a pillow in the seat of my overalls, dreading the worst. He never showed up. Anxiety ruled until four o'clock that day when I could get away for home.

Most parent/teacher conflicts were ironed out peacefully. One mother, who was a good friend of ours, had a red-hot temper. More than once, she came banging on the one and only school door, right in the middle of classes. She got the attention, all right. Every pair of ears turned toward the woodshed door. We could hear the loud complaints but could not quite hear the words. Teacher was somehow always able to calm her down. If it was called for, the teacher would agree to reasonable corrective action. So, the old woodshed was a good arbitration room, not to mention sufficiently soundproof by all that stove wood.

On our very last day of school at Frogpond in 1932, Art Stewart and I dug out the school ladder to climb up to the peak of the roof. There, we carved our initials in the ridge board for posterity. We wanted old Frogpond to know that it would always be in our memories. It was a day of loving and sober departure from wonderful pages in our lives. Art, Charlie, and I all went on to high school in Pickford and graduated. Charlie gave his life for our country in the Battle of the Bulge in Germany in 1945.

CHAPTER TEN

A Great Plenty of "Characters"

MODERN SOCIETY BOASTS that it has cast off the shackles of conformity. Really? As my dad used to say, "It all depends on how you look at it." In fact, we are held in the grip of a more tyrannical conformity than ever before. Thought police dominate in many American universities. Children must wear the right brand of sneakers. Every facet of our lives must be in step with the latest wrinkle. Television, Hollywood, and powerful advertising go after "the bottom line." However, in the name of nonconformity, they almost militarily conform.

We had no pressure to conform in our little one-room country schoolhouse or in our high school. My neighbor and friend, Art Stewart, wore an old leather World War I aviator helmet to school in the winter; it was very warm and practical to protect his ears in forty-below zero weather. Hand-me-down clothing caused no embarrassment, and unique getups were common. The same freedom of attire and manner of speech applied to every stage of growing up. We had an abundance of totally unique personalities—"characters!" The strange thing was, we did not recognize them as being peculiar or deserving of slight. They were genuine nonconformists. No molding by consolidated schools, TV, radio, CDs, fashion ads, or music. Here are a few examples:

Yes, Art Stewart in his World War I aviator's helmet. But laugh at him? Never.

Me, Clifton Nixon, eight or nine years old, still in knee-buttoned knickers. Funny? Not at all. Teased? No, but I do confess that I felt Mother was a little slack in letting me shed those for long pants.

Charlie Ames in his Uncle's World War I infantry cap? It looked nice on Charlie, and he was forever talking about his revered Uncle. Why not?

Harold Warren in what must have been his daddy's old head gear with the ear caps flopping down over his ears. Harold did not mind; it did the job.

My little sister, Vivian, in Marie's hand-me-down dress, which was a little loose on her. Any snickers? No, everybody loved my little red-headed sister.

There was a junior-high boy with a tattered old suit coat halfway down to his knees. Made you wonder if he had warm underclothes beneath that ragged outfit. Finger pointing? Remarks? None that I ever heard; I think we all felt understanding for him.

The pattern of natural uniqueness went far beyond clothing or prosperity level. The most unusual personalities emerged from this freedom of self-acceptance. The freedom to just be yourself. I am sure most of us were inhibited in many ways, but there were an unusual number of outstanding, unique personalities in Pickford Township. Let me name a few:

MR, HOPPERCOST: We never did know his first name, and no one ever knew much of anything about him. He never seemed to talk to anyone. He was a hermit who lived way back in the forest in a little shack all by himself. He made the long walk from Rockview to Pickford once a month with a burlap gunny sack over his shoulder to carry back his groceries. He was our "ghost man appearing out of the wilderness." He made the local scene interesting and stirred our imagination.

BARNEY NETTLETON: A legendary figure to us as we sat around the table listening to Dad and Uncle Ern's logging camp tales. His name came up repeatedly with a keen expression of admiration and mystery on their faces. Barney was a little man, but a giant among the most rugged men. It was said he could stand on one leg with the other around his neck. He could miraculously stop the flow of blood in a wound. We kids hung on every word. He rivaled Paul Bunyan as a champion logger, prankster, and nimble pike-poler, riding the log rafts down the river to Raber each spring. Barney was the merry-hearted chief storyteller of them all.

When I saw him, I marveled at the comical little man with fiery eyes. Once attacked by a buck deer, he wrestled and fought the deer for the better part of an hour before finally killing it. There could only be one Barney Nettleton among all those lumber camp heroes recorded in my memory. Uncle Ern was the one who liked to tell us all about the miraculous tales of Paul Bunyan. Just like Barney Nettleton, Uncle Ern, Sam Nettleton, Tanney Smith, and Billy John Clegg ranked right up there with Paul Bunyan too.

TOM PORTICE: My mother's brother was a genuine Irish storyteller. True stories, that is. The stories were often about some recent confrontation or exciting event. With snapping eyes in no uncertain terms, he would explain, "Sir, I said to him, I said, see here." This was his standard introduction, and his listeners would relive the whole thing—with Uncle Tom vindicated! We loved to hear him talk and laughed about the way he always came out on top. His kinfolk and friends had great fun among themselves, repeating his tales and mocking his quaint style.

There was the time he was working in his Uncle John's Dairy in the Soo. The train cut his horse-drawn milk wagon right slap in two at four o'clock in the morning. He just hung onto the driving lines while the wild leap of the horses saved his life. Milk and glass splattered the dissected wagon, railroad tracks, and the engine. To hear Uncle Tom tell it, there was no fault on his part. He gave the engineer a mighty dressing down, "Sir, don't come tootin' up behind me!" The train whistle had no doubt frightened the team and saved his life. In his eighties, he ran a red light and hit a school bus, but no one was injured. When the state policeman arrived on the scene, Uncle Tom declared, "Sir, where did that yella devil come from?" They say the officer could hardly suppress a grin to hear him tell his side of it. So unique was his manner of speaking, there could not possibly be another like him.

JIMMY GOUGH: He was an elderly man who often stayed at our place doing plowing for dad in the fall. He was a Scotsman and always referred to the other fellow as "yon jigger." Or it was, "By the jingles, yon jigger was quite a jot of a lad . . . quite a stout lad." And oh, the facial expressions that amplified the words. Every young man in his telling was quite a stout lad. Mr. Gough always "commenced" to do this and "commenced" to do that. "By the jingles," he liked to sing Scottish songs to us: "The Maid of Mohee" and "The Ship That Never Returned." We loved yon jigger, and he loved us young jiggers.

MELVIN AND KERMITH HANNA: These two were Aunt Mary and Uncle Sandy's boys. They just could not carry on a conversation without bursting out in laughter, belly-bending laughter. They found humor in everything with no effort whatsoever. They could put on a five-star TV program non-stop without any need for a script writer. Just turn them loose. Nothing off-color, no inventory of jokes or artificial applause, just bent over laughing about what happened. I have never seen the like of it. Two grown brothers who came up in poverty way back in the country and attended a one-room school. Honestly, today's TV comedians could not hold a candle to Melvin and Kermith.

Many, many others were given defining names for their outstanding characteristics or some expression that was associated with their name. Often this was done for amusement, but sometimes to distinguish their identity. "Old Eyebrows" is what the retired lumberjack cronies called Uncle Ern down at the cafe.

"Wobbly-geared Smith" was the man with a short leg who got along just fine as a good blacksmith.

"Mr. Dollar-a-Crate" was the man who grew tame strawberries and ranged the whole countryside in his old pickup, peddling the berries with his squeaky high-pitched voice for "a dollar a crate."

The young red-headed man with a hot temper who came to the farm threshing dressed in his brother's army jacket was named the "Little Colonel."

Uncle Sandy Hanna, the very relaxed farmer of Stalwart with the hearty, "My good land sakes."

Mr. Richard McConkey, who so often jovially exclaimed, "Well, I do declare."

Mr. Fred Ralph, the natural-born salesman who could sell you the Brooklyn Bridge.

Ken Smith, Pickford's radio scientist and nonstop, one-way conversationalist.

Leonard Anderson with his straight back and fast walking gait.

Mr. Walker in his big Chrysler with head thrown back and both arms straight out to the wheel.

The man we could identify walking down Townline Road like he was wading in deep snow.

The watery-eyed and sometimes tipsy bass drummer in the Orange Lodge parade.

Francis Nalley, who laughed at everybody while giving them a "hard time." Everyone loved his teasing—preacher, priest, whoever!

Yes, we had many wonderful and interesting characters per square mile in Pickford Township. They were truly nonconformists and certainly not the product of social engineering. They were unique and delightful personalities treasured by all.

SAYINGS I WELL REMEMBER:

"It's a long road that doesn't have a turn." Dad used this most often to mean that if some "clever" injustice had been done to you, do not retaliate in kind; leave it to the consequential turns in the road of life and in the hands of God. Or again, it could mean that another door of opportunity could open around the bend. Just be ready.

"Well... upon my word." This was Mother's response to surprising news or any puzzling development. She found it a good phrase for many situations. It could be spirited objection or disgust.

"Get that 'gurn' off your face." This was one Dad used. Now, get that pout off your face; change your attitude, and see the right and

good side of the matter. I looked it up in an unabridged dictionary. Sure enough, it is an old-usage term, probably Scotch or Irish. It was an effective healing tool with Dad.

"It's better further back." This was invariably Dad's response if he and a friend were looking at one of his bumper crops from the road, and the friend commented, "That's a mighty fine crop of oats there, Bert!" I used to tease Dad about this. He would just grin, but it often was true of a ten-acre field running back to our big ditch.

"Cabbageheads, rapscallions, young beggars, or little rascals." Mother would use these words when she was talking to neighbors and friends when we were within earshot listening to her. We liked it. She was sharing some good news about something or other we said or did. It told us we meant a lot to her.

"You little tear coats." We knew whom Mother was referring to and what she meant. It took a lot of mending, knitting, and sewing to keep us in operation.

"Barley top." This is what Mother called us if we needed a haircut. She had a lot of apt names for us, such as puddin' heads, punkin' heads, sliver britches, turnip tops, or young scalawags.

"If a man lies, he will steal." Another rock-ribbed principle Dad often planted in our mind.

"I don't chew my cabbage twice." This was to break us of the bad habit of not paying attention when we should have been listening. **"Hold your tongue!"** meant shut up and listen or ***"Shut up your head."***

"It all depends..." This was another of Dad's operating principles. If you asked his opinion, he was careful to think about all the angles. "What is involved? How do you mean it? There are two sides." Dad was slow to give yes or no answers.

"You mark my word..." This was Mother's Irish way of highlighting her opinion or advice in advance.

"Right fernenced everybody." I have never been able to check this one out, but with Mother it always went along with being embarrassed before others. Most often, it meant we were blabbing words or saying something best left unspoken. It could also be used when we were misbehaving in the presence of others. However, it could be an expression of humble pleasure if we praised her in the presence of her friends.

"Way up the lines." This was an expression Dad and Mother used for something west of us in the Upper Peninsula. Possibly the reference came from the one and only railway out of our peninsula to the rest of the USA. Copper mining was "way up the lines," and certain little towns were "way up the lines." It impressed us that it was a long way away.

"Well... common sense." This was Dad's expression of disgust and impatience with sloppy thinking, dumb decisions, unreasonable conduct, utter stupidity, or blameworthy irresponsibility. Dad was not so talkative, but he was a truly thoughtful man.

"It's a caution." This was another much-used expression of Mother's. Only three words, but it was applied to many, many situations. Here are a few: She said this when she was surprised by something new happening, and of course said it while relating it to someone else. "It's a caution what those little rapscallions will do." "It's a caution the job those men are undertaking." "It's a caution how that granddaughter has blossomed out." That phrase engaged all her Irish skills in showing surprise, satisfaction, commendation, or amazement. She used her eyes, voice, face, smile, laughter, or even a scornful look to go along with "It's a caution."

CHAPTER ELEVEN

High School Days

MARIE AND I GRADUATED EIGHTH GRADE at Frogpond School in June of 1932, and we looked forward to starting high school together in the fall. We would soon face problems of adjustment that neither we nor our parents had anticipated. Looking back now, I can see that we were taking large steps away from the comfort and security of our Frogpond world, away from our community and our old farm home.

For Marie it was overwhelming. She soon decided that high school was not for her. She lasted only two weeks. Mother and Dad realized how unhappy she was and finally consented. High school was still considered an elective to some extent in those days. My world took a nosedive when Marie dropped out. Here I was left to walk two and a half miles to Pickford and back each day, all alone. I had not realized how much I was depending upon my older sister. A terrible emotional decline began within my heart and mind.

The distance between our Frogpond home and Pickford High School became a wide ocean. I began to think about the future: *After high school, I'll be in college—another boundless leap away from Dad, Mother, and home.* This thought grew like a monstrous storm cloud in my mind, in which I could see no turnaround. It would be goodbye to my parents, my home, and the farm life I loved so dearly. Each day the weight of it grew heavier on my heart. Two or three weeks passed. I evaded my friends, Charlie, and Art as much as possible and brooded every step of the two and a half miles home. Each day seemed like the last time I would ever see home again.

Concern was written on Mother's face. She would give me some little chore to do for her, hoping it would help get my mind off whatever was troubling me. She asked me to go to the potato patch and dig enough potatoes for supper. I dug the potatoes for her but could not throw off the cloud that was descending upon me. I tried to shape up. Instead of getting better, my emotional state became more intense each day. I am sure Dad and Mother knew pretty well what was troubling me. They were at a loss to know what to say or do, lest I also drop out of school. My older brother, Forrest, had dropped out in tenth grade despite all their pleadings and bargains with him. All the restarts had failed. Another week or more went by in which I was often red-eyed. For the life of me, I could not put on a steady face.

Finally, this all came to a head one night after the chores and the milking were done while Dad and I were checking the safety chains on the milk cows. Dad started checking the neck chains at the stable door end of the stalls as I was checking from the far end. When we met in the middle between two cows at the passageway into the cream separator and feeding room, Dad looked right into my eyes ever so gently and asked, "Clifton, what's wrong?" I think he laid his hand on my shoulder. I completely broke down and began to blubber out of my soul, "I don't want to go on to high school." In the same tender voice, he asked, "Why, Clifton?"

He listened, and I was able to pour out all of my unbearable burdens: "Because it is going to take me away from home after high school. It will be farther away to college. It is taking me away from you and Mother—away from our home and our farm. There's no end; it will never be the same," I said, sobbing. Dad did not break in to my unloading. When I paused with a sense of being finished, he spoke very softly and slowly back to me: "Clifton, I want you to go on to school. Your mother only got through the fourth grade, and I only got through the third grade. We did not get the chance; we wish we could have gone further. Now, we want you to take advantage of the good opportunity you have. I want you to go on to high school."

A Farm Boy's Memoirs

Those were the magical words that I needed to hear. I have never been able to figure out how he was able to say them with no hint of rebuke or chiding. I knew he was sharing his innermost feelings with me. These were the deep yearnings of his own soul. A great responding relief began to rise inside of me: *If that is what my dad wants, then it is the right choice for me. That's the road I will take.* The heavy load was lifted. It was gone, immediately. I sniffled out that I wanted to do what pleased him and Mother. I trusted their judgment, but it went deeper than that. It was truly a miracle moment in my life. I never had an ounce of worry about it since. The greatness of my dad was welded to my heart. We closed the stable, walked to the house, and were soon fast asleep.

Four years later, with a five-mile walk each day, I graduated from Pickford High School as valedictorian of the class of 1936. The very next fall, I set out for Cleary Business College in Ypsilanti, Michigan. Alone and without wavering, I got on a bus with my single cardboard suitcase amidst the worst years of the Great Depression. Three of us boys from Frogpond walked together to high school in Pickford: Charlie Ames, who lived a half mile east of Frogpond school; Art Stewart, who lived across the fields from our house; and me.

I was small for my age as a freshman. One smart aleck kid gave me a hard time, always pushing me for a fight. A friendly town boy took note of it and coached me to stand up to the bully whom he said was a coward. At the tough guy's next "Come on, fight," I took Hallie's advice and waded into him, swinging. The coward broke and ran. I had no more problems. Hallie Harrison became my solid friend. His father was Bob Harrison, our town druggist. Other teens became good friends too: Keith Wise, Vern Leach, Gerald Harrison, Greeley Steele, Marjorie Beacom, Shirley Thompson, and many others. There was probably a tinge of stable on our boots once in a while, but none of those town kids ever mentioned it or looked down on us. We tried to be very careful about our clothes and shoes.

Shirley Thompson was a small freshman too. That was one reason she and I were selected by the senior class of 1932 for parts in their senior play in the theatre on Main Street. We were dressed up as two young kids and together sang the popular song, "Two Tickets to Georgia." Our song came up in the happy wedding scene where the two young lovers boarded the train for Georgia. A few lines linger:

> *"Come out and sing. Sing a wedding tune.*
> *For the Bride and Groom on their honeymoon.*
> *Hey there red cap,*
> *Take care of those presents. Yes, the lady goes too.*
> *Two tickets to Georgia,*
> *Two bits for you."*

Charlie and I tried out for the high school band. By the time I got up the courage, there was only one instrument left, the bass horn. It was huge. I lugged it home for practice between weekly rehearsals. After learning to blow the thing, I used to blast across the fields to Charlie; he would echo back with his coronet. We did not last too long. Those five-mile rehearsals were just too much.

Marie remembers how I first met Charlie: "It was shortly after we moved to our farm from the Old Gady Place. Charlie and his big brother Jack came over to visit. You and Charlie would not make up, so Forrest and Jack made you both stand on each side of the big tree in front of our house until you talked to each other. Then you and Charlie became the best of friends for the rest of his life. Charlie sure loved Mother's sugar cookies."

We remained great friends throughout our lives. We were drafted together in the very first call and boarded the train in Sault Ste. Marie on March 7, 1941. We were bound for Escanaba where we were inducted into the United States Army. Our paths parted at the huge induction center in Soldiers Field, Chicago. We corresponded during the war and were home on furlough at the same time once. Charlie gave his life for our country in the Battle of the Bulge in 1945. He was an artillery sergeant. When in Frogpond School together, Charlie often talked with great pride about his uncle, who was killed in World War I.

The walking distance shut Charlie, Art, and me out of sports activities also. I started on a running team in preparation for field day but had to drop out. At home, I practiced shot-putting with a heavy stone, dug out a broad jumping pit, and set up a homemade stand for high jumping and pole vaulting. It is a wonder I did not get impaled on that green poplar pole. We did get involved in other regular school activities, though, and enjoyed them very much.

Superintendent of Schools, Mr. Eno Honkanen was a Finnish man who grew up farther west on our peninsula, near Lake Superior. He was a fine person and a real blessing to me. I became the editor of our high school paper *The Munuscong*, and we got personally acquainted. He could correct you and make you feel good about it. The *Munuscong* was a monthly mimeographed issue several pages in length. Putting it together, I kept referring to the "stabilizer" and how to keep the thing working. Mr. Honkanen took me aside to explain to me that it was a "stapler." I appreciated his setting me straight. I had never seen one before. He used to tell us about how his father brought up the whitefish nets from the depths of Lake Superior and sometimes fish would burst open because of the sudden pressure change. We all liked Mr. Eno Honkanen.

Study came easy for me. Our good teachers in Frogpond taught us how to enjoy learning and how to express what we learned. Perhaps it was that third-grade experience I had of being held back that spurred me on to try harder. During high school, I seldom carried any books home. My programming was for chores and farm work with my family when I got home. I liked it that way. I always read carefully in study halls, especially when Miss Grant was in command. I can vividly remember what I read. Every book was an adventure to me.

Sometimes in planting or harvesting seasons, I would stay home a day or two to help Dad. The school accepted a written excuse and allowed me to read up on the classroom lessons I missed. One winter, I was down with the flu for a whole week and got back just a day or two before monthly exams. I crammed the textbooks and came up with the top grade in each study. My friends were amazed, but I knew it was a gift that God had given me. I never spoke about it or acted smart about it. Dad and Mother took a great interest in my report cards but never said much. I could read satisfaction and confidence in me on their faces. They always felt free to ask me about the pronunciation and correct spelling of words. One of them had to sign the report card before it went back each month. They did this in a slow, deliberate fashion because they were just learning to write. I liked to watch Dad sign his name. It was a rewarding accomplishment for him.

My freshman year was in 1932. The stock market had collapsed in 1929, which put our country into the throes of the Great Depression. There were times when we walked to school with cardboard in our shoes to cover the holes. It was painfully necessary to go in debt for winter footwear and clothing. We were fortunate to have sincere Christian merchants who were willing to give us credit. These great men were Mr. Ham Hamilton, Mr. Jim Watson, and his son, Mr. Otto Watson, plus Doctor Fox and two blacksmiths.

In late fall and early spring, we often managed with worn-out monkey-faced gloves all squeezed up in our fists because the fingers were full of holes. Bundled up like that, they did the job. Not so in winter, however, then we had to have Mother's double-knitted woolen gloves inside of leather mitts for below-zero weather. Elsewhere, I have written about frostbitten toes and chilblains from tramping through the winter snows to high school. It is very painful thawing out your toes inside your boots by the hot water register in the classroom. I also remember the difficulty of breaking through the frozen crust on snow fields with an egg crate on my bicycle. Even though I was lucky to get a bicycle for some of my high school years, relatively few trips were made to school by bicycle. Most of the time, I could not use my bicycle because of wet, soggy roads, snow, or flat tires.

There were no hot lunch programs in Pickford High School. We carried our lunches and came up with some unique depression sandwiches, which were surprisingly good. All on homemade bread with plenty of home-churned butter. I would bring either a peanut butter and jelly sandwich, a peanut butter with bread-and-butter pickles sandwich, a baked bean sandwich, a pickled beet sandwich, or a headcheese sandwich. Mother most always came through with home-baked cookies, cake, or pie, and usually a hard-boiled egg or two. There was no grumbling. We were well fed. We had excellent teachers who fed us a wealth of knowledge too. I well remember Mr.

Forbush, whose coat was a bit threadbare; I expect his paycheck was in the same shape. He challenged our minds by discussing things back and forth with us in the classroom. I had a couple of study periods each day in the high school auditorium. The school must have been pressed for space over all because the auditorium was chock-full of double desks with one lone teacher way down front at the foot of the stage. This brings to mind another remarkable teacher.

Her name was Annabelle Grant. She was a tiny little lady, but she certainly knew how to manage that big assembly. I will never forget one example of her total control. Right across from the desk where I was sitting, a couple of guys were whispering and talking with minds far removed from study. Their disrupting influence was growing. How Miss Grant got back to our area unnoticed, I do not know. I was hearing their disturbance well enough when suddenly everything got quiet. Over my left shoulder, I saw her. Straight as an arrow with her arms folded, she stood just behind the two boys at their desks. They had been taken by complete surprise. Every eye in the large auditorium swung around to stare at the culprits. The power of that great silence weighed down upon them. Miss Grant was just standing there, letting them squirm. The unanimous judgment of their four hundred fellow students fell upon the two cuties. Still, she stood there with arms crossed. The silence was awful. Finally, she spoke ever so softly. "Don't you think it is time you boys began to study?" She had no harshness in her voice of authority; it was like we all said it together with her. Then she turned about face quietly and took a circuitous route back to her distant desk. No eyes dared to follow her. We were all back into our textbooks. Miss Grant's study hall was study hall par excellence.

Four years of high school seemed to pass in a hurry for me. I enjoyed the summer planting, haying, and harvesting times right along with Dad. In hunting season, our uncles came to deer hunt, which we thoroughly enjoyed. I loved hounding through the woods and the excitement of the fireworks out ahead when we drove out a buck. Looking back, I wish I had been more aware of the uniqueness of those days and realized they would never be repeated. I was always looking ahead. I suppose all young people are that way.

I did get involved in school. At a class council meeting early in our senior year, the subject of a class trip to Detroit came up. No graduating class had ever undertaken a senior trip. They had talked about the idea, but finances were the great barrier. Discussion moved negatively toward the same conclusion: it was an impossible dream. It was at that point that I suggested an idea without much hope that it would go over: "Why can't we put on a mock WLS National Barn Dance show and sell tickets? Everybody is wild about it on the radio. We could give them the real thing. We have the singers and the musicians with a violin, banjo, harmonicas, and all. We could organize the Hoosier Hot Shots with 'Are you ready, Hezzie?' and his tooter, washboard, and one-string, tin-tub viola. Vern Leach would be our tap dancer. We could have a real do-si-do square dance with caller and all. A mystery drama like they have on the radio could be added. We could come up with our own sound effects?"

The meeting immediately began to warm up to the idea with, "Why not? I think it would go over." "Be sure to have Uncle Ezra!" and such. Somebody piped up and said that since it was my idea, he thought I should put it together. Before I could get up an objection speech, they had me named the director and were gung-ho for Detroit. Within a week, all senior class members became imitators of the WLS National Barn Dance. The program was roughed out, and rehearsals set with clearance received from our class sponsor and Superintendent Honkonen. One night, a drama plot came to mind. I sat right down and put it on paper, right then and there. In a few more days, it was mimeographed for rehearsal. By early spring, we were ready. Tickets were printed, but I do not remember how much we charged.

On opening night, the high school auditorium was jammed. The crowd enjoyed every minute of our version we dubbed WLS Barn Dance Hour and clamored for a repeat performance. Our gang was in high clover! The mock characters, hilarious costumes, dramatic surprise, excellent music, and songs went over great. The cash for Detroit was rolling in.

A Farm Boy's Memoirs

We put it on again in our Pickford High School auditorium and gladly put on requested shows in both the Cedarville and Detour high schools. They were all sellouts! Total receipts went over the $400 mark. That was a lot of money in the Depression years. The school board may have added a little to our effort. A hired bus and driver took us to the great city of Detroit for at least two nights at the fancy big Penobscot Hotel on Cadillac Square. Few of us had ever been across the Straits of Mackinac. For most of us, it was the first time we had ever slept in a hotel.

Our tours included the Ford Rotunda, the new moving assembly lines in Henry Ford's automobile plant, Thomas Edison's invention laboratory, and other wonders at Greenfield Village. It was true adventure for the Class of 1936 and a first for Pickford High School. It sure was a first for me; I had never been out of the Upper Peninsula. There was no Big Mac Bridge then; a large ferry took us across the Straits of Mackinac to Mackinac City in the Lower Peninsula of Michigan. It was only the second time I had ever been more than forty miles from home. The first time was with my 4-H Club, when we went to Escanaba for a showing at the Upper Peninsula State Fair.

My senior year in high school was a whirlwind. After the WLS Barn Dance money-raising venture and our senior class trip came the traditional senior class play, to be presented in the Cameron Theatre. That is mostly a blur in my memory, but I did play a role. This was my second senior play. Before scarcely knowing it, the 1936 spring flood had come and gone. We were into planting season on the farm, and it was graduation time. There was plenty of work to do. Many hours were spent behind our draft horse team, disk harrowing and drag harrowing. Most of the planting was done with a horse-drawn seed drill, but the very tiny clover seed was sewn by Dad with his hand-turned cyclone seeder.

I had been named valedictorian of the 1936 class and had to make a speech at our "graduation exercise" at the Pickford Methodist Church. My speech was all written up and ready to go, but something happened that day, and we were late getting to town. The church was full when we arrived. I made it there just in time to go up front and give my speech. I am ashamed to admit that not much time was given in preparation and it showed, but it was sincere. Truly, I was not adequately aware of the gravity and preciousness of that event in my life. I did not give it the effort it deserved. I should have gotten some guidance, but none was offered. I should have sought it. Looking back, I wish I had.

Still, it has entered my thoughts that possibly the Lord was in it all. Giving the valedictory speech was an honor bestowed on me. I should have appreciated it more highly. I felt badly that my speech was more like an off-the-cuff sermon. Was an unknown and higher priority involved? Was this God's way of hedging me toward the ministry and away from who-knows-what? Was there a connection between this event and the shock I felt as a junior or junior high boy when Marie swung that floor mop at me and called me "preacher?" I had run across her newly scrubbed kitchen floor. She swung with temper and missed me, but what she called me hit me hard. I was stung and taken completely by surprise. *Why did she call me preacher?* I'd wondered. I did not take it seriously and thought it was a mean blow, but I never ever forgot it. I now believe Marie was prophetic with her mop, and I accept the fact that God may have been at work in my sermon-like speech too.

Soon after graduation, I got my first off-the-farm job at the Islington summer hotel near Cedarville. The inevitable launching away from my beloved farm home had already begun. Those high school years were good years. Full appreciation of their epic nature came to me in subsequent years.

Clifton and high school friends

CHAPTER TWELVE

JANUARY
Better Than Black-Eyed Peas

NEW YEAR'S DAY WAS NEVER a big day for us. We had not heard of hog jowl and black-eyed peas or New Year's parties. January was the grand entranceway to real winter. No more mud. Winter had come to stay. All the earth was white as far as the eye could see. The heavy snows were falling, often two feet at a time and sometimes four feet or more. Windblown snow drifts piled up like miniature mountains with sharp cliffs. Buildings blocked the driving wind and snow, leaving the ground almost bare on the downwind side because a vacuum was formed. On the other side, snowbanks could form overnight and stay all winter. Most storms came off Lake Superior from the northwest, so huge snowdrifts formed on both the west and the east ends of our house.

Our wellhouse had a collar of snowbanks. Likewise, the old henhouse on the way to our barn. These mountain collars of snow made it rough walking to the well or the barn. Many winter mornings we awoke to find a snowdrift just inside the kitchen door. A windy night drove the snow in because we had forgotten to put the old rag rug across the bottom before we went to bed. Most mornings, Dad would be up early to have the kitchen stove roaring and the snow swept out before the rest of us got up.

Dad would be sure to put the teakettle and the oatmeal water on the hottest lids of the range before going off to the barn to do his pre-breakfast chores. It took quite a while for the reservoir on the range to get hot. Mother was up next, fixing breakfast, while we kids were getting up and dressed for school. When Dad got in from the barn, we all had breakfast together. Oatmeal and hot tea were items we had every day. Mother came up with lots of variations to go with that: fresh eggs, fried pork, fried potatoes, toasted homemade bread with thick butter and jam, pancakes, cornmeal mush, canned fruit, or fried cakes. After breakfast, Mother and Dad would do the milking while we went off to Frogpond School.

We accepted winter with joy. No more mud oozing through the holes in your boots. No more losing balance and slipping off the single end-to-end boards to the barn. When that happened, a cold disaster occurred when your bare foot came out minus your stocking. Off balance on one leg, you either fell flat in the slop or recovered by shoving your dry foot back into the gooey boot, struggling until you got it free.

By January fifteenth, the ground was frozen solid. The Model-T had made her last trip and was up on blocks for the winter "to take the weight off the tires." We traveled to town by horse and cutter, team and sleighs, dog sleigh, skis, snowshoes, or walking on "Shank's pony." Winter was always so clean and dependable. No more rain—just clean, white snow. So clean, you could eat it with cream and sugar. We kids invented many fun things to do in the snow. We would always keep cozy warm playing and come back to the house with rosy cheeks and happy faces. It was fun to ride in a cutter with a fast horse. It felt like flying. Bits of snow and ice peppered us from the horse's heels, making you long for a windshield.

The risky, muddy board walks to the outhouse and barn had all vanished—good riddance. Herein lay a fun challenge for us. We boys imagined we had the prime contract for keeping those highways to the pump house and barn open for traffic. After a night's snowfall, you had to wade knee-deep in the snow, hoping to stay on the narrow track. Good paths to the well house, outhouse, and barn helped all of us. It was never demanded of us, but we made it our job to keep those highways open for traffic, no matter what. The pathways we made must have been four hundred and fifty feet to the barn, fifty feet to the privy, and another hundred feet to the pump house. We took our road "contract" seriously but had great fun.

First thing after Christmas, we boys began making a new, improved snow car from the apple box Uncle Ern and Aunt Nellie gave us. The platform was a twelve-by-eighteen-inch wooden sled with two wooden runners curved up at the front. These were rubbed with candle wax to improve speed and wear. On top of this, we mounted the stout wooden apple box. A twenty-four-inch wooden pushing bar was nailed across the top rear edge, and two reversed tomato cans were mounted on the front corners for headlights. Our little sister, Vivian, or little brother, Dougie, were always ready to jump into our apple box wonder car for a wild roller-coaster ride to the barn and back. They always hollered, "Do it again!" Each year's new model was a rear-engine job with increased power. Automatically, we simulated ignition, engine roar, shifting gears, and acceleration to wide-open speed followed by deceleration and braking to a grinding stop. We knew all the authentic sound effects.

Blasting off from the kitchen door, we would be at full throttle by the time we hit the four-foot drop at the old henhouse snowdrift. It was a giddy plunge that garnered squeals of delight. Then we bore left on the straight-away to a double curve around the garden. We pushed on to the old log stable, taking a sharp right curve at the horse stable door. There the engine was cut as we slid the last thirty-five feet to the cow stable door. By then, the engine was panting and steaming, so a barn break was necessary. It was one busy highway with morning chores, noon chores, before-supper chores, after-supper chores, collecting eggs, special runs, and requested fun trips. In a full winter's time, the engine got a lot of wear. Vivian and Dougie were always game for more, and we loved it.

Somewhere along the line, Dougie and I got the idea of converting our snow car into a snowplow. Two pieces of board were tailored into a V-shape with Dad's old horse hoof rasp and attached to the front end. Tomato cans were flattened and bent outward, then nailed to the top edges of the V to thrust snow away from the path just like the huge county plows. Power and speed were on our side to make it work, so it was all pleasure when it did! The next day, we started a new concept by adding dual fans made from those marvelous tomato cans. Rotated by flying snow up each plow wing, we supposed the spinning fans would fling the snow farther up and out. The results were considered satisfactory at maximum speed. That was, of course, our standard operating speed, except when we had to do some shoveling on the first trip through after a storm. Soon, we would be running free and could clear the banks back to the full twenty-four-inch standard. What a thrill to watch that snow fly.

It is no wonder we were good eaters. Lots of sweat and toil kept the paths cleared for solid footing and high-speed commuting to the barn. Mother always helped Dad milk the cows both morning and night. Their other chores were overseeing the cream separator in the feeding room and teaching the young calves to drink from a bucket. Mother had a special pair of tall rubber milking boots. They were easy to get into and out of with wide tops and no laces. We boys took pride in keeping the road in good shape so that snow would not get in over Mother's boot tops.

Temperatures in our winter wonderland went down to forty below zero in January and February. Special care had to be taken to prevent frostbite. Now and then, we would get a few "melty" days, which allowed for more outdoor fun. We made snowmen, snow forts, or whole rooms dug into snowbanks. By sundown, it would freeze again to preserve our snow engineering. We liked our snowball fights. Days ran mostly in the upper thirties and forties but could plunge below zero for a whole week sometimes. That did not force us inside, but blizzards did.

When the temperature dropped to forty below, remarkable things happened. Telephone lines started their high-pitched humming, day and night. Tiny snowbirds would line up in long, unbroken ranks on those lines. How they kept their feet warm, I do not know. There were no electric lines out our way until 1940. I also remember certain strange atmospheric changes. Not a breath of air would be stirring across the white fields, but you could see smoke from neighbors' chimneys rising straight up toward heaven. Never a wrinkle, just pencil-straight smoke columns going hundreds of feet into the snapping air as far as the eye could see.

Setting out for school, I was surrounded by sparkling crystal. I could still see way passed Frogpond School, possibly to a farm in Stirlingville. For some reason, the road bent upward with sections of it turning into a reflecting pool of water. I knew that road was perfectly flat! Was it a mirage? It has never been explained to me, but I beheld it many times when the temperature was far below zero. Of course, I was cozy and comfortable as I turned in at Frogpond School, but what I saw and what I felt was permanently imprinted upon my mind.

In addition to humming telephone lines, the air was literally filled with eerie sounds. The snow grinded under our boots. There was a constant crackling of ice under the snow. Fence posts and telephone poles snapped. Frost set in motion tremendous powers of expansion and contraction. Water expanded and solids contracted. Water trapped in rocks often broke those rocks apart. On those cold winter mornings, everything was bathed in frosty flakes that transformed into dazzling jewels reflecting the morning sunlight on fence wires and last summer's spiderwebs.

The most awesome sight of all is the Northern Lights on a cold, frosty, moonlit night. The Aurora Borealis makes the hair on the back of your neck stand up. Such a sight would stop me in my tracks. More than once, I took a small New Testament Bible outside to confirm that one could easily read by the brilliance. To the north, a huge band of living light stretched across the upper heavens, much brighter than the surrounding moonlight. Perpendicular shafts of light shot up and down within the huge band. Simultaneously in right to left waves, these light shafts moved swiftly across the expanse like legions of angels dancing in the sky. Could the psalmist David have witnessed the Aurora Borealis when he wrote, "The heavens declare the glory of

God"? I can tell you that my thoughts turned to God, His Glory, and His Greatness. I was longing for His Love and His Grace in my life.

You may wonder how in the world we ever kept warm in below-zero weather. We had not heard of wind chill factors, but many times it felt like it was twenty degrees below zero. We could get actual temperatures of minus forty degrees below zero. The answer was threefold: heavy clothing, plenty of good food, and plenty of action. Dad and Mother watched out for us and gave lectures on what to do and what not to do. Mother was fast with those big twelve-inch knitting needles. She knitted gloves, muffs, scarves, and sweaters. She double-knitted wool socks and mittens. She could look all around and carry on a conversation while her fingers were flying. We kids would question her: "Mother, how can you go so fast and not even look at what you are doing? How do you form the thumb and narrow the wrist of the mitts and make the different color band changes so even?" She would just give us a happy Irish grin and keep us dangling in curiosity. We felt like the young farm lad who once protested, "We don't have much money, but we are not poor." That was our stance too.

Each winter the quilting frames would be set up in the front room for a week or two, getting ready for the quilting bee. Those fancy designed eight-inch quilt squares were made from worn-out dresses or shirts, remnants, and Pillsbury's Best flour sacks. Each square was a masterpiece of several pieces of cloth sewn together on her Mother's Singer sewing machine. The Singer was powered by a foot treadle, and Mother could make that Singer sing. Marie and Vivian got their training on this machine too. They learned from Mother, and both became expert seamstresses.

By the time the famous "Quilting Day" arrived, Mother had the frame up with three layers stretched on top and ready: the material for the bottom side of the quilt; the thick, one-inch batting for the unseen middle part; and all those sewn together squares formed the top layer. Eight or ten neighbor ladies would arrive for the quilting party, gathering around that frame to quilt it down. It was a huge undertaking seasoned with laughter, news, gossip, and good food. It really was a party, an all-important annual get-together. When Mother was very elderly, she amazed us with her ability to arrive at the exact date of these distant events. She could pinpoint it right down to the day with something like, "It was the winter of Aunt Martha's quilting party." On extreme below-zero nights, when all the fires had gone out, we would all be snug and warm under two or three of those fluffy quilts, "while visions of sugarplums danced in our heads."

In zero-degree weather, when you were driving horses and had to hold leather lines, large, heavy rawhide mitts went over your woolen knitted gloves or mittens. Without the heavy rawhides, your fingers would soon be frozen. If you were walking, you could get by with just thrusting your gloved hands into your mackinaw pockets. If the temperature got above fifteen degrees, you could get by with store-bought monkey-faced gloves or knitted woolen gloves. Those yellowish fuzzy gloves were fine, but the finger faces soon wore out. Many a time, I walked to high school in Pickford with fists doubled up in those gloves and stuck in my jacket pockets, which worked great.

We got our energy from wood, hay, and oats. Stove wood for cooking and heating came from the surrounding forests or bushes. We did not call them forests: Belcher's Bush, the Maple Bush, the Soo Cedar Swamp, and Armstrong's Bush. We grew the hay and oats to fuel Bess, Colonel, and Ole Ned, our horsepower. The milk cows, young cattle, hogs, and chickens also needed our hay and grain. Cold cash had to be put out to buy coal oil for the lamps and lanterns. Five drops on a tablespoon of sugar every time one of us got the croup worked well too.

What about bathroom facilities, especially in the winter? Well, if you insist, I will tell you. We had no bathroom, but we had a washtub, an outdoor privy, a Spiegel catalog, and a porcelain chamber pot dubbed the "thunder mug." The privy was a two-seater, but nothing fancy. There was an inside hook on the door and a wooden buckle on the outside. The snow path to it was not trampled much in the winter. In summer, boards were laid end to end for improved passage to and fro.

Vivian reminded me of a funny thing that happened when our younger brother Dougie was just a little boy. Our much-loved country schoolteacher, Mr. Forrest Haywood, had come to have supper with us. Just as we were sitting down at the table, a loud, embarrassing metallic clang sounded upstairs. We all flinched. Dougie had dropped the lid of the "thunder mug."

All our water came from our well out in the pump house. Daylight and wind came through the cracked wooden walls of this eight-by-ten-foot pump house. A hinged trap door let you down into the cistern. The humongous iron-handled pump drew the water up into your bucket on its spout. A trough was hung to the spout when the cattle-watering tank outside needed filling.

The main hitch was operating that heavy iron pump handle. Coming down was okay, but lifting that big handle was a tough job for a small boy. You got about a quart of water with each stroke. That watering tank outside for the stock held one hundred gallons. On most winter mornings, the ice had to be broken off the top of that tank. Each cow drank several gallons of water daily. Twenty or more thirsty cattle and horses would crowd around that tank, shoving and pushing as the water went down to the bottom. *Pump, pump, pump!* It always helped me to feel like progress was being made if I counted the strokes. It took about four hundred strokes to bring that tank back up to the full mark. Painful arithmetic for me, you might say. The tank must be kept full lest the freezing surface ice burst the sides wide open.

The pump would often lose its prime between pumpings. You had to pour water from a pot into the top of the cylinder with your left hand while you pumped the handle with your right hand. In winter it would freeze up, so you needed to get a tea kettle of scalding water out there. You had to pour hot water in there while yanking on the handle until it thawed loose. When pails of water were removed from the spout, water slopped out that built up a glacier of ice around the pump and over the entire pumphouse floor. At least twice each winter, a long spell of below-zero weather would freeze the pipe down deeper in the well. We had to chop ice off the cistern trap door to climb down in there with a torch of kerosene-soaked rags to get that stubborn feedpipe to the pump cylinder thawed out. That was an unhappy ordeal.

We had a little cistern pump in our washroom off the kitchen. This pump often froze up in winter, too, so we had another hard job. We had to trample down the snow path to the well to carry water back to the house in milk pails. You could carry two twelve-quart pails of water by holding them up high to clear the snow on either side of the track. If the path to the well house was in bad shape, we came up with a way to minimize water carrying on washdays. We would cut blocks of pure white snow from the snowbank just outside our kitchen door to melt down in the copper washing boiler on the kitchen range. Snowbank blocks created softer water, which required less soap; although, less water lugging was the real bonus.

In the early years, Mother scrubbed all our clothes on her wash board with rough Fels Naphtha bar soap. Then she wrung out the soapy clothes by hand and into the rinse tub they went. When that was full, they were soused up and down thoroughly before she twisted the water out of them again for hanging on the lines. Sometimes two rinses were needed, which meant more water to carry. Little wonder that Mother's wrists were strong. Milking six cows twice a day and putting out a washing should have left her huffing and puffing. Not so, she took it in stride.

White clothes, diapers, and sheets got a far more intense treatment. Therefore, the white things went from the scrub board into the big copper boiler with a red-hot fire under them to be stirred with a stick the entire time they were boiled. The whites were then ladled into the first rinse pan, wrung out to go into the bluing rinse pan, and then wrung out as dry as possible to be pinned on the outdoor clotheslines. Every farm wife vied with her neighbors to hang out the whitest possible wash each Monday morning. Cleanliness and pride were sterling virtues taught by Grandma Portice. Mrs. John Ames and Mother always raced to see who could get their washing on the lines first on Monday mornings. The Ames family lived a half mile across our open northeast fields. They were good neighbors and our good friends. Charlie and I were the same age and best friends.

As we kids grew older, we were commissioned to help on washday by carrying water, cutting snow, changing tubs, or pinning up clothes.

We still had lots of time to play. One grand day, Dad brought home a fancy manufactured washing machine with a wringer on it! Forrest and I nearly got into a spat over who got to operate the magic machine. After a couple of washdays, the newness of pushing that scrubber handle back and forth and turning the crank on the wringer became old stuff. Little brother got to operate the handle and crank many a washday, but I cannot remember ever feeling put upon or unhappy about helping Mother with the washing. Several times each winter, the wash would freeze stiff and had to be brought inside. We hung clothes on folding racks or lines strung up in our front room with the big woodstove going. It was fun to stand the union drawers in the corners. Warm clothes were a must. Woolen underwear with a buttoned-up flap in the back were called "union suits." It did not mean union made; it did mean the top and bottom were united. The whole family wore these suits. Dad wore his in the summer too; he claimed the sweat evaporation made them cooler. Shirts were made of wool or very heavy flannel, so were pants. Extra heavy "foldcloth" pants came from the Soo Woolen Mills. They were almost like felt. That is what I was wearing when I fell through the ice in the big ditch.

Jackets, mackinaws, and overcoats were made of heavy wool. Boys wore woolen caps with fur-line flaps that covered the backs of our necks and both ears. Toward spring, brave young upstarts would step out with a felt hat and shout, "Look, no ear flaps!" Sometimes these guys carried a set of portable earflaps (earmuffs) just in case. I thought they looked silly. Girls wore felt tams and woolen scarves. Everybody, and I mean everybody, carried a scarf for zero-degree weather or a blizzard. Ears, fingers, and toes were the most vulnerable. You beat your hands together, then put them under your arm pits or stuffed them into your pockets. If that failed, they quit hurting, turned white, and were frozen. If they were stinging with pain, you were still okay.

We figured that Eskimos had fur-lined boots, but we did not. The cold would come right through rubber. We boys were usually equipped with pants tapered into twelve-inch leather boots. They were the "in" footwear for boys and men. If you had the money, you could have the wool socks with fancy collar-bands folded over the boot tops. That is the kind Mother knitted for all her children. It was costly to wear regular shoes with cloth-lined overshoes or galoshes. That was dress-up gear, unsuitable for work or school. You could pay a high price for your pride if temperatures dropped and you had a long way to travel in the snow. I learned from experience. Toes began to sting in those laced leather boots sometimes, despite everything you did right. Your toes stopped stinging when they became frozen. The real pain came in the thawing-out process. A few days later, the chilblains, itching, and peeling began.

When we boys got out of knickers and into high-top leather boots, she put splashy red colors on our sock tops. "Keeping up the agony and puttin' on the style." Marie and Viv also liked those colorful sock tops folded down over their galoshes. 'Twas our folly that usually got us boys a touch of frostbite most every winter. Woolen mitts alone could not stand up to the bitter cold of winter. The wind would go right through them if you were driving horses with leather lines. For this kind of exposure, you had to have oversize leather mitts with Mother's knitted liners inside. Now, let the twenty-seven, below-zero weather come and let the wind blow, but watch your feet! At the first stinging, get off the sleigh and walk, or jump up and down on a cleared hard surface to get the circulation going—immediately!

How was it possible for all the animals in the barn to keep warm in below-zero weather? No problem, ceilings in the horse and cow stables were only seven and a half feet high and insulated with tons and tons of hay over them in the mows. The exterior sides of the stables had tar paper and cedar shingles, just like our house. Thick single-width doors opened to the outside from each stable. Between each of the stables was a long, narrow feeding room with the cream separator and, most important, the hay shoot midway. The four-by-four-foot shoot went way up to the top of the hay mow and was filled each day from above. A single sharp-pointed pole was the stopper. Pull out the pole and gravity brought the hay down for distribution to all the mangers facing the feeding room for twelve milk cows, calves, young cattle, horses, and el Toro. The feeding room had a single interior door to the big threshing floor where you could climb ladders to fill the hay shoot. The whole stable area had only three small windows. They remained frosted most of the winter.

Feed grains for the animals were in the granary, which was an enclosed part of the horse stable side. You had to go into the ice-cold threshing floor and make a U-turn to open the sliding granary door. There you got ground mixed grains for the cattle called "chop." The horses' daily whole oats and bran where also in the granary. Pigs had a pen on the horse stable side. They got chop and/or shorts mixed with slop. Shorts was a derivative of flour milling. Slop was a mixture of kitchen scraps and leftover skim milk after the calves were fed.

The body heat of twelve cows, a half dozen young cattle, eight calves, three horses, el Toro, a sow with twelve piglets, Ole Buster, and one tomcat put out a lot of BTUs. On a forty-below morning, it was amazing to open one of the stable doors. A great cloud of steam would burst out and ascend higher than the peak of the barn. It was always comfortable in the stables, no matter what the weather. Lots of times, we would come in with cold, stinging fingers and put them between a cow's udder and leg for a quick warming. Old bossy did not mind.

We had still another source of heat that was natural and renewable, the two large manure piles. One mountain was a few steps outside the horse stable door, and another mountain was just outside the cow stable door. They grew all winter long. Each represented hours of labor already accomplished, and each would demand many more hours of energy before spring planting time. But there was a bonus, the horse pile emitted a thin column of steam in the dead of winter. That giant compost pile made a handy foot-warming station for our stinging toes. It felt so good and was not messy on your boots. Friendly bacteria were at work in that giant methane furnace.

The morning chores were always waiting to be done. First, we cleaned the stalls, put down fresh bedding straw from the straw mow, and refilled all the mangers with hay. Then we measured out the proper portion of chop, oats, bran, shorts, boiled flax seed, scratch feed, and what have you to the milk cows, calves, young cattle, horses, el Toro, pigs, sheep, chickens, geese, and turkeys. Next, all those thirsty birds and animals had to be watered.

In the winter, the big stock watering tank had been brought into the cow stable. That was in the years after we had dug the water line from the pump house to the barn and converted to a force pump. Before that, we had to turn the cattle and horses out into the cold and march them clear out of the barnyard to the ice-covered tank by the well house. Now, with a force pump putting water into the barn tank, two or three cows were untied at a time and they automatically turned around and helped themselves to the open water tank. Then came the calves and young cattle. While they were drinking, we carried pails of water into the feeding room and set them before the horses and el Toro. Pigs had to have their slop mixture in their very own trough. All the feathered foul out in the henhouse were watered. Young calves were served individually measured amounts of milk with shorts. Weaning calves had to be taught how to drink out of a milk pail. Ole Buster and Ole Tom, our dog and cat, got good faithful care. In fact, Ole Tom came by for a well-earned squirt or two at each milking.

Someone had to climb up the long ladder to the hay mow far above the stables to refill the big hay shoot. It got empty so quickly; those animals baled a lot of hay by day and by night. When we got old enough to climb up there and pull out the packed hay, we would do this while Dad and Mother milked the cows. It seemed like it took a ton of hay to fill that shoot. Your heart would be beating in the back of your neck because that hay had been packed down so solid by tons of grain sheaves on top of it before threshing day. It was chilly climbing up there, but you always came down sweating. Vivian declares that one time she climbed the ladder and helped me fill the hay shoot. It must have been near spring when the hay mow was about empty. Anyway, she says she stayed up there and got on top of the hay in the shoot, while I went down and pulled the stopping pole out. Down came the hay and Vivian, spilling out into the feeding room! She remembers it as great fun.

When the milking neared completion, the De Laval milk separator was slowly cranked up by hand to required bell-ringing speed. That took some "doing." When the bell rang, you turned the tap on the upper pan so that the milk flowed down through the separator, allowing cream to come out one spout and skim milk out of the other. All the while, you had to maintain the high rpms of the inner centrifuge and switch skim milk pails. On the farm, chores were more than taking out the garbage once a day. Chores were a fundamental part of our lives that had to be done every morning and repeated every night before we went to bed. Dad took care of the brief noontime needs. The evening chores were sometimes divided into "before supper" and "after supper" chores. But oh, it was hard to get into barn togs again after a wonderful suppertime and head out to that barn again by lantern light in the cold. We preferred getting them all done at once, but that made it more difficult for Mother.

Believe it or not, most every farmhouse had winter flowerpots. Ray and Mary Dodd's eighty-acre farm bordered our farm on the north. Mary was famous for her houseplants. They were exceptionally good neighbors. During fieldwork, Dad and Ray often chatted over the fence and always traded hands for threshing and hay pressing. Mary's kitchen window was full of flowers all winter long. I always admired her beautiful geraniums, begonias, and bleeding hearts. We tried growing geraniums and begonias, but sooner or later our "no all-night fires" policy got them. Even the "Old Witch" in the warming oven froze up a few times.

Hay Pressing Day rivaled Threshing Day in excitement and color, becoming a wonderful bonding time for good neighbors to celebrate. Dad traded hands with eight or ten neighbors, so he had lots of threshings and pressings fellowship. I think it was a Frenchman from Kelden named Lamoreau who came with his monster 10-20 Titan tractor and hay press machine. It had huge iron wheels five-feet high with iron bars welded crosswise all the way around them for traction. I may be getting the machinery and personnel intermixed between threshing and pressing. It was a long time ago.

By January, the grain sheaves on top of the hay mows would be threshed. Now it was time to get the hay baled for the winter market. First class racehorse hay with the ideal timothy content was an Upper

Peninsula cash crop, one of the very few we had. If a hay buyer from the rail head at Rudyard came through buying hay, we wanted to be ready. Coloring and content were crucial. Of course, most of the hay in the two mows over the stables must be reserved to feed the stock through the winter. Ordinarily, that feeding hay would have lots more clover in it—the more the better.

Two more mows on the other side of the barn's threshing floor held many tons of hay. The mow paralleling the threshing floor would have been pressed down considerably by the heavy grain that had been piled upon it. If a bumper crop of botch hay and grain were coming on, Dad would opt for a temporary haystack just outside the threshing floor entrance, thus reserving adequate space for the grain inside. The threshing floor itself had to be kept clear to accommodate hauling in and unloading into the mows. This open floor space also allowed room for the threshing machine and hay press later. Long ladders were built into the barn framing in order to get way up to the top of the mows. We kids liked to climb clear to the top from the threshing floor. Best to keep your eyes closed tight as you climbed and to not look down!

A thick ten-inch drive belt transferred power from the big Titan engine some sixty feet out in the barnyard to the hay press inside on the threshing floor. That engine was magnificent, a joy to watch and hear. It had large flywheels on each side with a belt pulley on the right. The engine went "Choo-choo-choo . . . ha-ha-ha. Choo-choo-choo . . . ha-ha-ha" over and over and over by the hour. The *choos* were power strokes, and it sounded like the *ha-ha-ha* was just it coasting. The idea was to keep those big flywheels spinning at the right speed. Sometimes there would be power gaps and the complicated "governor" would call for more *choo-choo-choo*. The belt was twisted a little, which I supposed helped keep it on the drive pulleys. Alex McKenzie got his arm caught in the belt one time and was seriously injured.

The hay press made a terrible racket. Men way up in the mow would pull out hay and throw it down to men on the "table" beside the press. They fed it into a vicious iron jaw with teeth on it, which swung up and down, feeding the hay into a narrow chamber. While the jaw was up, a powerful plunger rammed the hay into the baling chamber. I shivered at the thought of a man getting caught in that thing. It took several men to operate it. Separating blocks had to be inserted between bales; baling wire had to be fed into it to bind the individual bales before they popped out the other end. Men with hay hooks grabbed the bales to make room for the next one.

The south end of the threshing floor could be used for piling up the bales. Up by the tons the bales went. Men with hay hooks hoisted the bales up from tier to tier like they must have built the pyramids. Eventually, a tongs rope, pulleys, and a horse would lift the bales up to top off the stacking. It sure was a day of action. Men were like ants, building a humongous kingdom in one day. Each bale weighed well over a hundred pounds and was carefully weight tagged somewhere in the process. Hard work, fellowship, dirty faces, unique personalities, and the big dinner-table feast made for an unforgettable occasion. When I got old enough for Dad to let me on his crew, I would get all covered with hay dust too. Getting to eat at the table with all those unwashed pressers was great. Wow, what a thrill!

One Pressing Day when I was about eight years old, my life savings came into sudden jeopardy. I had accumulated a quarter pint of dimes earned from rat-tail bounties. Where to hide them? The dimes, that is. *I know! I'll pour the sugar out of that fancy sugar bowl of Mother's. She hardly ever uses it! Put the sugar back on top. No one will ever know*, I naively thought. Now Forrest would not be pestering me for a loan anymore. 'Twas done. *It's secure now*, I thought. As soon as we got seated at the big presser's dinner table, I saw with alarm that someone had placed Mother's fancy sugar bowl right in the middle. I panicked: *Sure as I'm livin', one of those neighbor men is going to dip into my life savings!* Happily, it never happened; no one touched that sugar bowl. I snatched it up fast as I could, setting it back up in the cupboard where it belonged.

Baling wire was an indispensable item for the general farmer in our day. Always, you carried bale wire on every wagon, sleigh, mower, or binder. You can mend most anything with bale wire. Dad would say, "Cobble it up, and keep going. Carry on somehow; keep the job moving." We had no yellow pages, no one to call for service. You would have to take it to a blacksmith in Pickford. The blacksmith would probably have to send off for a part. So, "bale-wire it up and keep going!" Even as an adult, I used bale wire. Several strands of baling wire were always on my four-wheeler, and I kept a set of spare keys bale-wired underneath our car. At Thanksgiving in the Smoky Mountains, my son Wendel bale-wires the turkey for outdoor roasting.

CHAPTER THIRTEEN

FEBRUARY
Our Winter Wonderland

IT MAY SEEM STRANGE, but many of the most memorable events of my childhood took place in February. The auto license tag designers surely had the Upper Peninsula in mind when they proclaimed Michigan the "Winter Wonderland."

One Valentine's Day, a terrible blizzard came up suddenly out of the northeast. In these blizzards, we did not dare set out for home lest we get disoriented in the blinding snow. You could not see three feet ahead of yourself and could not face the blast. We had been carefully instructed by Dad on what to do. He would come for us with the team, pulling sleighs and plenty of blankets. Ole Buster, our dog, came too. Nearly every winter there were tragic stories from the Western Plains about the blizzards that caught children coming home from school. They became lost and froze to death while their frantic parents searched in vain. We kids were well warned about northeasters.

In our part of the world, we were not given to outward expressions of love and affection, but we went all out for Valentine's Day. Unless you were mad at someone, you bought a valentine for everyone in school, boys and girls alike. Of course, the finest card would go to our loved and respected teacher. No one begrudged laying out the price for that card. We shopped all over Pickford for the best card deals with the best wording. A penny would buy a very pretty valentine card; two cents would buy a much bigger, better card with more touching verse. There were ten-card bulk packages that saved money, but you had to examine the quality on those specials. The wording had to be measured by how much you cared for the person. I had a special liking for Effie Everleigh, so she got a three-cent valentine. My best card had to go to her, other than a special five-cent one for my teacher. I would have blushed if I had ever gotten up the courage to tell Effie with words. Valentine's Day was serious business emotionally. Dad and Mother always found the money to finance our shopping spree. Each of us got fifty to seventy-five cents; how we spent it was up to us.

Teacher always made a large valentine depository box with a big heart on it for us. On the afternoon of Valentine's Day, recitation bench work ceased and drawings began. When our names were called out, we proudly went forward to accept; the more trips the better. That evening, we would have a big viewing in our front room with Dad and Mother. We read all the names and verses to them. Those precious cards were carefully preserved for years.

February was prime time for outdoor adventures in the snow. Forrest and I decided to make skis and challenge the wide expanse of snowfields around us. The old Armstrong house to the south of our farm had been abandoned for years. Half of the eighty-acre Armstrong homestead had never been cleared. We called that the Armstrong Bush. The doors of the old, unpainted house were either unlocked or gone. Dad said we were to keep our hands off anything in that house. There were old fashioned dishes, a variety of carnival glassware, and bottles—untouchable treasures. We boys strictly observed Dad's commandment.

However, we spotted ceiling boards hanging down. They were the narrow wainscoting type with a groove down the middle, just like real skis! It was sad to see that good lumber falling down, just going to waste. We both agreed that to use the loosened stuff could not possibly be considered stealing. Happy finders were we with four unbroken pieces exactly right for skis. With Mother's cooperation, we melted snow in the copper boiler on the kitchen range to a good, rolling boil. We whittled the ends to a carved point like the "real McCoy." Into the boiler went the shaped ends. After an hour or so, we took one out to see if it would bend up without breaking. Sure enough, it worked! Soon, all four were bent and bound in some kind of a contraption until they would thoroughly dry out in place. We were proud as peacocks. Now we just needed shoe attachments.

All was going according to plan until Dad saw our project. Right away he asked, "Where did you get those boards?" He had always told us that anybody who would lie would also steal, so we fessed up with full-blown explanations. Certainly, we did not want to be hailed as liars; we could hardly be called thieves. Dad cut right through our rationalizing and showed us that we had no business taking those boards. We accepted his rebuke; it showed all over our faces. We should not have touched those ceiling boards. It got noticeably quiet. *What to do now?* we thought.

After a little bit, Dad turned to us and said, "Well, the damage is done; they're cut up and bent now. Maybe they would never be used again, but that does not give you the right to take them. Go ahead and keep them, but do not ever take another thing from that house. The Armstrongs moved out of it years ago, but it is not ours." We were thankful for Dad's decision and learned a never-to-be-forgotten lesson. Dad was a quiet-spoken father who never yelled at us; his spoken rebuke was a powerful discipline.

In the days that followed, Dad helped us find old spare pieces of horse-harness leathers, straps, buckles, and screws for shoe attachments on each of those skis. I would love to know Dad's thoughts when he saw us set out across the fields on those skis. I think he was glad for us and proud of the adventurous spirit in us. We made ski tracks all over acres of white, clear to the distant green forest walls. If a foot got out of the strap and you fell, you wallowed in twelve to eighteen inches of dry, cold crystals. That skiing enhanced our imagination and confidence in ourselves. Most importantly, we still had our Dad's loving approval.

Ears and feet were the most vulnerable in below-zero weather. The danger we faced was being caught in circumstances where it was impossible to prevent frostbite. My toes and ears were frostbitten a little almost every winter. Frostbitten from unavoidable situations, but mostly because of some foolishness on my part. The most serious example happened on a crystal-clear, far-below-zero morning in February. Temperatures had been running below zero at night but warming up to slightly above freezing in the day. About a week earlier, I foolishly put my winter cap with fur-lined ear flaps in the warming oven of the range to dry out. Wouldn't you know, I forgot all about that cap until the next morning. The rabbit fur was baked and fell out; the hide cracked into pieces. Scolding could not fix the cap, and there was no money to go buy another. Not a breath of air was moving. Smoke from all the chimneys in sight was going straight up about forty feet. After breakfast, Dad and Mother bundled up to do the milking. Mother cautioned, "Now, don't you kids leave early. Be sure to wrap your scarf over your head and ears." She knew the teacher needed to get the school stove going.

It was so cozy and warm inside our house. Outside looked calm and innocent to me at eight years old. Suddenly, I heard my good friend, Art Stewart, call from the road. I threw on my coat and cap, put on my mitts, and ran to join him at our road gate. There was no studied intent to disobey; I was just excited to walk to school with my buddy. Art wore an old leather aviator cap that came down over his ears and fastened under his chin. Within three minutes, my ears began to sting. I noticed a round, white spot in the middle of Art's forehead, and the hair sticking out from under his cap was white with frost from his breath.

My ears were really stinging. Looking back, we saw my older sister, Marie, running after us. Dumbly, we thought she was trying to outrun us, so we ran harder. It is hard to run like you are on a horse track and keep your hands over your ears. A few minutes later, I told Art that my ears had stopped stinging. Marie was not gaining on us. We only had another eighth of a mile to go. We burst into the schoolhouse in record time, but the damage was done.

Teacher had the wood stove going strong. She gasped when she saw me. "Clifton, your ears are frozen!" She immediately had a student hurry outside with the wash basin for snow, set me in a chair beside the big barrel stove, and began rubbing my ears with snow. The feeling soon came back, and severe pain set in. If you think cold fingers sting and hurt, try thawing your ears out after they have been frozen beyond feeling! Marie arrived, puffing for breath, and got all over me. "Why did you run when I yelled at you? I had your scarf! Mother came in from milking and sent me to catch you!" I squirmed in tears of pain far worse than Marie's well-deserved wrath. Mother was alarmed immediately, knowing that my ear flaps were useless and that only the wool scarf could save my ears. She knew I had misjudged how far below zero it was.

(front) John Pennington, Earnest Stewart, Vern Warren, Vivian Nixon, Billy Shobrook, (rear) Clifton Nixon, Marie Nixon, Effie Everleigh

Finally, the sharp pain began to let up. Teacher said the color had returned to my ears; the blood was flowing back in. At least a half inch of each ear had been frozen white as snow. My older brother, Forrest, rushed in the school door. Mother had him harness Ole Buster and hurry to the school to see if I was all right. When the thawing ordeal was all over, Teacher was still worried. She wrapped me up and packed me off with Forrest to go home on the dog sleigh. We made that half mile in three minutes or less. All I could see was Ole Buster's heels and feel the bits of frosty snow flying up in my bundled face.

Dad and Mother were genuinely frightened and made me stay home from school at least a week. Mother wrapped white dish towels around my head to keep my ears from sagging. She was afraid they might permanently flop down. I do not remember Dad and Mother being cross with me. I was taught a hard lesson. Even as an adult, the upper half of my left ear remained hard as a rock with only a little feeling in the outer skin.

One Christmas, we got a long factory-made sled with steel runners. It was a beauty. With a steering bar on the front end where the runners were flexible enough to be twisted, you could steer while going down a hill. That was a great winter sport! Climbing back uphill for the next run made rosy cheeks and got up a sweat under the union suits, wool clothes, heavy coats, and chooks. The driver, with sled in hand, ran as hard as he could and hit the sled full length at the very top of the hill. The rest of us would pile on his back for the wild plunge, faster and faster with every jolt a thrill. Down, down, down with loud yells and sometimes spills. Away we went until finally coasting to a stop. What a sled ride!

Dogs and sleighs came in a great variety in our winter world. All our dogs were eager to get into the sleighing act. The annual racing contest was a big event. Forrest gained attention with Ole Buster. I became his harness maker and all-purpose flunkey. My brother dreamed of that championship, but he would need a more powerful dog.

Making a dog harness was no easy task. Strands of baling wire were twisted into a strong circle and wrapped round and round with strips of cloth so that it would barely squeeze over the dog's head and rest comfortably on his furry shoulders. Two thick leather tugs were attached to the collar with a back band and belly band sewed onto the tugs just behind the dog's shoulders. Each tug had a snap for hooking onto the sleigh. Dad came up with the spare leather strapping, leather punch, harness needle, and heavy waxed thread. Forrest was very exacting, which made my job all the more important. The custom fitting made the dog proud of his harness. There was no struggle getting Ole Buster's cooperation. When we called, he would come running to get his head into the collar. A control rope was fastened to the dog's collar also. All steering was done by word commands.

Clifford McConkey stayed with us one winter, and he had a team of German Shepherd police dogs. How they loved to run. Clifford had to haul back on their lines while we all got aboard the double sleigh. Those canine racers were charging, barking, and raring to go. A wild ride we had with bells on the harness, the dogs howling and bouncing over the horse tracks, and icy snow flying up from their heels! It only took one minute to arrive at Townline Road. Mother even trusted us to take the ten-gallon cream cans to the school corner for pick up. Clifford's sleigh was big and sturdy.

In our growing up years, we had three famous dogs. They were a valuable part of farm life and each was loved and cared for by our whole family. I barely remember "Old Nick" of whom Forrest and Marie so often spoke. Dad and Mother had a good word for Old Nick too. He was of medium size with black fur and no pedigree papers but had a great record for usefulness and remembrance in our family. Marie told Vivian and me an experience she and Forrest had with a sleigh dog. The sleigh ran up on the dog's heels, then he turned around and bit Marie. She showed us the small scar on her arm—eighty years later! Marie was not sure whether it was Fido or Old Nick.

"Ole Buster" was my chief growing-up dog. It would take a whole book to contain his history. My dad knew how to train dogs for farm management. Buster was an A-one scholar, a faithful worker, and a loyal friend. "King" was our great German Shepherd police racing dog. Forrest brought him home as a pup. He grew by leaps and bounds so that by his second summer, he was a loving giant. King took to the harness and sleigh. He literally flew whether one or two of us were on board. Weight load was no problem; he just stretched out and ran with all his might and never slacked. Forrest knew he had his champion, and we delighted in telling all our friends. That was a mistake, a tragic mistake.

Near dark one summer evening, a rifle shot rang out toward the back of our farm. Forrest was the first to hear King roaring, coming up the lane. He cried out in alarm; King was badly hurt. Dad shouted for all of us to get into the house. Forrest only made it to the milk house, fifteen feet from the house door. What a horrible sight! King's head was a bloody mass. He was howling and crazed with pain. It took all of us holding the door with all our might to keep him out. Still, he got his head in; we knew not what he might do. The struggle lasted several minutes before he weakened, and Dad was able to push his head out of the door. For an hour or more, he lay groaning at the door and then moved away in the darkness out of sight and earshot. Mother was calming down; only then would she hear tell of Forrest rushing out of the milk house to join us inside the kitchen door.

Later, Dad ventured out with the lantern and found King lying quietly by the old henhouse. He came back with a somewhat comforting report; our dog had settled down. Now, we must wait till morning. When we got up in the morning, Uncle Tom Portice had come with his rifle. We knew what that meant. He and Dad examined King and agreed that he must be put out of his misery. It was a sad, sad day at our farm home. It helped lots to still have Ole Buster for our sleigh dog, but all interest in competition dog racing was gone. For years we lived with the question, "Who killed our friendly and harmless champion, King?"

My second serious frostbite incident happened when I was a teenager. I set out for high school, taking a shortcut across snowfields that had a frozen-hard crust. No problem, it held me up fine; I made good time until I came out on Townline Road. Snow had drifted into the plowed roadway, causing the teacher of Frogpond School to get stuck. She asked me to give her car a push. I pushed and pushed, but we were making little progress. In that loose, frosty snow, my toes began to sting. I told her that I must kick away a clear spot and begin jumping up and down to increase the blood circulation to my feet. She thought just a few more backups and runs would get her going.

It took too long to get her going. When I turned toward the remaining mile and a half to Pickford High School, no amount of jumping up and down would drive away the stinging. I opted for running and walking instead. My feet were numbing. When at last I reached the snow-free cement sidewalk going to the school, there was no more stinging. It felt like an inadequate amount of blood was gushing in and out of my frozen toes. Worried and late, I slumped into my desk seat located right beside a steam heat radiator.

In minutes, I was squirming in pain; my frozen toes were thawing out inside those high boots. Our good teacher recognized my agony and came straight to my desk: "What's wrong, Clifton?" I told her what happened and that my toes were frozen. She said, "Quick, let's get those leather boots unlaced and off right now!" Together we got them off fast; I sure was thankful for her kindness. She was not angry because of the interruption to her class. Within ten minutes, the pain began to let up. My toes and feet were red and swollen. It took a month for the frozen skin on my toes and heels to dry up and peel off. During that process, the itching of chilblains drove me to pawing the back of one shoe with the other shoe, which only helped slightly. We had no thermal shoes in those days. Almost every winter brought some chilblains symptoms on my ears, toes, and heels, but usually it was to a much milder degree.

By midwinter, days grew short and dark came early. Chores were done by lantern light. We shooed Mother off to the house and worked hard to help get everything done before supper. She could then put the finishing touches on a steaming hot supper of home-canned meat or venison, plenty of creamed vegetables, and homemade bread. What a good feeling it was to be in for the night. No rush to get up from the ole kitchen table to go back out to do barn chores. The feeling I got at those suppertimes was wonderful. One great warming consolation was that we would not have to get all dressed up again and light the lanterns to go out into the cold.

This was prime time for lumber camp tales of Paul Bunyan and his Big Blue Ox, or honest-to-goodness stories of real lumberjacks like Barney Nettleton, Sam Nettleton, Billy John Clegg, and Tanney Smith. Stories of Uncle Ern's prowess as a champion log decker, my dad on the decking line, and other men famous with pike poles on the river drives and log jams. When Mr. Gough would stay with us, he and Dad traded tales of camp life, the steam railroad in the woods, Dad's great decking team, water wagons, river rafting, memorable storms, filling the lake with logs, lumber milling, and a million other things. The camp cook got high praise for fabulous meals and pie any time of the day. Pie unlimited! Bunkhouse pranks brought many a laugh, like the night they sewed up Bill Brindley's hat with bale wire. It sounded like dawn-to-dusk good times.

Mr. Gough was elderly and a charming talker. The preamble description of every character in his tale was, "Yon Jigger was quite a stout lad." It did not matter that Yon Jigger could be fifty years old. The third finger on his right hand was permanently injured years before; it was stiff as a poker and turned up a little. When he "commenced" to saucer his hot tea, yon finger would stick out beyond the saucer while the others helped him cool his tea. He talked with both his tongue and face. We kids got a great bang out of both listening and watching him. We hung on his every word.

One evening we were all at the table when Dad and "Ole Jimmy" commenced to discuss the marvelous flavors of chewing tobacco. They allowed that there must be molasses mixed in with the tobacco and probably many other unknown ingredients. Whereupon Mr. Gough summarized the subject: "Yon plug of Yankee Girl must have gone through quite a 'pro-cess'." Forrest piped up, "Yes, it goes through quite a 'pro-cess' when it goes through you." Dad's hand flew out like lightning and rapped Forrest up beside the head for his smart-aleck remark. My older brother and Ole Jimmy were always at it. Forrest loved to catch him climbing through the strands of a barbed wire fence. He would pull on the wires a bit to get the ole gentlemen tangled. It was not harmful, and I do believe the old gentleman enjoyed the game.

Forrest and I often got into wrestling matches in the open space in front of the kitchen range. Mother would be sidestepping around us, refereeing, and often warning, "Watch that oven door! Forrest, you're going to hurt him!" Then she would call time and get into the ring to open and shut the oven door. After which, the battle continued. We never damaged one another and never did bust the oven door. It was great entertainment for all. Forrest must have gone easy on me, but I gave him a good battle just the same. He was four years older, and a good brother to me. I would like to ask Mother which she was worried most about: me or her oven door? She would have a good laugh.

By and by, we were all worn out. Dad was winding the clock and yawning out his "hoy, hoy, hoy" bedtime ritual, which meant it was time to climb the ladder, undress down to our union suits, kneel by our bed, and say the Lord's Prayer aloud. In short order, we would all be under the quilts. The fires were banked downstairs so the house would soon begin to cool down, but we were all safe that way.

I was prone to get the croup in the middle of winter nights, and my coughing would awaken Mother. She would shake Dad awake: "Bert, get up! Hurry down and get the kerosene. Clifton's got the croup." Out would hop Dad to go down the ladder, and in nothing flat, he was back with a rounded tablespoon of sugar with four or five drops of kerosene on top of it. "Open up, swallow," he instructed. Down it went. The taste was terrible, but it worked like magic; the coughing stopped and soon I was back to sleep. No matter what the weather, with hay ticks under us, flannel sheets, and three quilts over us, we were snug and warm.

During the winter, Dad and neighbor Jim Stewart sometimes took our draft horse team to work in the Wonnacott lumber camp, cutting and hauling pulpwood. He and Jim shared a tarpaper shack during the week and drove the ten miles home on Saturday nights, often in below-zero weather. Ole Buster would be first to sound the alert; then we threw open the door and heard the jingling harness bells: "Dad's home!" We hustled into heavy jackets, caps, and gloves to get out there with the lantern when he turned in at the gate. What a sight, with steam puffing out of Bess and Colonel's nostrils and their leather harness creaking. Dad got off the sleighs, trotting to keep warm with steam-frosted hair stuck out from under his cap. How glad we were to see him. We jumped right in to help get the team unhitched, into the stable, and unharnessed so Dad could come into the house. I've often wondered how satisfying it must have been to Dad when we gave him those hearty welcomes home.

Mother and Jim's wife, Emma, decided to make a surprise trip to camp with a load of food for their lumbermen in the tarpaper shack. Bread, cakes, cookies, Boston baked beans, stewed prunes, and potato salad would be part of the fare. Emma arrived with her famous horse, Sorrel Jewel, and the equally famous "cutter." Emma was forever railing against that old, broken-down horse about how worn out, weak, lazy, shiftless, and no count he was. He looked it too. Their son, Art, was my age and had designed the cutter contraption. A contraption it was with oversized, heavy sleigh runners underneath a big, ugly boxed-in seat arrangement with shaves for Sorrel Jewel. It was one sorry excuse for a cutter. Dad hauled two tons of hay to Rudyard on a double set of sleighs identical to the set under Art's conveyance.

Emma arrived on schedule and got down over a snowbank positioned right by our henhouse. Loading got underway—baked beans, stewed prunes and all. Emma and Mother boarded and got their lap robes tucked in just so. Of course, they had to get up over the big snowdrift to get out to the road. Emma commanded Sorrel Jewel, "Giddyup." Tragedy struck! Whether it was the snowdrift, too much horsepower, or some defect in Art's cobbled up cutter, over it went—Emma, Mother, robes, beans, prunes, cake, and all. A total collapse into the new-blown snow. Emma scrambled to her feet still clutching the lines, yelling at the old nag to stop. Lying on her back in the snow, Mother was all covered with groceries and baked beans.

"Get up, Selena, get up! Sorrel Jewel's gonna kick the stars out of the sky!" That got Mother tickled. The hapless, no count Sorrel Jewel "kicking the stars out of the sky" was just too much! What a miracle that would be; Emma's old plug of a horse had become a powerhouse. There she lay, laughing so hard she could neither speak nor get up—piled over with snow, blankets, and baked goods. Emma kept right on belaying the poor horse and "that dumb mutt of an Art" for the faulty state of the cutter. Poor Sorrel Jewel stood stone still and knee-deep in the snow drift. He had no notion of moving. Possibly something did give way on the cutter. I never did hear a final report on the cause of the incident; it may never have been discovered. Neither Sorrel Jewel, Emma, nor Mother were injured, but everything else was ruined. The mission was aborted. That was in about 1933. For the rest of her life, Mother delighted in telling the story to family, neighbors, and friends. She would always get to laughing until tears rolled down her cheeks. I am laughing while writing this.

A blizzard is a powerful windstorm mixed with a heavy snowfall. Blinding blizzards from the northeast were the most dreaded winter storms because visibility becomes almost zero. You cannot open your eyes and face it; your nose is closed by the driven snow; if you open your mouth to breath, you choke. The only alternative is to wind a heavy scarf around your head with a tiny peephole or turn your back to the storm and try to walk backward. If you are far from shelter, you are in grave danger. Dad would not even let us venture to the barn alone at chore time during blizzards. These shut-down times had a remarkable effect, bringing a strange thrill. It was a feeling of isolation from the whole world and a special identity with our home and family as we bonded with our brothers, sisters, Dad, and Mother. There was something about the powers of nature and our security in the midst of it all. A good feeling to remember.

State and county snowplows kept the main roads to the Soo, Rudyard, Cedarville, and Detour open. Side roads like ours had no such benefit, but the access roads to the country schools were snowplowed. On snowless days, the plows would push back the road banks to the marker stakes. In the fall of each year, these ten-foot poles were put in place to guide the snowplow drivers when everything became a level field of white. One winter, we were snowed in for two solid weeks. Not one road into Pickford was open from any direction. Snowbanks had built up seven or eight feet high. The plows were battling day and night to push back the road tops and widen the roadway, when another huge snowstorm descended upon all of Pickford Township and filled those narrow trenches solid. No way could the plows push that mass of snow up and out with their blades. They were absolutely useless; we were snowbound.

All the townsmen turned out with shovels to begin digging and pitching the snow up and out of the roadway over the high snowbanks on each side. Farmers from the whole countryside tramped their way into Pickford with shovels to try to help open the roads to town. When they got some narrow trenches dug for a hundred feet, they were hopeful the biggest and most powerful snowplow with its big blades and momentum could get under the snow to pitch it out—at least for a stretch. The Chippewa County snowplow man cranked up and charged from as far back as he could get. We held our breath. When he hit the snow, it just mushed ahead and absorbed all his impact; no snow went up and out. He made no more than a ten-foot dent. What now?

In a couple of days, the county came up with another idea: put the largest truck they had loaded with gravel behind the snowplow and tie the two together with two steel railroad track rails. Where they found two rails in Pickford, I do not know; we had no railroad. They succeeded in fastening the two monsters together, one behind the other for maximum thrust. Considerable hope was rising. Again, the men were summoned to dig some room for the snow to go up and out. Once the engines were started, they hoped it might keep on going!

Nearly everybody in town was out to see the action this time. People were getting worried. Once again, the powerful motors were warmed up and the two great machines charged forward to ram the snow blockage with all its might. Surely it would work! The big roaring of the engines and the forward flashing steel behemoth struck the snow with a heavy thud. Nothing went upend and nothing went out; the dent was about fifteen feet this time. It was an alarming defeat. The county road supervisor and town leaders were stumped. There was nothing more they could do. Perhaps they prayed. We had been snowbound for a week; food supplies were going down, and no answer was in sight. One day, from out our kitchen window, we saw a man riding a large sled and dog team across the fields to the southeast in the direction of Detour. We learned later that he was taking emergency medicine to that small, isolated village down on the point of the peninsula.

A Farm Boy's Memoirs

The men of Pickford turned to the State Highway Department for help and were able to get one of the new "snowplow" machines from somewhere. It was a lifesaver and a marvel to watch. Instead of trying to force the snow up and out, it had a rectangular boxlike cage on the front with internal augurs pulling the snow into the box and feeding it into a deeper box where a powerful interior fan blew the snow out a nozzle some sixty feet into the air and out into the adjoining fields. It reminded us of the pictures of Old Faithful we had seen in Yellowstone National Park. It crept slowly through the night with a light reflecting off the column of snow, arching up into the sky. The marked stakes were important now. By and by, cars and sleighs could move again, and teachers got to their country schools.

During the winter, Mr. McGinnis, from the railhead at Rudyard, would come through buying baled hay. He and Dad would talk and talk, bargaining until they finally settled on a figure of so much per ton. The poor farmer in our sparsely populated peninsula did not have much leverage. It was more often just take it or leave it. Dad tried to keep on the good side of the buyers. Cash was hard to come by during the Great Depression. From the mountain of baled hay in our barn, Dad would stack two tons on the double sleigh rack, readying it for the fifteen-and-a-half-mile trip to Rudyard. He would get underway about three o'clock in the morning. Bess and Colonel looked so small pulling that towering load, but the sleighs had heavy three-inch-wide runners with steel shoeing that slid easily over the snow. This was the ideal time to do the hauling because no gravel was poking up through the frozen roadways. Later, it could be too late.

When Dad pulled into Rudyard, he got in line to have his hay transferred into closed railroad cars bound for racehorse country. It could be late afternoon before he started back on the long trek home. Mother and we boys would have the chores done, watching for Dad's return, tired and hungry. Two days later, weather permitting, Bess and Colonel would be pulling another two tons to Rudyard.

Marketing our cream, hay, oats, peas, flax, barley, wheat, pork, beef, and chickens was always risky business. Many markets dried up completely in the Depression. There was no weekly paycheck. The grocery man would reluctantly take one dressed beef or one dressed pork. We could only get half of it in cash because the other half had to go "on the bill."

We raised our calves to two years old. Each fall, we hoped to sell four or five of them for cash. Mr. Billy Kirkbride was the chief cattle buyer; he ran a butcher shop in Pickford. Dad would call him to come out to our farm. Mr. Billy would circle around the critters several times, weighing in his mind how many steaks and how much hamburger he could get out of each one. It was quite a show to watch the bargaining. Both men were dead serious. Finally, the verdict came down: "Well, Bert, the market is pretty slow, but I could take this one for six cents on the hoof." That meant live weight and no butchering for Dad to do—a job we disliked. Of course, this would be the finest calf. "But I need to sell all five, Billy," said Dad. "They're well fed, and I need the money for winter clothes and taxes. Times are hard."

More circling and study. With a furrowed brow in the midst of risk-taking, Mr. Kirkbride allowed, "Well, Bert, I will take all five, but I can only give you five and a half on the foot. I really don't need that many; things are slow." Dad would hold off for a while, protesting that these young cattle were all first-rate and top-fed. "They're all worth six cents a pound when you consider all the pasture, hay, and grain that's been put into them." Negotiations stalled. Mr. Kirkbride had to walk some more, poke Dad's fine stock, and lick his lips in deep concentration. "Well, Bert, I'll go to five and three-quarter and take all five. That's the best I can do."

Dad believed Billy Kirkbride to be an honest man, and judging from his sincerity and willingness to take all five, he gave his nod of approval. The deal was closed. No papers to sign. A man's word was as good as his bond. Dad was satisfied—the farm was safe for another year. We would be able to pay that $108 tax bill. That was a great relief, but after buying winter clothes, we would still owe Uncle Ern eight hundred dollars for the annual payment on the farm. Uncle Ern would not foreclose; he and Aunt Nellie understood and loved us. Still, it was a heavy burden that year after year had gone by, and we were not able to meet that payment.

When we sold a beef or a hog to the Hamilton and Watson store, we had to do the butchering. Killing, skinning, and gutting a big beef cow was done on the barn's threshing floor. I think it was always done in cold weather so the carcass would freeze quickly for transportation to town. Overdue bills for the doctor, blacksmith, groceries, clothes, and footwear simply had to be paid first, or at least something on each.

Hogs were butchered in the fall or winter too. That meant building a fire under a fifty-gallon drum of water outdoors and supporting it at a forty-five-degree angle on the ground. Then you caught the pig, put a rope around one leg, rolled him on his back, and hog-tied him with half hitches around the other three legs. My job was to hold the rope while Dad shaved its neck and stabbed it with the butcher knife. I shut my eyes. In a few minutes, it was dead. Then the 135-pound pig was hoisted into the barrel of near-boiling water with the rope on his hind leg. This was a precise dipping process: into the water for a minute or so, pulled out for a bit, and back in again. This was repeated until the hair would shave off easily, but the hide was not cooked. When Dad judged it was exactly right, we pulled him out and strung him up on a pole rack where both of us went to work shaving off the bristles with sharp knives. Then "doctor Dad" would gut him and carefully set aside the heart and liver. In a few hours, he would be frozen stiff and stored in the milk house, standing on all four feet. The next day, we hauled the pig to Hamilton & Watson's. Sometimes they would only take half a pig.

Forrest had a new automatic twenty-two rifle, and he talked Dad into letting him shoot the hogs for butchering. Forrest fired away, hitting the pig just below the eyes, but the pig ran away. We cornered him again so Forrest could get him for sure this time. No good, the twenty-two-caliber bullet bounced off his snout. That pig-headed pig just kept going. After three attempts, Dad called it enough; we went back to our standard method. A general farmer had to do a lot of doctoring when castrating calves and hogs, getting bottled medicine down horses bloated with colic, assisting cows giving birth, or dehorning cattle. Dad could do it all and sometimes performed animal surgery for a neighbor. I wound up assisting and learned a lot about farm biology.

One winter when Dad was away working in Wonnacott's lumber camp, the grocery store called Mother for a dozen dressed hens—right away. Mother knew how to scald them and get the feathers off, but always shied away from the killing. Vivian and I declared we had watched Dad do it and could manage it for her. We caught the hens, tied their legs, and hung them over the clothesline. Next came the sticking. "Just get the sharp, narrow-bladed knife into the chicken's throat and twist it so that it bled quickly and soon stopped kicking," we'd been told. Our technique was flawed. We had an awful time of it. I am not sure, but I think we wound up chopping their heads off on a block of wood. Never again.

Vivian reminded me: "One time, Dad was at Uncle George Portice's threshing, and Mother was sick in bed. I guess I was about sixteen and I asked Mom what I could fix her to eat. She said, "I could eat some chicken soup." I said, "I'll have to kill the chicken first." She replied, "No, you don't know how to do that. Wait till your Dad comes home." I had watched Dad lay its head over the block of wood, nothing to it. I got the axe and wood block, then ran down one of the old hens. Everything was going right except when I gave it the axe, I missed part of the neck and off the old hen went. I ran her down again and finally finished the job. I got the feathers off after dipping her in a kettle of hot water, then got her all dressed out, washed up, and into the pot to cook. I asked Mom if she still felt like having some chicken soup, and she did. I told her it was in the pot cooking and all about my ordeal. She got so tickled and laughed till tears came down her cheeks. "Upon my word, what will you try next?"

Winter evenings were happy times for our family. We moved a step up into the front room when the suppertime dishes were done. Mother would carry in the Aladdin lamp. We all followed the light. The Victrola lid was lifted, and the gabbing began about what records would be played, who was to wind up the spring, and what songs were to be sung. Many of these songs described things that happened in the old days.

I can only remember a few of our favorite songs: "The Wreck of the Old Ninety-Seven," "When It's Lamplighting Time in the Valley," "The Strawberry Roan," "Back in the Saddle Again," "Birmingham Jail," "Thirteen More Steps," "The Bum Song," "Twilight on the Trail," "The Old Chisholm Trail," "Out Where the West Begins," "Home on the Range," "They Cut Down the Old Pine Tree," and "Golden Slippers."

The Victrola was a marvelous machine. However, it had two weaknesses: the spring could break, or the needle could get dull making ruts in the records so that lines of the song would keep repeating over and over again. When a needle jumped a track or rutted, a warning command rang out: "Be careful now how you reset that needle." When a record got hopelessly rutted or so worn that the words turned to mush and ran together, it would be stored away for a long time as a valuable keepsake.

Mother and Dad often requested that we sing school songs that Mr. Haywood taught us from the *Golden Favorites* song book. When we finished one song, they were always ready with another request. Dad's foot would be keeping time.

One winter day, I brought home from school a book titled *Heidi and Her Goats* and read it each evening to Mother and Dad. How we enjoyed it. They had little schooling. Mother could read some, but Dad could not read at all. They were so thirsty to learn. Dad learned to read from us kids. They both would ask us how to pronounce words and how to spell them.

Every scrap of printed material that came into our house, Dad would tackle. You would see him working his lips as he figured out each word. If he got stuck, he would ask us what it meant or how to say it. Mother became a great reader of poetry. She could remember many poems she had learned at the old Sunshine log schoolhouse on the bank of the Little Munuscong River. She also remembered mottoes that the teacher had placed on the walls of the schoolhouse. In her nineties, she could still reel off these old poems and mottoes.

Mother loved to sing around the house as she worked, mostly hymns from her youth. She was in no way inhibited by the presence of family members. When just a little tyke, I used to go around singing,

"Carry me across with a smile." No one ever corrected me. I thought of it as someone carrying me across a stream and was happy about it. Years later, I discovered that it was a hymn: "Carry Your Cross with a Smile." I copied Mother's habit of singing to herself. I still do it and am sometimes embarrassed by my unawareness.

When we were building our house in the Smoky mountains, my good neighbor, Jim Hall, came down to help me almost every day. After it was all finished, he would tease me in the presence of our mutual friends about having to endure my hymn singing while we put the plywood sheeting on the steep roof. I must have gotten this trait from Mother. My kids also used to chide me about my singing and humming. Vivian recalled that "we used to sneak out to the barn when Dad would be feeding the cattle in the barn before supper, and he would be singing all to himself or humming a lot. Dad could really carry a tune well." I had forgotten this. It comforted me to know I was not the only one. Vivian also added: "Our neighbor's daughter in Brighton tells me now how when she and Sue were little, they used to sneak in the house and listen to me singing and whistling away like crazy. Jenny laughs now and says, 'You were great.' That was at least thirty-five years ago." It must be hereditary, or early culture imprinting. We just cannot help it.

You may wonder what we did for indoor fun on shut-in blizzard days or long winter evenings without a radio or television. If you had been there, you would understand that we were not bored. I have already mentioned our singing. We invented lots of other activities. Nothing was programmed. We just did what we enjoyed doing, and you would have enjoyed it too. The mechanical toys we got for Christmas soon wore out. "Cheap stuff from Japan" was the truth in those days: five-cent harmonicas, cap pistols, spring-loaded cork guns, and wind-up toys. Marbles, jacks, and lotto were more enduring.

One winter, Forrest and I each got a pair of boxing gloves. We had been sparring with socks and rags over our hands. Forrest could clobber me, but I always came back for more and gave him a good fight. When the battles got lively, Mother danced around the kitchen, holding her breath: "Forrest, be careful. Shut that oven door!" "Watch the corner of that table!" "Now you'd better stop." We usually did not stop because we could tell by the tone of her voice it was not a command, just advice.

We made card games out of the dividers in Nabisco Shredded Wheat boxes by cutting them up into little inch-and-a-half squares. One game had four cards each of various kinds of flowers like roses, violets, or pinks. We made our own rules. The winner was the person who wound up with the most "books," a book being four of a kind. That game had several versions with animals, birds, and other items.

We made an action toy that was especially good for in-house weather. It got reinvented every winter just like our snowplow did. Fred Galer's buzz saw inspired our rubber band model. He came early each spring to buzz our log pile into stove-sized wood for splitting and piling. On "buzzing day," Dad and other men hoisted the logs and fed them to the saw table where Fred pulled the whirling blade back and forth, cutting them to size. Here is the spec sheet for our model: One of Mother's empty sewing thread spools was put on an axle attached to a sturdy wooden frame. A tomato can lid was attached to one end of the spool. That was the spinning saw blade and was notched to form sharp cutting teeth. A thirty-six-inch stout string was anchored to the hub of the spool and then wound around the spool with a loop in the end for the operator's finger. You would be surprised how fast and continuous the rotation. It was a two-man operation. One to pull the string steadily back and forth without stopping, the other to feed the paper to the saw. Of course, sound effects were part of the fun—the growling engine and the ripping of the paper. You'd better not get your finger in it. Rotation speed was maintained by just pulling the string to its full length and then letting the momentum of the whirling blade simply rewind the string in the opposite direction. It took some skill. Your fellow laborer, the "sawer," was trained to shove in the paper wood for cutoff on the pulling stroke. We spent many a winter hour perfecting that buzzing machine. The original paper shredder. Dougie liked to feed in the paper logs.

CHAPTER FORTEEN

MARCH
Kite Tails & Remedies

THE LION CAME WITH SNOW in his whiskers! We only dreamed of springtime in March if there was a rare warmish day. March often brought one of the wildest northeast blizzards of the winter. Now was the time to get into the woods. We would cut down and haul out the stove-wood logs for next winter's heating. Time to build that huge pile of logs in the barnyard in preparation for "Buzzing Day."

Buzz pile logs came from trees we cut down three miles away in Grandpa Portice's woods in the Sunshine School community. On his higher ground, the trees were better for stove wood: maple, birch, and tamer. We would set out after the morning chores on a Saturday morning or when we had some days off from school. For this job, the flat bed was removed from the double sleighs and high stakes were inserted in the ends of both the front and back sled bunks. Heavy cross chains connected the two sleds. Logs would be piled on these bunks inside the stakes. Dad and I could cut down, limb, crosscut to proper length, and pile on a full load of logs in four to five hours.

Eighteen inches of loose, frosty snow covered the ground in the woods. The horses and sleighs had to tramp down a road into the woods where we were cutting the timber. On the hard road to the site, we would take turns driving the team with those cold leather lines, walking behind the sleighs to keep warm. Leather mitts with woolen liners were worn at the first cutting with those ice-cold saw and axe handles. But within fifteen minutes, off came both the mitts and heavy jackets. The blood was circulating. The temperature was just right. Dad and I were having a thrilling adventure getting the heating wood for next winter. We thoroughly enjoyed working together.

By twelve o'clock, our stomachs were growling. The sandwiches were frozen solid, and a thick coat of ice covered the tea. Mother always made up a dinner for us of sandwiches, hard-boiled eggs, cookies, and a half-gallon Karo syrup can of tea with cream. Our dinner became a winter picnic. With birch bark and dry twigs, we soon had a crackling fire going. Crossed layers of dry tamarack soon had the Karo tea can sitting on top with hot flames surrounding it. Our sandwiches shoved close around the edges were toasted by the time the tea was steaming. We ate and talked, relishing every moment of our picnic by the fire. Food never tasted better. Indeed, those were moments to remember. Dad and I became a good "getting up wood" team.

Some of the logs we had to load were twelve or fourteen inches in diameter. We got them up on the sleigh bunks with teamwork and ingenuity. First, we would roll the big twelve-foot log up parallel with the sleighs with prying poles. Next, we used those same poles to leverage one end of the log up out of the snow. Then the bunk stake was removed. Those big logs needed to be loaded on first. Dad would ask, "Do you think the two of us can put her up there? I don't want you to lift too hard." Dad knew very well what my answer would be: "Sure we can; let's go." When we got our arms under the end of that log, he would once again caution: "Now, don't lift too hard; if it's too much for you, we'll just leave it here. I don't want you to hurt yourself?" The question mark was in the way he said it. We reviewed the situation again, then agreed. Together, with a mighty heave, the log rolled onto the front bunk. Now the stake was replaced and the back-bunk stake removed. This end was easier because the counterbalancing front end stuck out over the front bunk.

By four o'clock, the big load was rounded up above the height of the stakes with much longer poles above the heavy logs on the bottom.

Logging chains were fastened to the end of each bunk and over the top to the opposite ends. It was time for Bess and Colonel to head for home. By now, the sun was at the treetops, and the temperature was falling. We soon got back into our mackinaws and wool-lined mitts. Dad was anxious about getting the load out of the woods and onto the hardened road as soon as possible so that we would be sure to get home in reasonably good time. If we arrived a little early, we could even unload some logs. Those were memorable days.

By early spring, quite a mountain was ready for Mr. Galer's buzz saw and the "Buzzing Bee" date was set. Dad traded hands with neighbors for this annual event too. It only took one day for the buzz saw to convert that big log pile into a mountain of round block stove wood, enough for the next winter and summer. Now, all those blocks of wood had to be split into sizes for the kitchen stove or the front room heater. We split and stacked them in rows four feet high against the barnyard fence near the henhouse gate. It was a monstrous task that was spread out into early summer. Even in July, you could dig into the sawdust at the buzzing machine location and still find ice.

In March, the days were still short and the nights long, so we continued to enjoy our extended suppertimes by lamplight. One filling of kerosene gave us many hours of light. There were always delightful new insights in the retelling of the timber stories about Uncle Ern and our dad working in the Gogomain Swamp lumber camps when they were young. Cedar swamps and cranberry marshes were only a small part of the whole Gogomain tract of forest. Millions of board feet of prime lumber came from the higher sandy soil areas there—maple, birch, white pine, tamarack. hemlock, spruce, and basswood. Dad worked his own team of draft horses in those camps for several winters.

Around that supper table, we would go back to Mud Lake Camp cookhouse where the lumberjacks could get hot pie anytime of the day. It was smart management; lots of high-calorie meat with gravy and pie generated plenty of lumberjack energy for their labors from daylight till dark. The huge logs were rolled up into great piles as fast as the teams and sleighs brought them in from the forest. An ingenious rope arrangement rolled the logs to the top. Dad and his team of horses pulled the rope, and Uncle Ern was one of the "deckers" on top organizing the logs. A decker must be extraordinarily strong and nimble for that was a dangerous and skillful job. The standard wage was a dollar a day. Deckers and pike-polers on the river drives would get as much as two dollars per day. Dad would get good pay for his team too.

The logs were later loaded on railroad cars and steam pulled to Raber, a bustling sawmill town on Mud Lake. From the Raber sawmills, the lumber went into the maw of six-hundred-foot lake freighters and down the St Mary's river into the Straits of Mackinac. From there, the lumber went either westward into Lake Michigan toward Chicago or southward down Lake Huron to Detroit and worlds beyond. Wood was important in those days. They were producing lumber for the homes of America. Wood fed the steam railroad engine and fired the sawmill engines. Maybe the early lake steamers burned wood?

Those lumber camp men entertained themselves in their tarpaper bunkhouses each night, becoming gifted storytellers, pranksters, and champion liars. Uncle Ern's tales about the two Irishmen, Pat and Mike were a close runner-up to his many Paul Bunyan tales. We kids never tired of hearing them. Even when we heard again and again about their prank sewing up Billy Brunson's felt hat with bailing wire during the night, we enjoyed it. How they roasted one another. A spirit of camaraderie reigned in lumber camp life. Good pay, plenty of food, and hard work. Never a dull moment, and plenty of memories for them.

Fifty years later, I heard old-timers carrying on in Gough's cafe in Pickford, belaying one another with words. You would think they were arch enemies and about to come to blows. I knew the history. It all went back to those happy days together in the lumber camps. They always came up with unflattering names for one another. No offense taken. They could dish it out and they could hand it back.

Two animals were respected and well fed for one important reason beyond being fine pets—rat control. Ole Tom and Ole Tiger were famous cats on our farm. Our granary had a wood floor with divided grain bins on both sides, and at the far end of the center aisle sat the fanning mill. Each bin had removable boards on the aisle side that were put in place one by one as the amount of grain was poured in from the threshing machine. On Threshing Day, all bins were heaped full of oats, wheat, barley, speltz, peas, and flax. Peas and flax were often put in Bemis bags to make more room in the bins. They were cash crops and would soon be run through the fanning mill and sold.

If our resident tomcat took off on an excursion, our defenseless granary was ripe for an invasion of robber rats. One winter, we had a hundred or more of them strike. I think it was during Ole Tiger's reign. He had disappeared for a couple of weeks, and the rats somehow discovered that we were defenseless. First evidence was a depressed cone in the grain level of a bin. We knew they were under the floor, gnawing holes to drain out the grain. There were so many varmints that they not only bored holes under the bins; they invaded all the bins from the top. We sacked some of the grain and nailed tin from tomato cans over the rat holes in the floor. Fortunately, Ole Tiger came back just in time for our own invasion.

We held our cat back so they would come out wholesale, covering all the bins in the granary. Dad, Forrest, Ole Tiger, and I made surprise attacks about every thirty minutes. Dad had the five-tined dung fork to spear them. Forrest carried Ole Tiger and the eighteen-inch iron horse-hoof rasp. I held the kerosene lantern under my coat. We snuck out of the feeding room onto the threshing floor in the dark. When we all got in our agreed positions at the sliding granary door, Dad yanked the door open; I unsheathed the lantern while Forrest released Ole Tiger. There were ten-inch rats everywhere when we blasted in, ten or fifteen in the very first bin. Dad charged with the dung fork, and Forrest slashed with the rasp. Ole Tiger's one crushing crunch on the neck of a big rat never failed. Dad usually nailed two with the dung fork while Forrest got one or more with the rasp.

At least three raids could be made per evening. One night, they got rats cornered in a half-full grain bin. Forrest made a mighty rasp swing at a rat but hit Dad's foot covered by grain. Dad let out a yowl you could hear at the house. We retreated to see what damage was done. The grain, heavy leather boot, and double wool socks saved Dad's foot.

I really cashed in on the rat war that winter. Pickford Township paid a ten-cent bounty on every rat tail you turned in. Tails would be laid out in the barn to dehydrate and then went into my glass jar bounty bank. Sometime later, I opened a thirteen-dollar savings account at the Pickford bank.

City folks had iceboxes, and the iceman brought blocks of ice regularly. We had no such modern gadget, but we learned that ice could be cut out of the river and preserved with sawdust. Ike McDonald's sawmill had lots of free sawdust. They were glad to get rid of it. Ice cream could be made in July if we had ice. On the way to the barn, we had an old log stable that was falling apart but sometimes used as temporary shelter for young cattle in the spring or fall. Another brilliant use for that old log stable was discovered—storing ice.

By mid-March, the ice would be at maximum thickness on the Big Munuscong River at the Pickford bridge. We hauled sawdust from MacDonald's sawmill and laid down a foot-thick carpet in the old stable. There was no floor there, just dirt. We went to Pickford with Bess and Colonel hitched to the double sleighs with the long flat rack on top. Holes were cut in the sixteen-inch ice near the bridge with a spud. Then you cut out sixteen-inch squares of ice with a one-man crosscut saw. As the blocks floated free, they were pulled out with ice tongs and hoisted onto the sleigh rack. Backbreaking work pulling that old crosscut saw, but inspiring us were the thoughts of ice cream in July!

When the flat rack was full, we headed for home. We tonged and skidded the heavy blocks into the old stable, setting them in a row on the sawdust carpet with space all the way around each block. We had plenty of sawdust in the pile from the sawmill. We carried grain tubs of that free insulation to fill all around each block with a ten-inch topcoat over it all. By that time, we were ready for supper, but at least one chore had to be done first: feeding the stock. "Old bossy gets hungry, too, and she makes cream." Next day, we did it all over again and added another generous amount of ice to the stable. The ice under the buzz saw sawdust out there by the wood stack had convinced us this would work. We had perfect blocks of ice in the late summer. The great homemade ice cream made it all worthwhile. Yes, we had to turn another crank, but it was a lark compared to that cream separator.

Pumping water for the stock and getting the stock to the water was always a major chore, especially during the long winters. In the early years, we had to drive all the livestock from the barn to a large watering tank just outside the well house east of our house. That path went five hundred feet across the barnyard, through a gate and on through the field to the pumphouse. I have written of pumping that water tank full and breaking the ice each winter, morning and night, so the cattle could drink. In approximately 1926, we dug a four-foot-deep pipeline all the way between the well and the barn. Four feet deep to keep below the frost line.

It was a long digging project that summer. I can remember how hard it was to push the shovel into the dry red mud. Dipping the shovel in a bucket of water helped slightly. Many an hour we dug; it seemed like it took all summer. We kept digging and kept asking if it was necessary to go four feet deep. "Would the frost go down that far?" I asked. Dad answered yes to both questions. Finally, we got our Panama Canal completed in time for winter, laid the one-inch lead pipe, and moved the cattle tank into the stable. At this point, we had to buy a new well pump that would, on the down stroke, be able to push the water all the way underground through that one-inch pipe and up into the barn tank. The cattle could be turned loose and just swing around to drink indoors. What a luxury for the cows. It was an ingenious idea, but we soon learned that hand-operating the force pump was no luxury. It took forever to fill that thirsty herd, every day of every week.

A neighboring farmer got a small gasoline engine geared up to his force pump. With just a little gasoline, he pumped all the water he needed. Dad got in touch with the International Harvester salesman, who gladly came to our place and sold Dad a "far superior stationary engine that was bigger, heavier, more powerful, of long-lasting cast-iron construction, and well worth the money." A special pump jack adapted the sturdy engine to the force pump. *Eureka, our pumping problems were solved. Over!* Unfortunately, after a beautifully brief span of easy starting and filling the big tank in the barn, the miserable engine refused to start. All efforts failed. Back to the hand pump, which had been well named the force pump. The easy part was lifting the heavy steel handle. Forcing it down was the tough part. I had to almost get my feet off the floor and ride it down. When the International Harvester expert came, surely our expensive engine would soon be fixed and pumping water again. Not so, he would get it to fire up for a minute or two, then it would quit. After an hour or more, he left totally frustrated.

We got Fred Galer, the buzz saw man, to come. If anyone could fix it, Fred could. After a very long struggle, Fred gave up in despair. Our fancy engine was a bona fide lemon. With heavy hearts, we went back to the manual force pump. I mention this because I did most of the manual pumping for several years. I was ten years old at the time. It was then I learned to count the strokes in increments of four hundred to measure my progress as I watched through the darkness for the distant cow stable door to open. Dad would step out into the light, signaling with a hand wave and hollering, "Tank's full."

During the winter months, darkness came so early. We usually fed, watered, and bedded the stock before supper. They drank the big tank way down low. After supper, I would pump it back full while Dad and Mother were milking the twelve cows. In total darkness, it was helpful to divert my mind to various subjects or events along with the counting. One event I thought a lot about happened in 1927 when I was nine. Charles Lindbergh was the first one to fly across the ocean to Paris that year. We had heard about it in school. I flew over that cold, watery ocean in the "Spirit of St. Louis" many times while filling that tank in the night. By counting, I got some encouraging sense of the water level rising in the tank. I've forgotten how many 400s it took to get the cow stable door to open. It was always a great relief when light burst out and Dad shouted, "Tank's full." We never did get another engine.

When winter began to mellow and there were more soft snow days, the March winds began to blow. We made our own kites. Art Rich, one of our favorite clerks at Hamilton & Watson's grocery, would always reel us off a good fistful of his grocery wrapping string, free of charge. We had plenty of wind and open space. Now we were ready for the challenge of our kite's design using that ball of string, wrapping paper, homemade flour paste, and kite tails made from rags. Excitement came with the test flights, crashes, and high-flying fun. The wrapping paper was too heavy and the cotton grocery string too weak; nylon string had not arrived yet. Often, we got up over the height of the barn and the string would break.

Strangely, the worst season of flu and pneumonia came not during the bitter cold months but when the temperatures began to tilt toward springtime. It seemed like most every winter, every one of us would get down with the flu at the same time. We were sick in bed; all strength was gone. Uncle Ern and Aunt Nellie, who lived in Pickford, always came to our rescue. Uncle Ern would do the chores. Aunt Nellie would be our cook and nurse. She had been a nurse out in the Dakotas before she married Uncle Ern. She was a mail-order bride. I can still see Uncle Ern filling up the wood box for the night. He had a huge leather belt or harness tug of some kind that he buckled around one great load of stove wood, enough to fill the whole wood box. He heaved it up on his back and headed for the house—our Sampson! We admired and appreciated Uncle Ern and Aunt Nellie. It took a week for all of us to recover.

When someone at Frogpond School caught the mumps, chicken pox, measles, or lice, sooner or later, we all got it. Scarlet fever was the most dreaded of all. That required the posting of a red quarantine sign on your house door by the township authorities and the burning of clothing and bedding. To my knowledge, there were no immunization shots. We had faithful Doctor Fox and his little black bag of bitter pills and castor oil. People often died with scarlet fever; thankfully, that is one we never caught. Of course, in our cold climate, the 1918 Spanish flu took many lives. Fortunately, our flu was a milder type. We survived all our flu attacks and the many childhood diseases. I was immune to the mumps even though I slept in the same bed with my brother who had them.

We also had doctors: Mother and Dad. They applied certain strict health rules and some powerful home-brewed remedies:

1. Never drink milk after swallowing wild choke cherry juice (stomach cramps).
2. Never eat hot homemade bread just out of the oven (acute indigestion).
3. Senna tea for constipation (cheap to buy, nasty taste, but thorough).
4. Castor Oil for the spring-cleaning of your system (worst possible taste).
5. Five drops of kerosene on one tablespoon of sugar for croup (it worked!).
6. Onion soup for colds and most anything else.
7. Hot lemonade for colds and flu.
8. Watkins salve on chest and neck for colds.
9. Overnight application of hot oatmeal poultice for infected cuts, slivers, and risings.
10. Turpentine on a rag around the neck for sore throat.
11. Short haircut and kerosene for lice.
12. Severe cuts and bleeding: Apply a rag and cold water with compression. If you could not stop bleeding, apply white flour and compact dish towel or torn sheet, bundle up, and head for Pickford or the Soo.

Boils hit us several times, and the remedy was a poultice. When it came to a head, it had to be lanced, or else you could fill a bottle with steam and put it right over the boil. When the steam cooled, the vacuum created inside would pop the boil out.

Our household often had sore throats, nearly every winter. They all laughed at my cure, but it did seem to work for me. I could never convince anyone else to try it: take one sweaty four-day-seasoned woolen sock right out of your high leather boots at night and wrap it firmly around your neck, fastening it there with a large safety pin. You will soon get used to it and wake up feeling good as new. It worked for me many times. Tonsillitis was another story; I had a couple of two-week bouts with that most every winter.

A Farm Boy's Memoirs

Mother suffered over a period of years with pyorrhea in her gums and would have to go to the Soo to have teeth pulled. Many times, she had to pack her jaw with flour to stop hemorrhaging. It was a great relief the day she had them all pulled and got a new set of teeth. Another time, Mother dropped a pair of heavy shears that stuck in her foot. We used flour on her foot to stop the bleeding. I believe we applied kerosene for a disinfectant after the bleeding stopped. No doctor was called.

Of course, there was the time that Dad got kicked by a horse named Bud and had to go into the Soo hospital for surgery. Dad did not blame the young horse because he had approached quietly as he had always done with Bess and Colonel. When the curry comb touched Bud on the hip, he was taken by surprise and kicked quick as lightning with his iron shoe, right on Dad's rupture. Bess and Colonel had grown old and were retired. The new team soon became good friends with Dad.

When Dougie was a tiny baby, only Eagle Brand milk would agree with him. Once, we ran out of both Eagle Brand and money. I remembered my secret cache of rat-tail bounty dimes in the sugar bowl and dug out enough to buy the special milk for Dougie. I loved our baby brother very much, and it was not a sacrifice. I liked to tote him around in my arms.

CHAPTER FIFTEEN

APRIL
Brought Hints of Springtime

EARLY IN APRIL, THE WEATHER pattern began to moderate, and thoughts of spring began to enter our heads. However, a bad blizzard from the northeast could drive all those happy thoughts away. For some reason, a sneaky April blizzard was especially vicious. It meddled with our expectations. When temperatures got above freezing for eight or ten days in a row, it was painful to have the trend violated. Near the end of the month, bits of gravel would show up on the roads that had been solid white all winter. Spring was just around the corner. If you had any hauling to do with the team and sleighs, you had better hurry up and get it done. That gravel could create sparks on the steel sled runners and chew them up. Plus, if you had on a heavy load, you could get stuck. Without enough snow, your sleighs would become motionless.

At this time of year, those two stinky mountains in front of the stables drew our attention. The smoking one was at the horse stable. All that excellent fertilizer had to be spread on the already plowed fields that would soon be planted in grain. The snow depth on the fields was thinning, but the surface was still firm. The old one-horse "jumper" could be loaded high and still slide easily. The window of opportunity for manure spreading had arrived. Two of us would fork on a load, drive to the field, pitch it off on a twelve-foot-wide swath, and be back for another load in short order. There were a lot of loads accumulated in those all-winter piles. It took several weeks of hard work to spread all that manure. It looked like clod-sized pepper on still, snow-covered grain fields. Satisfaction came knowing that this organic fertilizer would produce a bumper crop of grain. "Organic" carried no significance to us; we had never seen or heard of commercial fertilizer.

It really was a landmark year when the manure-spreader salesman came through our part of the country and sold Dad that amazing machine. No more flinging that stuff with a dung fork until your arms ached. The new spreader had an eight-foot rectangular box that held two jumper loads. Now, all we had to do was hitch the team to the machine, pull up beside the manure pile, and fill it up. Two pitching forks could round it full in about ten minutes. Then one or both pitchers mounted the driver's seat and hauled it out to the field. You stop to pull back the lever that engages the rear cleated wheels to drive the outward whirling tedders in the back end. These move the chain drive feeder bars that carry the manure backward into the tedders. In five minutes, the box was empty. One load covered an eight-foot-wide swath of that life-giving plant food for about two hundred lineal feet. It took many loads to cover one ten-acre field. We had an adequate supply—genuine and free.

Before the invention of that wonderful machine, it took many weeks of hard labor to scatter those two manure piles over the fields. Now we could reduce the piles to zero in a week or so of intense loading, hauling, and spreading. Let spring set in and the snow melt; we were ready for planting season. That rich fertilizer added to our clay loam soil produced bumper crops, year after year. Dad rotated his fields from grain to hay every three years. The manure was applied to the grain fields each year, but not to the hay fields.

Splitting and piling wood began shortly after the annual bussing of the manure piles and continued in our spare time. This was another long, hard-labor task that had to be completed before haying time. Swing that axe for a day and you know you have been somewhere. April was the time to get started at the mountain of wood blocks. It was much easier to split while still green and frosty. There is real art to whacking a block in two with one stroke. Just as the blade hits the block, you give the axe a twist with your wrists and *zing*, it flies apart! Nothing to it, just lots of it. A whole years' worth is a lot of wood to split and pile in neat four-foot-high rows. The maple and birch hardwoods were extremely hard to split if they got dried out. When still full of frost, we boys learned to pop them off into flat slabs, just like Dad. It was comical to watch a city cousin try to split wood.

Handling axes and saws was extremely dangerous. Here again, safety was pressed upon us by both Dad and Mother. You never chopped down with an axe if your foot was in the pathway. You did not rely on moving your foot. You had to *always* place your foot out of the path so when the axe drove home, it hit the splitting block you had leaned the slab against. Stovewood was slabbed first. Then each slab was cut into sticks that would fit into the kitchen wood stove. Wood for the front room heater was usually a smaller block left its natural size.

Larger, clear-grained blocks were slabbed and split—that is where your foot was at great risk. Probably 75 percent of our wood was burned in the Renown kitchen range. While slabbing and splitting took powerful down strokes, your shoulder and arm muscles got used to it. There was pleasure in whittling down that mountain, getting it into agreeable sizes that Mother and our sisters could handle in the house. You'd better believe that if it would not fit in the wood stove or if a chunk was too big for the heater, we would hear about it. There was a lot of satisfaction seeing those long, perfectly piled four-foot rows take shape up against the house-yard fence. I can honestly say I enjoyed this adventure of growing up on a farm.

Money being scarce, we kids read every ad in the *Michigan Farmer* on the lookout for some way to make a nickel. Vivian read a remarkable offer for some kind of fancy candy. The advertiser would send her a box of garden seeds. If she sold them all and sent back the cash, she could choose her own prize from a great list. Off she went with Ole Buster and the sled. He hauled her way down to Rollie Hill's toward Stirlingville. Then Ole Buster turned and made his way to other neighbors' homes: Arnie Warren, Dan Everleigh, Joe Hill, and everybody else on the way back home. They all liked my little red-headed sister and her spunk. She sold all the garden seeds, sent back the money, and selected Delicious Boles Rolls as her prize—"a lip-smacking box of candy!" Three weeks later, Earl Miller, our faithful rural mailman delivered the delicious prize. Turns out, they were laxatives! Poor Vivie was in shock and no doubt had a crying spell; but she recovered and has been laughing about the Delicious Boles Rolls ever since.

Vivian liked to go to school early; on the way, she would drop in to say hello to Ray and Mary Dodd at the farm next door. Mary made the best big ginger cookies and was always so nice to us kids. Vivian had a crush on Ray. Of course, she told Ray and Mary all about the Boles Rolls. They helped her turn it all into laughter. We loved the Dodd family. Their son, Junior, and Dougie became fast friends.

The weekly *Michigan Farmer* magazine got a hearty welcome at our house during the Depression. The first thing we went after was "The Song of The Lazy Farmer." It was a refreshing new poem in each issue that poked fun at the lazy farmer, accompanied by an equally amusing drawing of the old couple. Mother would get bent over laughing. How she enjoyed telling others about the Lazy Farmer.

That *Michigan Farmer* did give us a good lift each week. Forrest and I read about a company that offered to buy dried hides if you skinned and cured them on a cedar shingle. We had cedar shingles and muskrats, so we bought a steel trap. Dad must have furnished the capital. We each set up a trapping line and checked it every afternoon after school. Either our bait did not work very well, or those muskrats were super smart. We caught and skinned a few, but the enterprise failed. We never tackled skunks. Forrest did get a mink once and got five dollars for that hide. Muskrat hides brought less than a dollar.

Several years later, I bought four used tires for my 1935 Ford because of an ad in the *Michigan Farmer*. They wore just fine and pulled me through a tight financial place. It may have been one of their ads that got Forrest into selling men's suits. That venture proved successful, and Forrest sold quite a few. He had his cases of sample fabrics. He would custom measure the buyer and send off the order to the manufacturer. When he delivered the new suit, he collected the money. Forrest was a good salesman, strictly honest. It would have to fit just so, that is for sure. He was particular about his own clothes. I know because I used to press his suit pants. The press had to be sharp as a knife. Forrest grew up in the very worst of the Depression years. It was hard for any young man to get a job of any kind whatsoever, but Forrest came through okay.

By late April, the spring "breakup" had begun. The snow softened and started melting. We could see the ice in the road ditches from the school down to our place was breaking up, causing open water to flow on down into Uncle George's creek. From there, it went into the Little Munuscong River. I loved geography in our country school and knew that water went into Mud Lake, Lake Huron, Lake Erie, Lake Ontario, the St. Lawrence River, and finally into the Atlantic Ocean. Our fields turned to oceans of water. The big drainage ditch cutting through the middle of our farm would flood, washing out the wooden bridge to our backfields. Both the Big and Little Munuscong Rivers were soon in flood stage. This made the old wooden bridge on the Townline Road from Frogpond School to Pickford become completely submerged under water. Now, our only hope of getting to town was to go north to Stirlingville, left across its higher modern bridge toward the Soo Road, and back down south to Pickford.

The spring flood was an exciting time. We kids lamented all our woes, but underneath we loved every minute of it. It always took Art Stewart and me a long time to manage that half mile from Frogpond School to our house gate. The big ditch on our side of the road would be brim full but would ice over each night. Sometimes, that would hold for several days. Art and I dared one other to take running skids across that ice. It might sag and crack a little, but that was the thrill. Invariably, we would get home with boots full of water and complain of the bad conditions underfoot with holes in our boots. I doubt that our parents were fooled. They knew very well what we had been doing. They had been young once and experienced the spring breakup just like us. Fortunately, when water came in over the tops of our boots, the holes down below drained it out.

One of those evenings, we were almost up to our gate when I went through the ice, clear to the bottom. Heavyweight Soo Woolen Mill foldcloth pants and my water-filled boots anchored me right there in the ice water up to my elbows. I pawed and scratched unsuccessfully, but Art got hold of my arm and hauled me out. Shivering, I waddled toward our house in those ballooned-out foldcloth pants with water squirting out of the holes in my boots. Art headed on home too. With chattering teeth, I made it across the ditch plank, through the yard gate, and into our house. Our cousin, Esther Hanna, had arrived for supper that night via the opened-up Sunshine School Road. That was a delightful sight for me. Comedian Esther's good humor, Mother and Dad's gratitude that I had not drowned, and my sincere regrets somehow got me off the hook. Soon, I was into dry clothes, enjoying a good supper around our big kitchen table. Esther Hanna was a young schoolteacher and a one-in-a-million cousin to us. We kids all loved her and so did Mother and Dad. What a never-to-be-forgotten evening it turned out to be.

Spring fever was the best fever we ever caught in our Frogpond community. It broke out in a rash of yearning to be free from schoolroom bondage. It would get so bad that I'd just sit at my desk, staring out the window. Concentration on the geography book was impossible when real live geography was going on just outside the schoolhouse door. "The snow is melting all around us; water is trickling everywhere; you hear it under the crust and see it running under the ice. The whole world is shedding its blanket of white and becoming water. Spots of bare ground are showing up. The pike are coming up the rivers; they will soon be up in Uncle George's Creek!" Such were our ruminations. We wanted to skip school and go fishing.

Looking out the north side kitchen window, twenty acres of our fields were underwater, clear back to the big drainage ditch and beyond. All the sea stories we had read in school came alive. We must set sail on this wide ocean. We had no boat, but why not a raft! Forrest and I found some old eight-foot cedar fence posts and scrounged up some rusty or bent spikes to nail rough boards across them, making a proper deck. We stuck up a pole and tied an old calf blanket or bedsheet on for a sail. By holding the sail out from the mast, we caught the strong west wind and were bounding eastward across the wide Atlantic. Our ocean was so crystal clear; you could see all the way to the bottom. No need for life belts; it was twelve inches deep. All went well until we hit the woven wire fence at the east end of the field and had to pole back the forty rods to the house. There we tied up until the next voyage. Even though we were wet and tired, our hearts were singing "Columbia the Gem of the Ocean."

As soon as that same field became open water, the first flock of Canadian geese would arrive. At sunset, they would settle in for the night not more than seventy-five feet from our home. From the north end window upstairs, you could look right down on them. There might have been four hundred big geese honking and gabbling all night long while I was sound asleep. Many a morning, we set out for Frogpond School and the geese were still over there in our "lake." Dad tried several times to shoot a goose, but somehow their thick coat of feathers would deflect the old .38-55 bullets. We had no shotgun, so we never did roast a wild goose. It was interesting to watch flocks circle over the area at dusk. Seemingly, on orders from a commander-in-chief goose, they would all put down their landing flaps and clatter into a landing. When they took off in the morning, they flapped their wings like crazy and rose like a squadron of airplanes. They did not seem to be afraid of us; we were never allowed to disturb them in any way. As I recall, these nightly stopovers continued for about three weeks.

One time, when the water had gone down some, Dad or Mother gave me permission to go visit the McConkey boys. Excitedly, I went down the lane to the far east end of our eighty acres, through the Joe Boer bush, and out another mile to see them. Clifford and I were good friends. We rambled and played together for hours. Before we knew it, suppertime had arrived. Mrs. McConkey asked me to stay and eat with them. *Why not? Mother knows where I am. She will know they invited me to stay for supper*, I thought. Supper lasted longer than I figured, and it became pitch-black outside. Mrs. McConkey said, "You can't find your way home in the dark, so just spend the night with us." There was no telephone; we were worrying about it together. It was decided that I should stay for the night; my folks knew where I was and would expect that I might be asked to spend the night. Just then, a knock came to the door. There stood Dad with the lantern, asking, "Is Clifton here?" "Yes Bert, the lads were playing," explained Mrs. McConkey. "We invited him to stay for supper, not thinking it would be dark and dangerous for him to go home. We were discussing what to do when you knocked."

"Well, there's lot of water in the fields," said Dad. "And there is a big drainage ditch running through our place. We feared he might have fallen into it on his way home. We were scared and imagined all kinds of things." I was listening, scared at what could have happened to me and thinking, *How great it is that Dad came all this way in the dark with the lantern, looking for me.* They had Dad come in to talk for a while. As I recall, they agreed that I should spend the night with Clifford and come home the next morning. Dad had to walk back through the woods and water alone. He did not scold me in any way. I have often thought of that night and how it probably contributed to the close bond we had across the years.

Sugar maple trees were plentiful in the forests on the higher ground southeast of our farm. Uncle Sandy and Aunt Mary Hanna lived on a sand farm in the Stalwart community. The soil was not so good, but sugar maples were plentiful. In the later part of April, the sap began to run. Uncle Sandy would make a small incision on each tree and hang a small tin bucket to catch the steady drip. Each morning, he would go through the woods with his one-horse dray and barrel to gather the sap. I had the opportunity to watch firsthand. Near his house at the edge of his maple forest, he had a long, metal boiling pan. It was about four feet wide by sixteen feet long and perhaps eight inches deep. Metal legs held it up high enough for a full-length wood fire beneath. When I arrived, there was a bed of coals under the boiling sap. Uncle Sandy was just finishing his morning rounds of collecting from the tree taps. He dipped the clear sap out of his barrel into the vat. To increase the heat, he put new pieces of wood to the fire underneath where needed. If the syrup began to boil over, he would dip in a pork rind just long enough to settle it down. That acted like oil on water. This process went on for hours until the sap boiled down to a thick, tasty golden maple syrup, fit for a king's table. I was so taken up with Uncle Sandy's maple syrup that I tried to make syrup from the bark of a maple tree we had cut down for firewood, but it did not work. Must not have been a sugar maple.

Uncle Sandy was a big, laid-back chubby fellow with a jolly laugh. He never seemed to have a worry in the world. No supply of winter wood was laid in, he just cut off a green maple log as needed. His speech was dragged out as he chuckled, "Ha-ha-ha, my good land sakes! Mary, could you make some biscuits and applesauce?" Aunt Mary was Mother's oldest sister. A dear, easygoing lady she was, with the sweetest smile. Seeing a touch of amusement in her Irish eyes, we knew her biscuits would soon be on the way. Vivian recalled a sweet memory: "Aunt Mary was the most humble, sweetest person—and loving. She'd go out to the little old milk house and get a jar filled with cream and shake that jar till the cream turned into butter. Then she would mix up a batch of biscuits with raisins in them. Never have I tasted biscuits as good as them. And when they were baked, we would have a meal of hot homemade biscuits with butter and lots of applesauce."

Uncle Sandy's hay and grain crops were very thin due to the sandy soil. But they were sure able to raise a wonderful family. I was closely acquainted with three of them. They were the funniest people I ever heard, natural born Red Skeltons. Melvin and Kermith found humor in everything they talked about. Just listening to those two, you would soon be in stitches. Esther was their match in any yarn. We claimed she was full of devilment; her Irish eyes twinkled when she laughed. Those three could easily make your day fun. Mother always got us on April Fool's day with some outlandish event that was going to happen. We all got revved up and spent the whole day trying to April fool one another for fun.

Clifton Nixon

CHAPTER SIXTEEN

MAY
Spring Mischief

IT WAS ALWAYS FUN TO DISCOVER the very first flowers of springtime. The ditch from Frogpond School went under a culvert into the headwaters of Campbell Creek. I discovered blue flagons growing right up from the bottom. Just a little way farther into the bush, there was an old, decayed stump where the very first arbutus peeked out of the cold earth. I remember taking my sisters there to see that miracle flower.

Some seventy years later, I wrote these nostalgic lines about Springtime:

> Look at the morning, look at the day
> Look at the ole farmer turning his hay
> Look at the roses down by the mill
> Turning all sour thoughts into a thrill
> Look at the swallows carving the sky
> Gracefully teasing my wishes to fly
> If all the city kids could just only see
> All this 'Disney World' so attractive to me
> At a rotting old stump way deep in the woods
> Where the very first flower of springtime emerged
> 'Twas a tiny arbutus, so beautiful to me
> If all the big city kids could just only see.

As the floodwaters abated in springtime, the pike, mullet, and suckers came up to spawn. Only the pike came up into the shallower creeks like Uncle George's. With pitchforks poised for action, we would tiptoe along the edge of the creek to spot a pike at standstill in waving underwater grass. Down would come the back side of the pitchfork. You were hoping to just stun the fish so you could reach down and pull him out. Dad was an expert at it and usually brought home eighteen-inch pike for supper. I never could do it like Dad.

For the mullet and suckerfish, there was a three-pole "stand" across the Little Munuscong River by Jim Stewart's farm. Two poles, eight inches apart, were the walkway. The third pole was three feet higher for a handrail and seat. Two fishermen took positions in the middle, thrusting their six-foot-wide net of chicken wire stretched between poles. When the fish hit, they would holler, "Lift!" Up came the net with often two big fish twelve to sixteen inches long. The suckers were not fit to eat, but mullet were tolerable. Good netters could swing their catch over to the riverbank without budging from the stand. We took turns netting and by ten o'clock at night, we would have a washtub full of mullet. The pike were bony and the mullet oily. One meal of mullet was enough. The rest became garden fertilizer. Years later, Art Stewart told me his mother pickled the mullet in vinegar, and they were good. That was the extent of our fishing. Except, delicious smelt fish was given to us by people who lived on smelt spawning streams. I think we had fried smelt at Aunt Mary's one time. They were great compared to mullet or bony grass pike.

Springtime could bring out the mischief in us. Vivian recalled this fun memory: "They used to tease me about Ernie Stewart, and we called him the clothespin. I pushed him into our front ditch of water. He ran home, screaming, and shortly thereafter Mrs. Stewart called Mother. Oh boy, I'm not sure what was said. I was about eight or nine." My sister Marie told me about another springtime adventure. From school, Forrest, Ellsworth Lordson, Jack Ames, and Mervin O'Brien saw all the floodwater from Shobrook's fields over the road to the Nixon house eastward, as far as the eye could see. Only one thing to do if they got the chance: ship and set sail. They became a raft and scurvy crew that soon got into trouble. Big Mervin O'Brien pushed Forrest overboard into the icy brink—heavy woolen shirt, britches, leather boots, and all. When they got back to the schoolhouse, our teacher, Millie Gough, immediately slapped restrictions on Forrest. He was to sit there in those soaking wet clothes until six o'clock. Dad was just getting ready to go to school to get Forrest when he saw him coming. What a tale of innocent adventure, persecution, and unreasonable punishment Forrest told Dad. Next morning, Dad went to the school. Marie put it this way: "I don't know what all Dad said to her, but there wasn't much love lost between her and our family. She had pets in school, but we sure weren't one of them."

Early May was repair and blacksmith time, getting ready for summer's work. Horses must be shod, hoofs trimmed, loose shoes re-nailed, and worn shoes replaced. Most every spring, I spent a whole day with Dad and our team at the blacksmith shop. We had three of them in Pickford. Mr. Oak Roe was our favorite. His face would be blackened with soot as his strong, brawny arms worked. By the hour, I watched him work, thrusting the metal into the fire and turning the air crank to fan the fire until the piece was red hot. Sometimes he would sprinkle what looked like pepper on the glowing steel and shove it back into the fire for more heat. Then he would lay it on the anvil to hammer it thinner, wider, narrower, or rounder. When he was satisfied, into the water tank it went. You could hear the sizzle when the tempering process began. Mr. Roe would lift the horse's foot between his knees while he chiseled, rasped, and shaped the hoof to fit the shoe. He would drive nails from the underside up through holes in the horseshoe into the bone-dry part of the hoof. He was a man to be admired. A lot of teams were waiting their turn, so I had many hours to watch. He never seemed to mind. I guess that was why we liked him so much.

Seeding the fields, haying time, and harvest lay ahead of us, so many things had to be checked and fixed. We made sure the Pittman drives were good to go. Broken axles got welded. Dull blades on the six-foot mower bar were sharpened, and missing or broken blades replaced. Sickle blades had to be riveted in place. Dad could do all of that, and I learned to help him. There were many things to be replaced: broken tines on the hay rake, broken handles on pitch forks and worn-out cogs, weak harness tugs, worn out horse collars, cracked wagon tongues, and broken whippletrees. Lost bolts, kingpins, bent levers, burrs, and spikes on the drag harrows also had to be replaced, just to mention a few.

Our two wagons had to be worked over. Each wheel had to be pulled almost off so axle grease could be smeared on the hub, pushed back in place, reburred and locked with a key. The hay mower, seed drill, manure spreader, grain binder, and hay rake disk harrows had to be greased. There was a never-ending list of oil cups to fill and keep full on the grain binder, the hay mower's Pitman bearing, and the cream separator.

Planting was the beginning of the hard work. Try driving a team of horses pulling a ten-foot spread of tooth harrows up and down a forty-rod stretch on a ten-acre field. You walk behind and steer with the long lines, stumbling and bouncing over clods of dirt. Engineer the turn-around at each end of the field and be careful you do not upend the harrows on yourself or the horses. Both team and driver were hungry by noon, then tired and hungry by suppertime.

My dad was a good farmer and nearly always had bumper crops of hay and grain. He was, I thought, thorough to a fault sometimes. First came the disk harrows that cut only a six-foot swath. Thankfully, it had a riding seat as you crunched over the plowed ground. There were a lot of turns in a ten-acre field. Then the drag harrow was used to break up the clods. If that did the job, you planted. If not, the drag harrow was used again.

We had good appetites. Mother had her own dinner call that could reach us at the back of our farm. Here's Vivian's description: "We used to call Mother the Old Mill Whistle. She and Dad had an arrangement when he was out in the fields and dinner was ready. She would go out, get lots of air, cup her hands, and then yell 'B-u-u-r-r-r-r-r-r-r-r-r-r-r-t.' Then he would wave back at her, and she knew he heard. Even our neighbors could hear her, and they, too, knew it was dinnertime." Old Colonel heard too. You might as well drop the traces and head for the barn. It was a near perfect imitation of Ike MacDonald's sawmill whistle. I loved to hear it too.

When the soil was properly "mellow," as Dad would say, we used the seed drill up and down the field with six-foot coverage each way. Afterward, the drag harrows were used; we walked behind them with the depth gauge set shallower to harrow the seed into the soil. The next five or six ten-acre fields were waiting for us. We also farmed Uncle Ern's "old place." If Dad planned to switch a given field to hay the following year, he would plant grass seed as well as the grain seed for the current year. This was done with a hand-turned cyclone, the coverage measured by the speed of his walking and the speed of his turning. It took a skillful ten-acre grid walk to sow this expensive red clover and timothy seed.

The potato patch and garden were always planted after the major fields. The Upper Peninsula soil and growing season produced good potatoes, cabbage, rutabagas, beets, beans, carrots, and tomatoes. Tomatoes would not ripen, but the green ones were made into "governors," a pickled delight we ate year-round. Corn was grown for ensilage, but the season was too short for ripening. We planted half an acre of potatoes. Irish potatoes were a year-round dinner staple at our house. Mother saw to it that our pantry shelves were well stocked with pickled beets and governors. In the hard Depression years, mashed potatoes with governors was a tasty dish. Beet tops and "pigweeds" were the only greens we ever ate. Later, I learned the technical name for pigweeds was "lamb's quarters." They came up as weeds do in the spring but had an excellent, mild flavor. Only when Uncle Sam took me south did I learn about some other vegetables, like turnip, collard, and mustard greens.

About this time of year, we sent off for spring chickens. They came in a pasteboard box by Stage. It was a touch-and-go business to keep them alive until they were big enough to transfer to the henhouse. Our kitchen was the nursery. Intensive care included lantern heat at night, blue vitriol in their drink, and special mash food. You had to watch closely lest they crowd up and smother, or peck and kill one another. As I recall, about twenty-five of those leghorns would make it through the pullet stage and eventually join the egg-laying flock in the henhouse. What a thrill to gather those beautiful white eggs from the row of nests in the henhouse. Mother would quickly ready them for delivery to Hamilton & Watson's Grocery store in Pickford in exchange for groceries.

We always had some Plymouth Rocks and a rooster or two. These were a self-propagating variety and made their nests in the haymows or some secret place. It was a happy surprise each summer when the mother hen trotted out her little flock from the land of nowhere. Hawks spotted these little fuzzy broods, too, and would dive down to snatch them up. However, the mother hen would let out a warning squawk, sending the little chicks running underneath her feathers until the attack was over. No hawk would tangle with the wrath of a mother hen.

Sometimes we bought turkey, duck, or a special variety of chicken eggs and slipped them under "setting" hens. It worked. Oh, the delight we kids had watching the nest and waiting for the first chicks to peck their way out of the shells. New life right before your eyes! It was always fun searching for eggs and new nests. If the hen was setting, she was not to be disturbed. We found lots of eggs in the hidden nests of these ingenious freelancers. We ate those brown eggs. The stout Plymouth Rocks made good baking hens. That is how we got our Thanksgiving and Christmas turkeys—free enterprise production!

My years on the farm were in the pre-tractor age. Bess and Colonel were our powerful draft horses that turned the sod, cultivated the soil, and cut the hay and grain. They hauled all the harvested hay and grain into our big barn. After the hay was bailed, they took it all the way to the railhead in Rudyard. In the winter, they hauled a years' worth of logs from the woods for our woodpile. Some winters, Dad took them to work with him in the lumber camps. Our old retired spare horse was kept busy too.

I have talked about "Doctor Dad" earlier, but praise of his veterinarian skills is worth a double mention. Horses have many medical problems, like colic and fatal bloating if they drink too much water when sweating. Dad kept a quart-size bottle of kerosene handy if a horse went down; he would lift its head to force it down their throat. Relief came in a few minutes. Our lathering draft horse team coming in from the hayfields was only allowed a short drink of water until they had cooled down. Liniment must be applied to spavins on the hocks and feet. Shoulder sores could develop under their collars from sweat lather and chaffing, leading to infection. Thick pads under the collar, close inspection, and care were a must. They must get a complete grooming every night with a curry comb and brush to remove all remnants of dried lather. A horse was never to be overworked. If they began to lather under their collars in hot weather, it was time to stop and rest until they cooled down. Otherwise, the horse could develop the heaves, something like asthma, which ruined the animal beyond repair.

Dental and foot care of our horses was vital. Horses' teeth need to be filed, so Dad was also a horse dentist. Foot injuries, overgrown hoofs, a loose shoe, a stone, or something caught between the shoe and hoof—all required "Doctor" Nixon's attention. Off came the shoe and the source of the limp discovered: the hoof was trimmed, rasped, ointment applied, and the shoe renailed in place. Then, he observed the foot closely before putting the horse back to work. Dad guarded the health of our horses with just the right mixture of oats and hay, doctoring, grooming, and loving care.

Surgical operations had to be performed on young cattle and hogs. Dad did it all. I watched him do it. His disinfectant was turpentine, I believe. If a cow needed assistance to have her calf, Dad would roll up his sleeves and get to work turning the calf around in the right direction and attaching a rope to help pull the calf out. I would be on the rope learning Biology 101, indeed. It was a unique experience to wash up, see that cow lick her calf, and watch the calf soon struggle to its feet, wobbling around alive. Neighbors sometimes came to get Dad to help them save a cow or other animal in serious trouble. In the earlier days, there was no vet available. As a family, we developed affection for our animals and received many years of faithful benefits from them.

Seeding always began by Memorial Day, but that was a time to lay aside all other interests and spend the day at the Bethel Cemetery where our loved ones were buried. It was about four or five miles north of Pickford on the way to the Soo, a seven-mile drive from our home. Mother always fixed a royal lunch basket. We boarded the flat hay wagon pulled by Bess and Colonel for many years. Later, we went in our Model-T Ford. Dad always insisted on stopping at Hamilton & Watsons Grocery in Pickford for some bananas and cheese. That was a must for every picnic.

Upon arrival, all hands began pulling weeds and grass, planting flowers, and fixing up the gravesites of our dear little brothers, Clarence and Merlin, and sweet little sister, Eva. We were cautioned to walk only on designated paths lest we step on someone's gravesite. We also took care of Grandpa and Grandma Nixon's gravesites. Uncle Ern and Aunt Nellie joined us, and we worked together. At noon, a blanket was spread under a shady tree for the holiday feast. Many people had gathered. It was a day of celebration and remembering with respect. Scriptures and words of affection were read with contemplation of each person and date. Looking back to those Memorial Days, I see it as a wonderful event for both our families and our community.

CHAPTER SEVENTEEN

JUNE
Pick'ns

BY EARLY JUNE, ALL THE GRAIN fields would be planted. The hay fields grew taller and thicker toward a two-ton-per-acre crop. It was also wild strawberry picking time. The whole family got involved during this brief lull before haying time started. Harvey Campbell's unoccupied farm across the road from us was a gold mine for wild strawberries. Harvey lived in Fairview and welcomed our picking. The bigger berries grew in older hay fields where the clover and timothy grass were thinned out quite a bit.

The standard berry bucket was a two-quart Karo syrup can. In two or three hours, one good picker could fill a can. Even Dad would get into the berry-picking fun after the evening chores were done. Mother did the canning and got into picking some too. Competition was keen as to who could fill his pail first. When Mother got fifty quarts canned for the pantry shelves, we could pick and sell strawberries to the "wealthy" matrons of Pickford. We got twenty-five cents per two-quart pail. The two-and-a-half-mile walk to Pickford would jostle the berries down badly. This was solved by covering the top and shaking it upside down. Equity was restored, and our pockets jingled with cash as Depression-era entrepreneurs.

The wild berries lasted about fifteen or twenty days. After that, we older kids went to Jimmy Ralph's tame strawberry patch. He paid us twenty-five cents per every twelve-box crate we picked. More competition. More cash. Another strawberry man in Kelden would let you pick your own berries for a dollar per crate. This is how we stocked our pantry shelf with tame strawberries. That jolly man had a peculiar high-pitched voice. We always just called him "Mr. Dollar-a-Crate."

Our old rhubarb bed in our house yard never failed to yield us some scrumptious rhubarb pie and preserves. Mother knew how to get the best flavor out of them! I can still taste her rhubarb pie.

The hops bush was beside the small gate to the mailbox. It was one of our most important plants that sprouted back to life in June. Mother used the hops to start her "Old Witch" yeast jar, a year-round source of yeast for bread making. The two-quart glass jar contained the powerful yeast concoction. When she used it down for a six or eight loaf batch of bread, all she had to do was add more potato water. In just a week, the yeast would be as powerful as ever. Just keep it from freezing in the winter!

The mosquito invasion came in June. Each evening as darkness approached, bloodthirsty millions arose from everywhere. There really was no defense. We could see deer driven out of the woods, trying to find relief. Our screens were absent or torn. Lamplight drew them in by hordes, so we sat in the dark and went to bed with the chickens. Next morning, all was clear; but come evening, they were all over us again. The plague lasted ten or twelve nights. Thankfully, it never came at strawberry picking time or else we would have had to do our picking in the hot sun. No one could pick berries while trying to fight off those mosquitoes.

Then, those meddling beavers started threatening our grain crops. The very same generous spring rains that helped the grain sprout up and grow turned into a nightmare. Those enterprising beavers would build a big dam to form their own private lake down in the Armstrong woods. Water would back up all the way into our "big ditch," overflowing into acres of our tender, young six-inch seedlings. We were not planting rice. A couple days of water would kill our winter wheat, oats, barley, or speltz. You did not dare touch the beavers or their super dam. They were protected by the law! They built their own ecosystem for propagation and food storage with underwater entrances beneath their dam. It is a sight to behold a family of beavers chew down large trees, cutting them into pieces to build a dam with wood, limbs, debris, and mud all pounded into place by their big, flat tails. They work at night and disappear by day into their domed house in the middle of the lake. Joe Hill, the game warden, had eagle eyes. We knew the fines were high; my Uncle Webster got caught trapping them. Our only hope was to reach Joe in time to have him come and dynamite a hole in the top edge of the beaver dam. This would quickly lower the water level while preserving the beavers' priority project. Joe Hill was a good and highly respected man. He always came promptly but had to make many return trips. Those beavers could have the rent repaired overnight with the water climbing again. Oh, the excitement a farmer enjoys!

Up until we kids were about ten years old, we started going barefoot sometime in June. In a couple of weeks, our feet would be so tough we could run freely on all the farm surfaces. Now that's real freedom. It sure cut down on the footwear budget. Amazing how tough your feet get that you have no trouble at all running through a stubble field. In the fall, a heavy frost on the cow pasture would be hard to handle barefoot. When a cow gets up to head for the barn, you run to that warmed spot. Now you know, it is about time to go back into shoes. A cut or two on our feet each summer did not slow us down much. I once got a bad gash wading in the ditch in front of our place. We boys used to scrub our overalls out there to help cut down on Mother's wash load. I do not recall ever getting a serious infection. If it started getting red around the cut, an oatmeal poultice was applied immediately.

Yes, we had time for lots of summertime play while we were growing up. Hoops were a lot of fun. A cross piece was nailed on the end of a stick with a ten-inch metal wheel rim that became a motorcycle or automobile complete with all the sound effects. You kept the wheel rolling with the stick and ran real fast. The fenced lane from our barnyard clear back to the back forty was our speedway. The cow, horse, and wagon traffic made it very dusty. We tied something around our waist to drag behind raising dust. We had two fourteen-inch spoked iron wheels left over from some worn-out machine. We inserted a stout stick into the one-inch hole of each axle to simulate high-powered cars for racing up and down the lane. Later, they might be made into a two-wheeled dog cart. Old, worn out metal became something great for us.

There were slingshots for target shooting, and attempts were made to kill crows or rabbits. Rubber band guns of all kinds allowed us to play cops and robbers. Stores were set up to make mud pies you could purchase with make-believe money. Eggs mixed with mud made an unusual pie. Long wooden spears turned us into African warriors. Bows and arrows made us ferocious Indian fighters. Sports included softball with homemade bats and every imaginable substitute for a ball, custom designed. Everything was homemade except for the two wheels and iron hoops. Believe it or not, a wilted beet made a long-lasting ball. Sometimes, hammered cans were wound around with cord-cut leather from an old boot. High-jump and pole-vault stands were easy to make. A young, green tree trunk made a flexible pole for vaulting. All this, plus rambling around in Campbell's bush made us very tired kids. By bedtime, we would be well fed, exhausted, and soon sound asleep. Mother could see around corners and even up the ladder to our beds. Often, she would call up to us, "Boys, did you wash your feet?" "Noooooo, we're so sleepy." "Well, you get out of that bed and get right down here and wash those feet. Get down this minute." Down the ladder stairs we came, half asleep and dizzy. The lesson would last for quite a while. It was so hard to come down the ladder just to wash our feet; what a waste of time. We sometimes nearly fell asleep saying our prayers. Mother would wake us and pile us into bed.

Dad had a winsome way of getting us boys to be his happy helpers. Life was not all play. It was a joy to be taken into partnership with him on all kinds of projects. Fence repairing was a two-man job. One on the handle of the wire puller at the end of the field to hold the wire tight. The other man went along driving "steeples" in each post of that long stretch. For one man, it would be like a one-armed paper hanger with the hives. Dad made you feel special to be his helper. On a rainy day in town, we would hear him telling a neighbor how "we" finished up the fencing. We felt indispensable; often, he would have to tell us to go back to play.

Cedar fence posts rotted off. Cattle reaching between the barbed wire would finally stretch and break it, or the wires would rust and break. By night, the neighbor's cattle would cause a disaster in our grain field. It might even be our own cattle, such as the "Old Batho Cow"—one of our best milk cows. If a gate were left open, she would find it; if a fence sagged, she went over the top. She could jump over a low gate. How she loved to get out of the pasture and come down the lane into our garden at night. The row of beets would be cut off like somebody did it with a knife. We could see her tracks as she innocently stood where she belonged—in the pasture field.

We put a wooden frame around her neck. That did not stop her. We hobbled her by tying a rope from her back foot to her horn, pulling her head to one side. Still, she laid back her head and got over the lane fence into the barnyard before heading out to the road. From there, she lifted the little latch on the mailbox gate. She must have quite a brain to get into our house yard garden. Our prize beets were trimmed again. Still, we appreciated this gentle cow for giving us a twelve-quart pail of milk twice a day.

When haying started, everything else halted. One summer, there was one big "in between" venture I will never forget. Picture Dad and me climbing way up on the barn roof to put on new cedar shingles. Now there is a slow, tedious, and hot job. Very exacting, the rows must be straight, right to the string. Each bundle of cedar shingles must be carried up. They were made up of assorted widths—four to seven inches. Imagine laying shingles one hundred feet to a line. Each one must be carefully selected to straddle every gap in the previous row. Each shingle must be nailed in at just the right place. Our big hay and cattle barn measured forty by one hundred feet, so each side of the steep snow-bearing roof measured twenty-five by one-hundred-four feet That translates to one hundred rows of shingles! Each row advanced only six inches. Small wonder Mother always spoke of "the summer we shingled the barn." There was not much slack time that summer between the seeding, haying, and grain harvest.

While still in my teens, Uncle Ern put up a new barn on his place. I had gained enough climbing and shingling experience to be allowed on the purlin plate, twenty feet above the ground on that barn-raising day. I also helped Uncle Ern shingle that barn. I am sure he must have paid me something, for he was always good to us. It was a great feeling to be unafraid and trusted by Dad and Uncle Ern. I could lay my row of shingles right on the chalk line and keep up with the men. A Barn Raising was an epic event. All the neighborhood folk were present, and a huge dinner was spread. Professional barn hewers had all the bents, plates, and rafters laid out and bolted together for raising into place by many men with long pike poles. The mammoth skeleton put up and strongly fastened together in one day. This was a festive event with wonderful community bonding, another milepost for Mother's historical measuring system. When Mother was asked when such and such happened, she could zero in on the exact year, the month, and often the exact day. "It was the day of Uncle Tom's barn-raising. It was the year the sawmill burned, and I remember my sister Mary wore that new dress Grandma made her for Christmas. It was the year the river rose clear up to our door." "Eureka, it was in 19 xx because Mary was xx years old and she was born in xx." Mouths gapped; mine did too.

We walked the five-mile round trip to the Presbyterian Sunday School and Church a few times each summer. Vivian says Mother would put cardboard in our shoes to cover the holes so we could go. Mr. Ham Hamilton often invited us to come to church; I was always impressed with his earnestness. Viv also remembers Mrs. Jack Gough taking us to vacation Bible school at the Methodist Church where we all got little black Testaments. "I believe it was our first year back at Frogpond School after they took us to Pickford School for one year, so that would have been about 1928," Vivian recalled. I distinctly remember going from the consolidated Pickford School over to the Methodist Church to hear the sky-pilot evangelist.

Our road from Frogpond School to Sunshine School was a county road, but there was little maintenance done on it. We got one dollar off our taxes for each wagon load of gravel we spread out on that badly rutted road. Late June was the window of opportunity for this. The gravel box was put on the high-wheeled wagon. Dad and I went perched on the two-man seat atop the box with our draft team, Bess and Colonel. It was four miles to the pit. We snaked down a steep grade to the bottom and shoveled on our gravel load by hand. Colonel was properly threatened lest he slacken on the heavy pullup out of the pit. The four-mile trudge back home was comradery time for my dad and me. We chatted together on all kinds of subjects as we helped cut down our tax bill. I was in high clover.

When we got to our road, we straddled the worst rutted places and stopped. The bottom of the gravel box was made up of close-fitting four-by-fours sticking out a few inches beyond the moveable end "gates." Each four-by-four was fashioned on each end so we could get the big iron crowbar in place and pry up. First, the end gates were pried out, then each four-by-four one at a time, thus dropping the gravel. I moved the horses ahead a wagon length per third of a load. When the floor pieces were put back in place, the gates inserted, and the seat reset, we went for dinner. We hoped to make another haul that afternoon. It was extremely rewarding work, smoothing out our road. Dad had a way of making me feel like a main part of the project.

CHAPTER EIGHTEEN

JULY
Hay Days

BY JULY, THE FIRST HAYING would be underway. It was the beginning of the hardest and hottest worktime of the year. A high sense of urgency set in and lasted until all the hay and grain was safely in the barn. "Make hay while the sun shines" was no mere saying. With an extremely short growing season and early fall rains, whole fields of grain were sometimes a total loss. Hay curing was very touchy. If it got too much sun and browned, its sale value went down. If you put hay in the mows too green, it would get musty and "burn." I can remember hearing Dad and Mother moan about a few lost crops in former years.

    First, the hay was cut down with the horse-drawn mower. When it had dried just right, it was raked into winnows with the one-horse riding rake for more curing. Then, it was "coiled" for final curing before being loaded on the big, low-wheeled wagon and hauled into the barn. Coiling was my favorite place to shine. Each miniature must be properly built into a coned stack that would shed rain. At ten and eleven years of age, I could almost keep up with my dad as we built our parallel coils of hay. He would come over and help me catch up occasionally and caution me not to work too hard. During one haying time, Dad went into town for something and came back with a very special pitchfork for me. The handle was about two-thirds the length of the standard adult fork. It was my pride and joy.

The first three days of haying were the toughest. It was a struggle. It was just too hard. You would be huffing, puffing, and dreading each hour. But about the fourth day, the sweat glands got opened and all that sluggishness vanished. Bring on the hay! Literally, that was so. We would be wringing wet with sweat. We had no air conditioning or fans inside the house, and our favorite drink at dinnertime was hot tea! Hot tea seemed to get the body's cooling system working. The affect was cooling and refreshing. It was dangerous to drink any large amount of cold water when overheated. You could soon become deathly sick with stomach cramps. Our horses were only allowed a little sip of water until they had cooled down. Mr. Ferrack, a polish man from Goetzville, used to work for Dad in haying season. He always put raw oatmeal in his water jug when working in the heat. We learned to do the same.

It was always my lot to "build the loads" when it was time to "haul in." The hay wagon rack was eighteen feet in length with front and back six-foot, full-width ladders. The flat rack was eight feet in width and extended out over the low, wide-rimmed steel wheels underneath. The driving lines for Bess and Colonel were tied slack to the front rack so the "builder" could move about receiving, spreading and balancing out the hay as it was pitched up from the coils. Dad and Jim

Stewart both would be pitching on hay. Sometimes hay came at me from both sides at the same time from their separate rows of coils.

If heave-hoed from the same coil, they would insert their pitchforks and come up with a mountainous load together. I was scrambling to separate and spread it to fit the rack before another load came up to hustle into place. By that time, I was huffing, puffing, and wielding my pitchfork like crazy. The fourth and last lift from that coil came up at me with a command to move. All I could do was wade through hay to the front ladder, grab the lines, and say "giddyup" and "whoa" to Bess and Colonel near the next coil.

Before I could jolt to a stop, another whirlwind of hay landed. Four big pitches about as big and heavy as Dad and Jim can get off the ground. Four in a row! I remember being half-buried in hay, trying to unscramble it in order to make a balanced load. Once accomplished, it was time to move again! This time, Dad halted Jim so I could finish spreading past lifts of hay. Sensing I was done, Dad hollered, "When you're ready, Clifton." Loving a challenge, I hollered back, "Okay." Now, because they were having to pitch the weight higher, the workload was moderating. However, a new challenge lay for me. I needed to tramp the hay more. It also required deeper tramping, and the balance-of-load factor started to get critical. This two-ton load of hay was a fixed four-foot bunk over the low back wheels and a single point over the swiveling bunk on top of the front axle. The whole load had to be moved with caution over every furrow bump; turning around was a huge hazard.

We kept pitching, building, and moving as the load got higher and higher. I had to wallow through the hay way up there. Dad held Jim back somewhat, but they also felt the lift now, which gave me a little help. I looked down at Jim and saw the sweat running down his face in streams. The hay was up to the top of the ladders, so Dad coached me about balance. I tramped the load down all the way around the edges and moved side to side to check the balance. They were leaning on their pitchforks down there. Dad knew what it was like up there building the load and I heard him call up: "Take your time, Clifton. Call us when you are ready." I was about tuckered out. My arms and legs felt the stress, and my heartbeat was pounding in my neck. Being twelve or thirteen, gung-ho, and stubbornly proving myself, I soon hollered back down: "Okay, let 'er come."

Two more feet of hay came up, about as far as their pitchforks could reach. Now, each pitch must be distributed with great caution and the total load moved ever so gently. Every furrow crossing with those low wheels was critical. Dad would coach my driving until we finally reached the lane leading to the barn. What a wonderful break when I felt my heartbeat returning to normal. We would be turning to the left in the barnyard, heading right onto the threshing floor of the barn. Dad and Jim had walked rather than climbed up those wagon ladders. Dad would refer to all this as putting on "a little jag of hay." John Ames liked to laugh and get in a jibe about Bert's little jags of hay: "You could see them over the treetops!"

We were all ready for a water break. One of my sisters would be there with cool water from the cistern in the well. Jim Stewart was a big man who could down a two-quart syrup can of water in nothing flat. It never seemed to bother him. Dad and I drank slower with oatmeal in our jar of water. Mother would come out to drive Ole Ned on the "hay pull" line. Soon the unloading of two tons of hay began. If we wanted to bring in four loads a day, we had better get a move on. Dad and Jim climbed the long ladders to the hay mow we were filling. We had four of them, the threshing floor being in the middle. My job now was to "set the fork," sending up four to six huge bundles of hay.

Near the very peak, a one-hundred-foot steel rail ran the full length of the barn. On this rail ran a travel unit that we called "the car." A two-hundred-foot length of one-inch "hay rope" was threaded though pulleys on the car and a pulley on the hay fork. This same rope also went the full length of the barn and back down through another pulley at ground level attached to a big barn post. From the post, the rope went to the horse, who could pull out, making the hay rise. When a lift of hay went up, it automatically streaked toward the mow for which it had been preset. A long trailing rope was fastened to the hay fork. I had to drag the hay fork and car back to the center point where it automatically released the fork, allowing me to pull it right down. It was an inverted U shape with sharp points I could thrust about two feet into the hay. Then, I lifted a lever that turned four-inch jointed points on the ends of the legs, locking in the hay. I would then sing out, "Ready in the mow?" Dad would answer back, "Ready." I would shout to Mother, "Okay, go." Ole Ned would go out into the barnyard, making a big chunk from one end of the wagon tear loose and start up, pulleys squeaking. When it locked into the car, the whole thing went streaking toward the mow. At just the right second, Dad would shout down, "Drop." I would give a yank on the trip line and yell out to Mother, "Whoa." Down swooshed the mighty bundle of hay right at their feet.

Now it was their turn to wrestle and sweat before I had the next lift on their heads! Mother and Ole Ned heard me yell, "Come back!" and immediately swung around to head back to the barn. I pulled the now-empty car and fork back to the central position, then took it down to reset at the opposite end of the load for the next lift. Six of these lifts would empty the wagon, and away we would go to the field for another load.

One time, the wagon tongue broke into two pieces. It was dinnertime, and we were so hungry. Dad did something simple that time; we just stopped. One haying, we were bringing a big load of hay from the Old Place (Uncle Ern's farm a half mile south). We'd just come down the hill, over the bridge, and back up on the level road when the tongue broke again. We spied over in the woods an ironwood tree four inches in diameter, cut it down to size, and bail-wired a splint onto the broken tongue. We were soon on our way again. Dad always had emergency tools fastened to the wagon for this kind of thing. That axe and bail wire sure came in handy.

Getting up that hill from Uncle George's creek was always risky. With a heavy load, Colonel was prone to quit halfway up. Bess could not possibly hold the load by herself. It would be a disaster if the load ever started backward. So, Dad always commanded, "Whoa" on the bridge to give Colonel an urgent reminder. He would crack the leather line over him like a whip and lay a gentle tap on his back end. Colonel got the message: No quitting! Dig in all the way to the top!

A few summers, we had so much hay that we had to build a haystack just outside the barn. It was topped off with wild marsh grass, which would shed the rains. On the back forty acres of our farm, we had a low, mucky spot where only marsh grass would grow. That same spot caught fire once below the surface where it burned and smoked for half a summer.

The Fourth of July was considered a picnic day, but I only remember a time or two when Uncle Ern and Aunt Nellie invited us to join them down at Caribou Lake toward Detour. It must have been just after we got our model-T Ford because it was a twenty-four-mile journey each way. We had four flat tires on one of those trips, but "Old Henry's" car had a patching kit. After the Fourth of July came the biggest celebrated event around Pickford—the Orange Lodge celebration on the twelfth of July.

They had a great parade! Orangemen in colorful attire carried huge orange banners adorned with gorgeous fabric, gold braiding, and tassels. Ornate text was written on many banners, some so large that it took two men holding two standards to carry them. Men carried big Bibles on chapters suspended from their shoulders with more gold-tasseled ropes. Like our history books portrayed the American Revolutionary War soldiers, all the Orangemen marched in full array to the music of the fife, base, and snare drum trio. They sang too. The Orangemen were celebrating the 1690 victory of Protestant King William of Orange at the Battle of the Boyne in Ireland where he defeated Catholic King James II, the deposed king of England and Ireland.

As an adult, the orange, gold, and purple in those banners awakened colorful memories from my childhood. On a summer evening prior to July 12, we could hear the drums and fife trio rehearsing as they marched down Townline Road. I remember one line from a ditty we sang heartily: "The protestant boys are coming to town; the stink of their feet would knock a dog down." How we looked forward to the big event. Vivian told me that she remembers how Forrest used to take the receiver off the telephone to interrupt the party line with this same tune while beating it out on our old iron frying pan. Dad and Mother were out of earshot, probably in the barn milking cows.

Sounds authentic for Forrest; he liked to stir folks up! We were celebrating freedom from the tyranny of the Pope. I am sure there must have been speeches and prayers. There did not seem to be any expression of real hatred, just joyful identity and a sense of mistrust of Catholicism. I bring up this shameful subject in order to express thankfulness that in my lifetime those prejudices disappeared completely.

It is amazing, but true: the pioneers within a radius of twelve miles from Pickford separated themselves into six distinct ethnic communities. The immediate Pickford area and a few places in between were Protestant Scotch-Irish. Ten miles to the east, Goetzville was the heart of a large Roman Catholic Polish community. The women wore babushkas; their houses were painted in glaring bright colors, and their names often ended with "ski." Eight miles to the south, the Swedish Lutheran settlement began along the Straits of Mackinac and the Les Cheneaux Islands around Cedarville. Five miles to the southwest, away from the water, was the Catholic Italian settlement with their grapevines. Eight miles to the northwest, gathered around the village of Rudyard, were the Finnish Lutherans. Six miles to the northeast across the Munuscong River lived the French Catholics in what they called the Kelden area.

Of course, language barriers were a fundamental reason for the sharply defined communities, but it went much deeper. There were ugly discrimination barriers too. Back then, Goetzville was Roman Catholic and Popish with Priest-ridden heretics. They were called "Pollocks," or "Dogans." The Italians were "Dagoes" and off-limits for us because they were "knife-wielding and dangerous," or so we supposed. The Frenchies were "Catholic moonshiners pickled in wine." The Swedes and the Finns were okay Protestants, but you could not understand them. The Finns had all those funny little steam bath houses out back, separate from their regular house. Thank God, all those walls came tumbling down. Fear of one another has vanished.

Ethnic and religious discrimination was still raging in many countries of the world. I think it all ended quickly here in the Upper Peninsula for a variety of reasons. First, whole-hearted faith in God cured malice and hatred. Second, the Constitution of the United States declares every citizen equal and free. Our government is strictly neutral in the area of religion. The genius was that it did not get politicized; the barriers came down with no government involvement whatsoever. Third, economic commerce grew. Polish farmers would come to our place to buy piglets, and Mother would have them stay for dinner. Dad hired Mr. Ferrack during haying time. We all learned to love and trust Mr. Ferrack. Dad would load our whole family in the Model-T on a summer evening to go to Goetzville. Those Polish farmers sold us good milk cows and were always kind. We even learned a few Polish words. "Sand Farmers" were very likeable despite all we had heard about Catholics.

I am ashamed to say we were overly judgmental regarding all these unique communities. Cedarville was home to Protestant Swedish boatmen and fishermen with accents we could not understand. After high school, Vivian and I worked summers at the Islington Hotel in Cedarville. We got to know Mr. Shoberg, a Swedish boatman and fishing guide. He told us stories and sang Swedish boat songs to us. We loved it. Their son, Tigner, married the daughter of Mr. V. L. Lipsett and became a partner in Lipsett Chevrolet Garage. A second cousin of mine dated a Kelden boy, a French Catholic. She did not marry him but protested that he was genuinely nice and an honorable young man. Mr. Romeo from the Italian settlement had a large and fancy threshing outfit. Dad hired him to do our threshing for a couple of years or so. He turned out to be a good and reliable businessman, "even though Italian, and Catholic." The Finns out in Rudyard Way always got good marks for being peaceful, efficient farmers and great basketball players. It got so we could understand them. Some of the American boys married Finnish girls, and some married Catholic girls from Goetzville. They were all Americans!

By the time of World War II against Adolf Hitler, every Orange Lodge chapter had dissolved and faded away. The twelfth of July Orange Lodge celebration is gone. All references to King William of Orange and his victory over the Catholics in 1690 are gone. The Battle of the Boyne in Ireland so long ago is history, where it belongs. No more "riding the goat" for entrance into the Orange Lodge Chapter. They have vanished with "good Riddance," and no more *Rail Splitter*, the rabid anti-Catholic magazine. In its heyday, my dad joined the Lodge and had to "ride the goat" at the swearing-in ceremony. Although, he was never active and seldom attended its meetings. When I was a boy, I was solicited to join the Junior Orange Lodge, but it never materialized. Dad and Mother frowned on the idea. I believe they were "seeing the light." We all loved Aunt Stella, who married Uncle Dewey. She was a sincere Polish Catholic and a dear lady. One of Dad's brothers had resented their marriage and referred to Aunt Stella as a Dogan. We never felt that way. Even our uncle later reformed and repented of that hatefulness.

Early July was good raspberry picking time. Our best picking was in the woods east of Uncle Ern's old place, around Taylor's mill. We even went into cedar swamps or all the way to Rockview, five miles south of Pickford, to pick. Wherever there was logging, big brush piles were left behind. Among the brush, the raspberries would automatically spring forth like hair on a cat's back, yielding bumper crops for several years. Those were wonderful outings that gave us a break from the heavy field work. Ten-gallon milk buckets were our picking pails. Dad and I used to race to see who got their pail full first. That was real fun. When Mother hollered, "Yooooo-hoooo" for dinner, that ended the race. Win or lose, we laughed and made excuses for coming in second. My sisters and brothers usually had smaller pails, but we all had a holiday time centered around the big picnic. Mother spread it all out on white sheets that she put on the ground.

Vivian reminded me about the time we went by horse and wagon to Taylor's Mill. Mother was always scared of bears. Dad said, "Don't go rambling, stay close to us; there are bears up here." Mother insisted Dad bring along the old .38-55 deer rifle, just in case. He carried it right beside him as he picked the big raspberries. Sometime midmorning there in the woods, with us all wallowing in brush piles and raspberry bushes, Mother yelled out: "Bert, there's a bear! I hear him. Hurry, get the rifle!" Dad forsook his berry pail, grabbed the rifle, and came crashing to the rescue. He threw open the shell chamber and reached in his pocket for the ammunition. He got a jolt! The pocket was empty. The box of shells was back in the wagon! Fortunately, the bear fled. It could have been Mother's imagination. What an exciting day. We had a good berry patch laugh, went back to picking, had a merry picnic dinner, and came home with everything jammed full of raspberries. Dad got razzed for the rest of his life.

Mother and my sisters worked into the night, washing and picking over those berries. They must sugar them down for canning the next day. With fresh cream, they were a delicious winter dessert. Mother would "put up" at least fifty quarts of wild strawberries, probably seventy-five quarts of raspberries, and near one-hundred quarts of huckleberries. When she got done with canned venison, green tomato "governors," pickles, relish, and wild plum jelly, we had a mighty full pantry.

> Mother: "We always had plenty of canned green tomatoes called 'governors,' pickled beets, canned citron, potatoes, and pumpkin sauce for pies stored in the root cellar. We picked wild strawberries. Had to have enough canned for winter, Vivian. Ninety half-gallon sealers one year!"
>
> Vivian: "How did you fix pumpkin sauce?"
>
> Mother: "Lots of pumpkin. Peeled the pumpkin, sliced it, cooked it in a kettle with sugar. After supper, mashed it with a wooden masher, set overnight, added a couple eggs, some milk, and some spices. We just ate that. Sometimes we cut the pumpkin in cubes, made light syrup, and canned that. We made beet relish. Mash after cooking—vinegar, salt, pepper and sugar."
>
> —-from Vivian's hospital talks with Mother, November 23, 1985

Many other jobs punctuated our summers, such as pulling mustard. It grew up wild in our grain fields, so we all had to help pull it out before it went to seed. Fifty acres of grain had to be purged, and that is a lot of tramping. Dougie, had an eye for making money. He hired out to Harvey Pennington to pull the mustard out of a field for twenty-five cents.

The potatoes had to be hilled("scuffled"). Dad would hook our retiree horse, Ole Ned, to the scuffler. He could handle that and the hay rope. I had to ride Ole Ned and steer down between the rows of spuds. Dad hollered, "Watch out now! Where are you going? Careful!" I loved to read the serial stories in the *Saturday Evening Post*. Earl Miller, the mailman, had just brought the July issue; I was deep in a wild sea adventure. Our dad, down there on the handles, was a patient and understanding man. He told me I could read my sea story while I rode Ole Ned. I wonder how many taters got trampled.

I bring up July activities to say that Dad and Mother always made provision for us to get to our regular monthly 4-H club meetings, rain or shine. We were never kept home for any work in progress. Looking back, I think it was incredibly wise on their part. I remember one year I was president of our Pleasant Park 4-H Calf Club that held monthly meetings in John Ames' gravel box. Not very fancy, but we got a lot done. We were planning our fair entries and banners. Like many business meetings I have since attended, our meetings were productive and defining. 4-H stands for your Head, Heart, Hands, and Health!

The Upper Peninsula of Michigan should be named the thunder and lightning capitol of the world. Surrounded by the Great Lakes, our summer lightning storms were frequent and terrible. Many a night we were rousted out of bed and called downstairs to lay in the middle of the old kitchen floor for maximum security. *Clash! Boom! Bang!* It was like being bombarded from every side. The danger was real. Lightning struck trees and barns all around us. Forrest was stunned by lightning one time when he got too close to the front room stove. I guess it hit the stovepipe. Another time, the iron bed frames upstairs were jarred. That is why we went to the floor in the kitchen until the storm passed.

Mother was the security chief and enforcer of lightning regulations. We could never figure out why she acted so lightning proof herself. She would go from window to window on the northside of our house to watch the storms. They seem to generate in Lake Superior, follow around the St. Mary's River before heading into Lake Huron and Lake Michigan. Geographically, we were in the middle of all that water. We were tired and sleepy, wanting to get back up into our beds. In a half hour or so, we would be encouraged by Mother's storm report from the window: "It seems to be going around the lakes, but stay down now. Don't get near that iron stove." What a relief when she gave the all clear, and we could go up to our beds. Often the relief was short-lived when another storm of flashes and earth-shaking bolts brought us down to the first floor again. Jim Stewart's barn was struck one night, and his two work horses were killed immediately. If you did not have lightning rods on your barn, it would soon be hit and often burn to the ground. Lightning scars were everywhere. Our fears were well-founded. I have lived a lot of other places and have never seen such lightning fireworks as these, anywhere.

CHAPTER NINETEEN

AUGUST
While the Sun Shines

DO YOU REALIZE THE RUBBER BAND is a great source of energy? That genuine rubber had much more elasticity than the modern synthetic bands. It was excellent for our slingshot adventures. Each of us sought to be a Robin Hood at target practice with tin cans or old bottles. We began targeting sparrows, squirrels, stubborn pigs, or cattle. Next, it was telephone line insulators. They are tough and our small pebbles seldom, if ever, broke one. But it was fun to hear one hit it and bounce off.

Other times, rubber bands became the arms industry supplying our war games and banditry. Law officers and outlaws both had to have good working pistols and rifles during holdup. The rubber band was not only the power for propulsion, it was itself the missile. If you got hit with that rubber band, you had to drop dead, no cheating. Guns were designed so that a trigger made from bale wire would control the release of the band pulled back to maximum stretch. The rifle was developed with a longer barrel for greater stretch power. Of course, the variety of guns and gun games moved into bigger productions. Store operators, bankers, and a jail had to be created. Everybody had a role, and we took turns being the villain or officer of the law. We respected

Dad's old .38-55 hunting rifle that hung high on the wall in the washroom. It was absolutely off-limits, never to be touched. It was hardly ever taken down by Dad between hunting seasons. Fortunately, we all grew up on the right side of the law.

Grain harvest and huckleberry picking were on the front burner in the month of August. If we had a field of winter wheat, it would be the first to ripen and get safely put into the barn, weighing down a haymow. The fields of oats, speltz, and barley ripened later in August, so the harvest stretched over into September. I can see Dad plucking a handful of grain and rubbing it in his hand to break the kernels from the hulls. He would squeeze or bite the seeds to tell for sure that the crop was ripe and ready.

In August, dry spells caused the water level in the well cistern to get dangerously low, and the pastures began to dry up. Something had to be done. We put bells on the cows, opened the south fence, and drove them into the unlimited forest bordering our farm to find green pasture and water. They could wander away and be lost, so I wound up taking a lunch and tending our herd until late afternoon each day. Those were long, lonesome days that we hated. I kept the flock at grassy spots along the creek around the beaver dam area.

A few times, Vivian came along with me. She wrote me a note about that: "Remember how we took the cows down the lane into the bush past the beaver dam and on into Uncle Ern's place for them to pasture all day. We used to carve our names in trees and build tree huts. Dad would warn us not to play around that beaver dam, but we used to 'just a bit' on our way home in the afternoons." That is the way Viv remembers, but I know we never went out on that beaver dam. We may have waded in the backwaters. Those beavers had quite a lake for themselves there in the woods. Their houses were way out in the middle of their lake. Once, we forgot to take water and got so thirsty, we drank water from the creek.

When the grain was fully ripe, Bess and Colonel were hitched to the McCormick Deering binder and harvest was underway. Speed was the word. Now our song was, "Make Grain While the Sun Shines." Without warning, the fall rains could set in before we were finished and the whole crop would be lost. One reason being the loss of traction and footing for the horse team. They had to pull the big binder. It had a big, wide iron drive wheel with cleats that drove the five-foot cutting blade, turned reels that swept the stalks of grain up against the blade, and drove the canvas belts that carried the cut stalks up to the sheaf-making mechanism. The last part of the binder's job drove the apparatus that tied the sheaves with twine and kicked them out to the ground. It was a truly marvelous machine. If the big drive wheel skidded in the mud, you were out of business. Two days of sunshine were needed to dry up the mud and save your grain crop. The only other alternative was to use a hand scythe with a cradle and tie the sheaves by hand. You had fifty acres to do by hand if the fields turned muddy. It is no wonder that Mother often joined in to help us with the harvest by shocking up the sheaves, pitching sheaves onto the wagon, or driving Ole Ned on the rope.

That rich clay loam grew bumper crops of grain. Just as quickly as it was cut, the sheaves must be set up in "shocks" to dry and cure. About six or eight sheaves stood up, leaning their heads close together with a cap sheaf carefully positioned on top to shed rain. The binder spit its sheaves out in a row, so we made straight rows of shocks by gathering in the sheaves from the center of two parallel rows. This is where I fitted in with both joy and zeal.

Bess and Colonel, along with my dad, could bind five acres of grain in a day. No one picked up one sheaf at a time. They swooped up one in each hand, then swung to the centerline and plunked them down firmly into the stubble with just the right lean. Automatically, they'd swing to the other row and grab two more, setting them right next to the first two. In nothing flat, they'd decide whether the shock needed two or four more sheaves, squeeze the heads closer together, and flair out the cap sheaf on top of it lengthwise. Vivian claims she helped me sometimes so we could keep up with Dad's binding. Your work would be tested by the wind and rain. It would not cure lying on the ground. On to the next shock you would go until a row the full length of the field was completed. At that point, we'd be ready for a break because that equaled 330 feet! The heavier the crop, the closer together the shocks. They would average eight or ten feet apart. So, you formed thirty-three to forty-two shocks in each row.

There really was no break. We immediately started another row, took a water bucket breather, and kept right on going—till suppertime. Sometimes Mother would do all the milking so Dad could bind till dark or until that whole five-acre field was finished. Why? Because it was grain harvest time in Northern Michigan. Ruination could be days away . . . because it was the Great Depression. These crops were tax money to save our farm, money for winter clothes, money for groceries, and money to pay down some of our bills to the doctor, the shoe store, the drugstore, and the blacksmith. Besides all that, we were behind on our mortgage payment to Uncle Ern. He never dunned us, but the weight of it was there just the same. We loved our way of life on the farm, our family, and our home. Maybe that is why loving God came naturally to us.

When the grain was cured and dry in the shock, we used the big hay wagon to haul it into the barn. Only now, we had to lay down a rope "sling" for each projected lift. The rope sling was a ring with three ropes attached and the other ends of each rope had a loop. The load builder spread the sling down on one end of the wagon with the ring at one end and one rope in the middle and the other two out toward each side. It covered a half-length of the rack. As the sheaves were pitched on, I had to spread them out carefully on top of these ropes, building a "sling load" two feet high. After that, I flopped the ropes with looped ends atop the sling load and made sure the ring was visible at the front ladder. Next, I would lay down a corresponding sling on the other half of the rack with the ring at the back ladder this time. Grain is much heavier than hay. When six sling loads were built on the wagon, we headed for the barn.

Unloading grain sheaves is similar to unloading hay. Instead of "setting" a steel fork into the hay, you pulled a yoke gadget down from the "car" attaching the ring and the three rope ends from each sling. After you locked them in and yelled out instructions for Mother to get Ole Ned to march out of the barn, the sling of grain went up and over to the programed mow. You better never be under that sling load when the mow man hollered, "Trip!" I was the one who yanked the trip line from below, and down into the mow the grain sheaves went with a great swish. The underlying hay in the mow soon shrank downward. It is a good thing the grain crop came last, or we never would have been able to get everything jammed into the barn.

> Vivian: "Mom's on a talking spree again. She's talking away back about helping Dad to get hay in the barn and the 'apparatus' to put hay in the mow, helping Dad to shock grain. She tells how they milked cows, turning the separator to separate the cream from the milk. How they had cars to enjoy them if they wanted to go for a nice ride but didn't run to town every day. How they used to have snowblowers to clean the roads out. How her grandson, Donald Long, dressed her up for a ride once on the big snowmobile he drives. 'He took off; I really enjoyed it; it was Christmas day.' Oh boy, isn't this something for her to remember? She says, 'Now, I tell you, they get a lot of snow in Upper Michigan!' Neighbors used to get together and help one another get their crops off. Grain was very valuable. The gadget they threshed with gave us straw bedding for the cows."
>
> —from Vivian's hospital talks with Mother,
> November 26, 1985

One fall, we were hauling in the last of our crop after dark because rain was threatening. Mother was helping Dad pitch on. We got quite a scare when a car came down our road and turned a spotlight on us. They were no doubt "shiners" with the light attached to their rifle barrel. If they spotted a set of deer's eyes, they pulled the trigger. Sometimes cattle were mistakenly shot and left in the fields. We hollered out and waved our kerosene lantern. They moved on. What if they had first caught our horse's eyes?

Watching for cars was especially exciting when we were young. All the full activities on the farm made the summer days seem so long. We longed for someone to come visit us. We would watch a car turn down our road and hoped with all our might that they would turn in at our gate. Then at night, we would watch for car lights coming down Townline Road to see if they would turn down our road. We would sing out, "There's one coming!" The next test would be to see if the car turned in at our gate. If the car did turn in, we excitedly yelled,

"They're turning in! Mother, someone's coming!" Too often there was a groaning, "Oh, they've gone on by."

Lots of times, Uncle Dewey came out from the Soo to see us. Sometimes he came on Saturday and stayed overnight. There would be a kicking fight that night in our bed when we boys tried to push Uncle Dewey out. We usually landed out on the floor. Always, there was a riot. He loved to play with us and was a great tease. Sometimes Aunt Stella came along too. We thought the world of them both. I can remember many fun things we did. Often, he chased us round and round the house with a threat of a whisker rub if we did such and such. He called Vivian "Carrot Top." From his favorite perch on the wood box, he would threaten a whisker rub if she put that silly "A-Tiskit, A-Tasket" record on the phonograph. She always took the bait. Down he came from the wood box and the chase was on. Viv wound up caught in a whisker rub, promising, "I won't do it anymore." None of us were exempt from his teasing. Come bedtime, we all went overboard at least once before we were worn out. Dad would call out from their bed, "All right boys, it's time you were getting to sleep; we have a big day ahead." That brought about a peace treaty, and we were all three quickly sound asleep. I am convinced that Uncle Dewey happily remembered those battles, even though he landed on the floor sometimes. Our votes for Uncle Dewey's playful teasing were unanimous; we all loved it! He was a true highlight in my childhood memories.

He and Dad loved to talk. I enjoyed listening to these brothers—a city man and a farmer. It was late Sunday afternoon and Dad turned to our dog and said, "Well, Ole Buster, it's time to bring up the cows for milking." Then he went over to the porch and took a milk pail from the hook. Without another word, Ole Buster headed out of the house yard and went down the dusty lane toward the back of our farm where the cows were laying in the pasture. Within ten minutes, the cows were marching single file up the lane and into the stable. Ole Buster was trotting along gently behind them. Uncle Dewey just could not get over it. I dare say all his fellow workers at the Union Carbide Plant heard about Bert's brilliant dog.

A Farm Boy's Memoirs

Uncle Ern and Aunt Nellie liked to take drives on summer evenings. We could tell it was them coming down Townline Road. They drove their coupe about twenty miles per hour. Often, they dropped in for a while. Just as often, though, they went on past us to their old place a half mile down the road. They just roamed the country roads, enjoying the sunset and watching the deer come out. One summer evening, Uncle Randolph and Aunt Margaret Monck's family turned in at our gate. They had been on a trip out west and were on their way back to Muskegon. I was happy to know they had come, but I ran and hid under the bed to keep from being kissed. I could not face all that. But I have changed a lot in eighty years.

Once or twice each summer we would hear an airplane. Whatever we were doing came to a complete halt, and all hands searched the sky to locate it. We watched in awe as it crossed the sky in front of us and became a disappearing dot in the heavens. What a marvel! One summer day, a mammoth dirigible came from the northwest and passed right over us. I think it was the Hindenburg. *Who could build a thing like that?* we thought. A big bag of gas with motors attached, and people in it? What will men dream up next?

After we got our Model-T Ford, we sometimes went to the Soo on Sunday to visit at Uncle Herb's or Uncle Dewey's house. They both lived on Minneapolis Street in the Soo, one block apart. Pingatore's store was on that street too. Back then, it seemed like an Italian immigrant had planted a bustling and interesting grocery store in every neighborhood of the city. Penny candy unlimited! We had so little company, we kids always begged to stay longer. We were always invited to stay for supper, but that was a tough decision for Dad. A few times Dad agreed. We were thrilled, but there was a price to pay—the chores were waiting for us, and the cows would all be up at the stable doors, bawling to be milked. Sunday togs were shed and the feeding, stable cleaning, milking, watering, and cream separating got underway. No problem falling asleep after that exceptionally long day. Mondays were always filled with action, "making the ole farm pay." I enjoyed the farm, and the imprint of those days has never faded from within me.

A heavy rainstorm during harvesttime spelled blueberry picking. We called them huckleberries. This became an exciting holiday for us in late summer. We celebrated! The curing grain was all up in shocks, each with a cap sheaf to shed a maximum amount of rain. Bess and Colonel were hitched to the hay wagon, racks and all. We were off to Kibble's huckleberry plains. Dad would shift Bess and Colonel into trotting gear every now and then to make better time. Mother made a big lunch of fried chicken, potato salad, and cookies, even lemonade. Plenty of containers were on board for the berries—two ten-gallon cream cans, the old wooden breadbox with a hinged lid, milk pails, and half-gallon Karo syrup cans for picking buckets. Holes were punched in the cans for the rag strings you tied around your waist.

The Kibble plains were five miles north of Pickford and another mile west. By noon, we had established our picking territory. Mother had raised a marker pole with a white milk strainer flying from the top. We were instructed to stay in pairs and always keep the marker flag in sight. Dad and I often picked together, racing to see who could fill his eleven-quart milk pail first. We could usually fill those pails by the time Mother gave the dinner call. If Dad got his full first, he would help me fill mine and vice versa. It was humiliating to bring in less than a full bucket. Mother's mill whistle got a hearty response, bringing her hungry family out of the bushes from all directions. Dinner was spread on white bed sheets on the ground. It was a royal feast. The talk was about the huckleberries—the big ones we found. "Hanging in clusters, you could just pull them off by the handful; they were everywhere you turned."

It is funny how the ramblers had to range far and wide to find worthwhile picking. Dad and I preached, "Stick and pick. Don't ramble; your bucket will come up faster!" Forrest claimed it best to keep on the move for the bigger berries: "Find the black ones; they taste better." Mother would give forth on the quality of our picking. "No green berries. No stems attached. No bugs, leaves, or trash mixed in." Quality made Mother's job lots easier that night. She and Marie stayed way up into the wee hours cleaning the berries in a big washtub of water, skimming off leaves, bugs, green berries, and dead stems. Then, handful by handful, they carefully checked them before they went into big pans or crocks to be covered with sugar in preparation for canning the next day.

Before we scattered for picking again, Mother would caution: "Forrest, don't you go so far; you never know." Her fears were well-founded. One could soon get lost in those trackless plains of high bush huckleberries. They were ten feet tall and close together in clumps. The danger lay in rambling from clump to clump in search of the biggest berries. Throughout the day, Mother and Dad would keep calling out names, and each of us would answer: "Yoo-hoo, Berrrrt?" "Yoo-hoo, Forrrrrest?" "Yoo-hoo, Marieeee?" "Yoo-hoo, Selenaaaa?" We were expected to answer "yoo-hoo" right back. We younger ones were assigned to pick in pairs, *always*. Not one of us ever got lost. This berry patch was once thousands of acres of virgin white pine. Only lone, dead trees and stumps survived. Every few years, fires swept across the plains and rejuvenated the growth of these wild huckleberries.

We took pride in pouring a full bucket of clean berries into the cream can or the old bread box. Yes, we each kept count of the quarts we picked. Before we knew it, Dad would start spreading the word for leaving time. He had the only watch, so he would tell us the minutes left. The chores would be waiting for us. "Start picking toward the wagon." All too soon, it seemed, Dad would pronounce the verdict: "It's time to go." Don't you know, that's hard to do. It is uncanny how you always run into a patch of bigger berries than you had seen all day when it is time to go. *Grab a few handfuls on the way. No use being the first one back anyway,* Mother joined in the roundup calling: "Keep together now. Marie, is Vivian with you? Where's Dougie? Keep them close to you! Can you see the white flag? Start heading for the wagon!" Soon we were all assembled and the berries secured. Bess and Colonel were ready to hit the sandy trails toward home nine miles away. The chores awaited us, but what a wonderful day!

Just to think of those huckleberry picnics cheers the heart. Huckleberries with cream and sugar or huckleberry pies were so good. Soon there would be huckleberry preserves cramming the pantry shelves. We would all spread those preserves with home-churned butter and peanut butter on homemade bread all winter long. I loved the crusty end slice the best. There is nothing better than walking home from school to the smell of a freshly baked huckleberry pie and your Mother cutting you out a man-sized piece. Chore time was not such a chore after that. Here's Mother's memories of huckleberries at age ninety-two:

> "We always would go pick wild blueberries out in that old Kibble marsh. You know, they grow all that stuff now in Lower Michigan and in canning season they truck it up to the Soo. Marie used to buy lots of that stuff and can it and freeze it. Remember that jar of peach jam she gave us to bring home this fall? It was so good. She can really cook. That Marie is so fussy about her cooking and cleaning."

> Vivian: "She really is a good cook, isn't she, Mom?"

> Mother: "You better believe it. And a fussy housekeeper; cold packs tomatoes, pickles, you name it. She's got it, canned or in that freezer—peaches, carrots, strawberries, pickles, jam, some kind of pickle cut in long sections put in jars with salt, vinegar, and some kind of spices ... [two-minute pause] Are you still here, Vivian? ... Yes? Okay."

> Vivian: "Then away she goes again!"

> Mother: "Marie and Ford picked berries a lot of times."

In our pre-tractor days, salesmen came through the country going farm to farm: Mr. Jim Stirling with his Gypsy-like grocery wagon; the Watkin's Salve man with ointments for man or beast; the Fuller Brush man; Mr. Baldwin the insurance man from the Soo; the International Harvester Company man, selling binders, mowers or gasoline engines; and Fred Ralph, the Model-T Ford salesman. Unlike my mother, who steadfastly refused to buy a new range from the Home Comfort salesman, Dad was more vulnerable. Labor saving machines were attractive to all of us. Dad bought the manure spreader when that salesman came through. It was a landmark success. We had no credit cards, but Dad had good credit so we put it "on time." If only that International Harvester pump jack engine had worked as well as the manure spreader! It really was aggravating to work that old iron force pump handle up and down for a half hour with that fancy, good-for-nothing engine sitting right there by you. A thoroughbred lemon.

One summer day, Jim Stirling, the grocery man, came to our place. He had all kinds of goodies on board. I think he handed out candy samples. If he did not have what Mother wanted, he would take an order and deliver it on the next trip. Since we had oatmeal for breakfast, Mother thought we did not need fancy Kellogg's cereal and scratched it off her grocery list. Since we pestered her, and she wanted to please Mr. Stirling for stopping, she ordered a box of Kellogg's Cornflakes. The grocery peddler suggested the economy size. Okay, that would be fine. So long, Mr. Stirling. A month later, our cornflakes arrived—a huge twenty-four by twenty-four by twenty-four-inch cardboard boxful! We ate cornflakes and cornflakes on oatmeal for months. They got soggy and tough, but not a flake was lost. We had many laughs about this "big" purchase.

August was "convention month" for nasty bedbugs. I hated bedbugs. My mother hated bedbugs, and my sisters hated bedbugs; we all hated bedbugs. They literally came out of the walls at night. New wallpaper was always put on top of the old, faded patterns because you did not want to create a rough surface by pulling off chunks of plaster on the wood underneath. Across the years, many layers of wallpaper added good insulation against cold winter winds. Unfortunately, there was a serious side effect. Bedbugs took up residence in the cavities between the layers of wallpaper, at the curling ends and shrinkage spots in the corners. Nothing short of burning the house down could get to them. It was all-out war in August. We counterattacked with boiling water, a garden sprayer, and coal oil. The steel bed frames were knocked down and carried outside where we poured boiling water on them. The floor moldings and corners were sprayed with kerosene, especially where the paper was cracked or curled loose from flimsy lattice underneath. We fought them to a standstill but never could route them out completely. All winter they were hibernating or surviving on that homemade wheat flour wallpaper paste.

Vivian and I have one memory we would like to forget. It was late summer, and the crops must have all been in the barn. Dad was making a final night check on the horses and tapped one on the hip to get over in his stall. Apparently, the horse was taken by surprise and let fly with his hoof. He hit Dad right in the abdomen and he developed a mild hernia. He wound up in the Soo Hospital where the surgeon repaired the hernia along with the kick wound. Viv and I were doing the evening milking that evening. The cows kept switching at the flies, flinging their dirty old tails right in our faces. Even though she got walloped on her side a time or two, the old Izzard cow could not be persuaded to cease.

"I'll fix you," declared Vivian as she tied the stubborn critter's tail to the tail of the cow alongside her. That settled that; what a relief! We finished the milking, cream separating, and most of the other chores. Unfastening the cow chains and letting them out would be the last thing we had to do. Viv started at one end of the stalls, dropping the neck chains and I at the other. We had forgotten all about knotting the tails; our minds were on winding up the chores. At the same moment she loosened the adjoining cow, I dropped the chain from the Izzard cow's neck. They whirled around and headed for the stable door. We hollered out together, but it was too late. At the first tension on their tails, the two cows went into high gear to get free. The old Izzard cow was on the outside of the high doorstep, and the other cow was on the inside, pawing at the concrete floor in the opposite direction. Calamity of calamities, the knot had tightened solid. Hearing the commotion, Ole Buster came barking into the barn to see what was wrong. Fearing the teeth of Buster, the Izzard cow used her hind feet braced against the doorstep to give a mighty lunge. She tore the whole switch off the other poor cow's tail. There was a lot of blood, but no trauma center. Mother had gone to the hospital to see Dad. Somehow, I got the injured cow back in her stall and began yelling, "Vivian, run to the house! Get some white rags or milk strainers and a lot of flour! Hurry!"

Viv really made tracks to the house and back. She knew what I was going to do. Eight inches of that poor cow's tail was a bloody mess; the hide was entirely gone. We comforted her by name as best we could, while I did what I had seen Mother and Dad do on lesser wounds. We sprinkled on handfuls of flour until the bleeding began to let up; then,

I wrapped it with clean strips of rags and anchored the whole bandage to the remaining hairy hide above. Old bossy calmed down. Viv and I started to breathe again. We were two shattered people, but we knew we had to carry the news to Dad in the hospital. It was the next day, but we did it. He did not scold us. He knew we did not intend to do it. I suppose regrets were written all over our faces. Dad got home within a few days. The cow's tail healed up fine, but her switch never grew back. We got switched a few times with that bony tail, but we never retaliated.

It is often said that farmers had lots of meat for their table during the Great Depression. Not so. We were growing the meat, all right, but in August our pigs and beef were getting fattened on grass and clover to grow pounds of fall income for us. In the summertime, Mother would buy baloney and frankfurters. She could turn out delicious meals with fried baloney or hotdogs. It was the vegetable dishes and goodies from the pantry shelves that she added that made our meals memorable. Jell-O with sliced bananas was hung down in the well to cool and set. Out of that flour bin, she could turn out wonderful bread, cakes, pies, cookies, and fried cakes. Those grazing calves must be kept growing. Pigs, chickens, geese, and turkeys must all keep growing. If the wild deer were trampling down your pea field, you could shoot them. Dad and Forrest brought home some summer meat that way but never advertised the matter.

During the summer, Vivian used to let neighbor Ray Dodd's cows into the Harvey Campbell woods across from our place each morning. They would come down a cow path on our side of the road between the ditch and Dodd's fence. When they got that far, it was her job to go open the gate and get them back through it again at milking time. He paid her a dollar-fifty per month. She was the apple of Ray's eye. Little Vivian was such a special little girl. She remembers Dad used to rock her while waiting for Mother to finish getting dinner on the table. Years later, Dad and Mother gave her that same rocker, which she treasured. I remember Dad often sang "Hey Diddle Diddle" to little Vivian. When she got older, she would use a metal curling iron in the long hair Dad used to comb across his bald spot while he sang,

Clifton Nixon

"Hey diddle, diddle!
The cat and the fiddle,
The cow jumped over the moon."

CHAPTER TWENTY

SEPTEMBER
Competition and Jamborees

SEPTEMBER AND OCTOBER WERE GREAT, shining 4-H Club months. The fall fairs were crowning events for us. A rising challenge for all farm young people. Fortunately, Miss Corrine Ormiston, assistant to the Chippewa County Agent for youth had introduced us to the 4-H Club through the hot lunch program at Frogpond School. Mr. McMillan and Miss Ormiston won a great place in our hearts.

Forrest and I took the pledge and joined the 4-H Calf Club right away, with Dad and Mother's full backing. The official Pleasant Park 4-H Calf Club was now a reality; several from our school joined. Soon, Marie and Vivian took the pledge and joined the 4-H Sewing and Canning Clubs. Each is an expert cook and seamstress today. Dougie grew up to excel in the 4-H Handicraft Club. He became a superior craftsman and made fine furniture—a hobby he enjoyed all the rest of his life.

Forrest and I competed nose-to-nose in every available class at the fairs; he with his Betsy Ross and me with my Rose. We always won the first and second place ribbons. Sometimes, he took the blue ribbon, and at the very next showing, I would take it. It was a fifty-fifty race for the honors, the cash prizes, and the ribbons. Each fair had open classes for calves of various breeds and ages that anyone could enter. You could enter your 4-H calf in the Best-Groomed Calf and Best Calf Showmanship categories. There was a separate duplicate range of classes just for 4-H Club calves including the Best Groomed 4-H Club Calf and the Best 4-H Calf Showmanship in the ring. We entered them all. Each had a first to fourth place ribbon and graduated cash prize. Each fair published a book showing the classes and rewards.

Forrest and I never fell out with one another, but we sure did compete. We pampered, groomed, and special fed those calves all year long in preparation for September. It was indeed all about 4-H Club duties with our "Head, Heart, Hands, and Health" prior to and during fair season. We kept a growth log and weighed our calves each week. Fitted blankets went on Betsy Ross and Rose to make their coats slick. Now and then, we would add flaxseed and an egg to their food to promote a slick, shiny coat of hair. Horns and hoofs were carefully scraped with pieces of broken glass to remove rough ridges, then rubbed for hours with olive oil and pumice stone powder. Proper hair clipping was a must. No unseemly dangling strands. No bristled hair along the backbone or neck.

"Barber Bert" Smith in Pickford did not come up to Forrest's specifications. I had to turn the crank on the clipper stand for what seemed like an hour sometimes for Forrest. He would pause and ask me if the cut looked right. "Oh yeah, that's just right," I would agree. But he would study some more and find another flaw. We would go back to work on his Betsy Ross for another ten minutes. My patience wore thin after three or four reruns. "Now I've done it," he would groan and call for still another round.

I irritatingly replied, "You should have left good enough alone." By and by, it came my turn to fancy clip my Rose while Forrest cranked the clippers. Within ten minutes, his patience was exhausted. As kid brother, I had to make every minute count and stop before taking too long.

Vivian was watching the clipping one day, when suddenly she began to holler, "Ouch! Stop! Stop!" Her long hair had caught in the cable at a broken place in the housing. Her head was drawn down, almost to the clippers. We got stopped. What a fright! "Is she hurt? How will we get her loose? Don't cry, Vivian, we'll get you out. You'll be all right." I cannot remember how we did it. We must have gently turned the cable crank backward to disentangle her golden-red hair lock by lock from that greasy cable. We may have clipped some. Anyway, we got her free, all snubbed up, and our little freckled-faced sister was smiling again. Vivie was a dear.

Summer evening 4-H jamborees were planned and led by Mr. McMillan and Miss Ormiston. Young 4-H members and their leaders came from several clubs. Those were unforgettable times of fun, games, and food. Members took the 4H pledge, sang 4-H Club songs, and listened to Mr. McMillan. We made many new friends that expanded our frontiers in every dimension: mentally, socially, and geographically. Each big gathering would be at a different place heretofore unknown to me.

The Pickford Fair was the grand opening event of the fall season. We could not imagine where all the people came from, by the hundreds. There were horse barns, a sheep and goat barn, a hog barn, a cattle barn, and a special barn for 4-H stock only. Every breed of foul and animal had its enthusiastic owner: Holstein, Guernsey, Jersey, Hereford, Shorthorn, and Black Angus cattle; Poland China, Yorkshire Red, and White hogs; Barred Rock, Leghorn, and Buff Orpington chickens; as well as Percheron, Belgian, and Palomino racehorses. Besides all these varieties, there were turkeys, ducks, geese, rabbits, and guinea hens.

Grains, garden vegetables, quilting, needlework, dressmaking, canning, pies, cakes, and all kinds of stuff were exhibited for show and judgment. 4-H entries got special attention. Marie and Vivian did shine in their categories. A covered wooden grandstand with many tiers and concession stands of all description surrounded the racetrack. A calliope occupied the middle. There was even a Stinson airplane offering rides from a grassy airstrip. No beer or liquor of any kind was allowed on the grounds; no gambling and no off-color concession booths were allowed either. The horse racing, harness racing, and horse pulling contests were all won or lost right before the cheering crowd in the grandstand.

The horse racing and harness racing in light two-wheel carts were mostly entries from outside our township, and we did not know them. Now the heavy-weight pulling contest was another story. We knew the eight or ten teams and yelled for our champions. The most colorful action was the one-armed George Izzard show! Only an extraordinarily strong man can handle those snorting, raring-to-go, 4000-pound teams with only two leather lines. George Izzard, with one line wrapped around the six-inch stub of his left arm and the other in his good right hand, could teamster those jerking, prancing behemoths into getting hitched and moving the load quickly. His team seemed to understand everything he had to say to them as they pawed, scratched, and moved the heavy load. George kept on talking to them while the crowd cheered. Many a year, his team took the honors.

The 4-H calf barn became our habitat day and night. We boys put lumber up on the open ceiling joist and made a hay-mattress bed right over our calves. I painted a three-by-nine-foot Pleasant Park Club banner. The stalls had to be kept immaculately clean with lots of fresh clean straw. None got better treatment than Betsy Ross and Rose. They were watered and fed the best hay and grain, as well as brushed and blanketed. The night before showtime, we scrubbed them down with soapy water and gave them a thorough rinse. The switch on their tails received the final beauty treatment. The long white hair was divided into eight or ten strands with each strand tightly braided and tied. Then, the whole switch was wrapped with clean cloth and carefully tied so that no possible stain could contaminate this work of art. Blankets and neck chains were checked before we climbed up to our bunks for a good night of rest. Three days of showings and judges lay before us.

I cannot remember how we got food, either on the grounds or Mother brought it to us. Morning time meant that stall cleaning, feeding, blanket removal, and hair brushing began. Horns and hoofs got a final buffing with olive oil. If any contrary hair stuck up, it was carefully clipped off. Minutes before the first showing, the braided tails were unwrapped. They had dried and set all night. Now they were combed out into the fluffiest flowing white bundle of hair imaginable. Beautiful! We had put bluing in the final rinse the night before.

Then came the call for the one-year-old Holstein heifer general class. We were ready and led our calves in to stand in a row of eight to twenty entries. Each of us received a numbered tag. We feared the stern old cattle judge from the Soo. His name was Welch. He never smiled; he always looked sour to those whom he judged. Nevertheless, he was a fair man; his gimlet eye did not miss a thing. The circling crowd became silent when judgment began.

Judge Welch moved slowly back and forth between the rows of calves with never a facial hint of what was going on in his mind. He would meander from one end to the other for second looks. Finally, he made his way back to the edge of the crowd and turned toward us. With bated breath, we waited for his pronouncement of the winners: first, second and third place. Heartbeats slackened as a fair official stepped forward to present us with ribbons and record our names for the prize money. Now on to the next general class showing.

Marie and Vivian won prizes in the agricultural hall for their 4-H Club gardening, cooking, and sewing. Vivian remembers getting a blue ribbon once for white muffins. They would attend our calf showings, but I think their hearts were in their exhibits of homegrown and canned vegetables. All showing classes, showtimes, races, and the amount of the awards were published in the *Pickford Fair Book*. A full three-day ticket cost two dollars. All 4-H Club members with entries got in free.

Everyone got involved in the big Saturday night street dance during the fair on the newly paved main street of Pickford. Bags of cornmeal were spread over the cement to facilitate dancing. All three hundred residents of Pickford and the whole countryside were present, or so it seemed. Uncle Ern, the deputy sheriff, moved about among the crowd and quelled any pugnacious drunks with a gentle rap on the head with his billy club. I only knew about three of them, but I won't mention their names. We figured they got the moonshine down in Kelden. Pickford was dry. Local fiddlers, banjo, and guitar players made the music. Country music experts called the square dances. It was a rousing event.

Next came the Soo Fair, but it never had the charm of the Pickford Fair. We always entered all categories open to us and nearly always took first or second place. We did not know the people there so well. Somehow it was not as country as our very own extravaganza. Nor did the prizes add up so well. The Stalwart Fair, which came a little later in the fall, was an entirely different story. I will certainly be telling you about that.

> "It was September and Doug was going into Service; it had rained a lot, but when it dried up enough to put the grain in, Dad and I put sheaves in the barn while everyone else went to the Fair. I could drive the tractor. Dad was a good manager and a good man! I tell you. Dad never complained. He loved to get to go berry picking but work at home was done first.
>
> —*from Mother's hospital talks with Vivian, November 1985*

That tractor driving had to be after I had gone to Cleary Business College and been drafted into the Service. Immediately after the above, Mother's time frame advanced and she said: "That big program they showed on TV to raise money to help the farmers was wonderful. Reagan really knew what he was doing when he did that." It was a riot to hear Mother relate events, what with her Portice Irish storytelling heritage and a twinkle in her eyes. At ninety-two, in the hospital under medication, she still had magic in her speech and facial expressions. She had gracious Irish genes.

The Stalwart Fair was excitingly different to us. It was more remote. The fairgrounds were smaller, but people crowded in from far and wide. It was the crowning event of the fall season. 4-H Club work was just as active there as it was in Pickford. We entered every class available and always came home with the blue and red ribbons, plus the prize winnings. Like the Pickford Fair, they had horse pulling. One-armed George Izzard was exciting to watch again. Another special event at Stalwart was the boxing ring! One year, they had an expert professional in the ring who challenged anyone who dared to take him on. For a guaranteed one-dollar reward, Forrest jumped into the ring and put on the gloves. He was going after that cash and just might get in a lucky blow. He put up a good fight, and the guy did not hurt him. Of course, he did not last long. Forrest had the spunk though.

One year stands out. Forrest and I had to leave about four o'clock in the morning to make the seven-mile trip to the Stalwart fairgrounds with our calves to get them shaped up for the first showings. We backed the hay wagon into a ditch to get Betsy Ross and Rose loaded and tied to the front ladder. I had bought a young thoroughbred Holstein calf at the Pickford Fair and was going to show him at the Stalwart Fair. He would have no part of that wagon. He weighed about a hundred pounds, so we had to wrestle him on board. We tied him to the back rack and set out for Stalwart in the dark.

It was starting to get daylight when we came around the Diamond Springs corner. We were less than a mile from the fairgrounds. "We're in good time and we will soon have our champions in their stalls for feeding and grooming," I said excitedly. Forrest and I were standing up near the front of the wagon and gabbing. I happened to look back and let out a gasp. "The calf's gone! How could he be gone?" Looking back down the road, we saw there was a furrow plowed in the loose gravel going back as far as we could see in the early dawn light. "He jumped overboard!" Running to the back of the wagon rack, I saw that he had been dragging by his neck! "No! Stop the team! We've killed him. He's choked to death!" Forrest backed the team to slacken the rope. We were both on our knees beside the little calf, getting him freed from the rope. To our delight, he was still breathing. The rope did not have a slip knot, so he was not choked. However, his stomach was all swollen up like a balloon. We could not get him up. "What shall we do?" I asked Forrest.

We were right at Tony Dendigger's gate. Should we rouse him out at this time of the morning? Would he get mad at us? We decided that one of us must go and try to get help. About that time, his door opened and out came the old man. He was all kindness and went right into action. "Get him up. I will go for kerosene. He is bloating. But get him up, now! If kerosene does not work, we will have to stick a knife in him, else that gas will kill him." Away he went at a run to his barn. Forrest and I heaved and lifted him by the neck until we finally got his front end up onto his two front feet. He could not get his big stomach and back end off the ground. We tried everything we knew without success. In desperation, I grabbed him by the tail and on the signal "lift," Forrest pulled him forward by the neck while I lifted on his tail like it might pull off. Up he came! My poor little thoroughbred Holstein was a can; he looked like a barrel on four legs.

Mr. Dendigger was back now with a knife and a quart-sized bottle of kerosene. While we held the calf's head up, he shoved that bottle down his throat, forcing him to swallow big gulps of that horrible stuff. We had heard Dad tell of the wonders of the coal-oil treatment. He wobbled and belched, but we kept him on his feet. Soon, his sides went flat again, and "doctor" Dendigger was a happy man. Tony Dendigger went up to the top of the charts with us boys that day. We thanked him so much for saving our 4-H Club calf. Before long, we had the calf walking a little and wondered how we would get him up on the wagon again. I said, "Forrest, let me lead him the rest of the way to the fairgrounds. It's not far, and I will take it real slow." He kindly responded, "Okay, I'll go ahead and get them registered and get our stall assignments. I can get our show heifers off the wagon by myself. But take it mighty easy with him."

I walked beside my little bull to the Stalwart Fair. I patted and reassured him as we went along. It was so early; we still had the road all to ourselves. A happy streak of poetic inspiration took hold of me on that half-mile walk to the Stalwart Fair. By the time the fair was over, I had written down an epic poem, "The Spry Little Bull." As soon as we made it to the calf barn, we gave him a complete bath from head to toe, then fed and blanketed him. He flopped down on that fresh, clean straw bed like he was dead. He was plumb tuckered out. We supposed we would not be showing him. We were only glad we had not killed him. There would be other fairs ahead. Later in the morning, when the rest of our family arrived, what a story we had to tell. That day, we showed our big calves and won ribbons. It was late afternoon when the one-year-and-under showing came up. My little bull had recovered nicely after his long nap, so I entered him. He won a blue ribbon! We took courage for the other upcoming 4-H showings on the second and final day.

That night, I decided to shampoo and braid the little bull's white tail and commenced to groom him for both the open class and the showmanship class. That was a thrilling day. He took the blue ribbon in his age class and put on such a show that he won first place in the showmanship class. As they came to give me the blue ribbon, that little rascal snapped the leather leading line from my fingers and went gamboling around the circle of onlookers. He certainly lived up to the title of the poem. The long trip home that night was ideal for the completion of my poem as my little thoroughbred lay quiet and secured on the wagon. Mother dearly loved my poem and told everybody about it. It was a memorable fair by any measurement, but somehow the precious manuscript vanished. My mother would declare it a great loss.

In September of 1996, Francis and Vivian took me to the Stalwart Fair. My last 4-H showing there was in 1936. The Presbyterian church was open that day, serving up a great dinner for all the modern fairgoers. Chet Crawford's old Stalwart Store and the Stalwart School are boarded up now, over sixty years later. The Maltas Memorial Log

Church is still there right beside Pete Nalley's farm where Francis was born and raised. Dad's draft team helped with the logs for that church when it was built. The Fairview Cemetery across the road is well kept. A walk among the tombs brought back memories of neighbors and friends. I stood a long while by the grave of my best boyhood friend, Charles Ames, who was killed in the Battle of the Bulge. Freddie McConkey's grave is there also. Freddie was so young. He died in the Battle of the Bulge also. Oh, war is such a waste.

    A crowning experience of my 4-H Club days was when Mr. McMillan selected my calf, Rose, to go into the competition at the Upper Peninsula State Fair. He took me personally in his car to that far-away extravaganza. Though it was less than two hundred miles away, it was far away for this farm boy who had never been more than fifty miles from home. I won a state ribbon and felt highly honored for the opportunity. Now, I wanted to win the race to get every last bit of our grain safely into the barn in September before the rains came. Otherwise, the fields would become so soft that all our machines would founder in the clay loam mush.

CHAPTER TWENTY-ONE

OCTOBER
Rubber Boots and Barn Dances

THE NEXT CHALLENGE WAS THE THRESHING season. There were only two or three threshing machines in the Pickford area. Dad always got scheduled for one as early as possible. He got firm promises from seven or eight neighbors to "trade hands." This made for a great threshing season. Dad would go to each of theirs, and they would all come to our threshing. Mr. Phillip Romeo was our favorite thrasher. He lived in the Italian settlement southwest of Pickford near Rockview. He was always reliable and did a good job.

On the day before our threshing, the giant 10-20 iron-wheeled tractor came chugging down the road into our gate with the big separator hooked on behind. It looked like a mountain being moved. We kids watched every inch of its progress. First, Mr. Romeo swung round in the barnyard and backed that machine up into the threshing floor of our barn. Then, he unhitched from it and moved about forty feet out into the barnyard, carefully lining it up with the separator. Next, they dug out the biggest, widest, and longest belt we had ever seen. It took two men to carry it. The first man hung it around a steel drive pulley on the tractor. Then, both men unrolled it toward the barn and heaved the belt around a similar drive pulley on the threshing machine, tightening it by twisting the belt once and pulling the tractor forward. That eight-inch-wide belt was amazing. They brushed the inside surface with something they called "belt dressing." I guess the sheer weight of that belt and the dressing gave good traction on both pulleys. We kids were just dying to understand it all. We wondered what kind of man could have possibly built this big contraption. It said "McCormack Deering" on the side of it in fancy lettering. Two men must have gotten together to invent it.

Early on the first day of this two-day event, the big Titan 10-20 was snorting and puffing. Mr. Romeo was going about squirting oil on moving parts, filling glass oil cups, and final checking everything. He would not even think about touching the iron lever that engaged the drive pulley before all his safety checks were done. Meanwhile, the farm hands had piled in and taken their positions. Two or three men were way up in the mow to throw the sheaves down to two men on the "table" platform beside the open mow and the monster machine. One man had to manage the distribution of the straw as it blasted out of a fourteen-inch blower pipe. Two more men had to be ready with metal buckets when the grain came out and then tote that grain to the proper bins in the granary. There were odd jobs, like emptying the weed-seed refuse, that the big separator kept spitting out. The boast of a good thrasher was that he could get out all the enemy seeds (such as fireweed out of the grain) with his machine.

When Mr. Romeo threw the lever, the racket began. The titan snorting, the belt swishing and flapping, the pulleys rolling, and the whirling chopper blades were devouring the sheaves. Many cradles inside were shaking, pounding, and separating the grain from the stalks, from the straw, and from the chaff. A powerful interior fan at the back end was blowing the straw clear outside of the barn through an eighteen-foot pipe. Other shaking sieves took out the wild seed. Finally, moving elevator cups delivered the finished product out the grain spout into metal baskets. You just cannot imagine the motion, smells, dust, and cacophony of noise. Talk about excitement, that was exiting! The monster 10-20 machine with its drive belt was just doing its thing: vibrating, bouncing, grinding, chopping, rattling, and blowing clouds of dust out of every joint and cranny. Sheaves constantly swishing down from the mow above and the rattle of carrying tubs sounded out along with it.

The job required Mr. Romeo to stay on top of the tractor and wide belt. His second in command managed and harmonized the rest of the whole nightmare. Promptly at noon, the titan whistle blew, the great marvelous racket came to a halt, and weird looking men poured out of the barn, hungry as bears. Their faces were black with smut from engine and grain dust. When they removed their hats, you would see a white rim around their heads at the hairline. Mother provided wash pans with water, but they only washed their hands. What a sight to behold their faces jammed around Mother's festive outdoor table. Other neighbor ladies had come to help Mother prepare and present the feast. They pitched in, eating, talking, and laughing. It was quite the social event of the year.

From age six and up, I was involved in our threshing days. Helping carry grain, running errands, and "sidewalk superintending." By age twelve, I got a black face just like the rest of the crew with jobs like building the interior straw mow. After the sheaves were threshed, another task began over the stable hay mows. The blower was swung inside, and enough straw put in for stall bedding throughout the winter. The day I first got to eat with the threshing crew was a milestone. I had envied that spot. I appreciated the recognition Dad was sincerely giving to me by allowing me to help. Up to that time, all the children had to eat with the womenfolk after the main event. Dad never let me go along with him to threshing days with our neighbors. I think he felt like he needed to shield me from some of the risk factors.

I must tell you more about the granary, our treasure-house bank. It was built into the stable section under the two mows west of the center gangway. A twenty-foot aisle with four bins on each side gave us just enough room. The fanning mill equipment that turned the threshed grain into clean grain was in there. There was just enough space for us to get around it. For many abundant years, all those bins would be heaped full, clear to the ceiling. The surplus grain had to be bagged and piled in the feeding room. Speltz would be ground up to make "chop" for the milk cows and young cattle during the long winter months. The oats were a must for the horses year-round, but surplus oats could be sold for cash. There was barley, flax, marafat peas, and winter wheat. Leftover fall wheat was put there too. We took some fall wheat to the grist mill in Pickford to be ground into flour for us and "shorts" for our animals.

During the years of my pastoral ministry, I developed an annual Threshing Day sermon, which always brought appreciative comments from the congregation. Jesus spoke of harvest often: "The harvest truly is great, but the labourers are few." Luke 10:2. Most every fall, we sold our crops for cash, except during the Great Depression. During those years, prices for crops went down to rock bottom, making buyers both "few and far between" and miserly. This was a testing time—a bare existence time for Mother and Dad for many reasons. They had to get the Spiegel-May Stern catalog order in for winter clothes for the whole family. We had three or four regular monthly payments and taxes to pay. We had grocery, doctor, and blacksmith accounts to pay up. If we got the granary filled and a good crop of hay in the barn, we might be okay. If we added to that enough young cattle, hogs, chickens, geese, plus a turkey or two, we were in good shape. Slim markets and the annual payment on our farm always hung over our heads.

Campbell's bush was our forty-acre magic forest filled with all kinds of treasures. Down near a certain little branch of water leading into the creek, there was a wild plum tree. By the first of October, it was plum harvest time. We kids gathered around that tree, shaking it until the plums came down like raindrops from heaven. The ground was covered, and into a Bemis bag they went. We proudly lugged them home to Mother for plum jelly.

Cranberries were supposed to be down on the shores of Mud Lake in the Gogomain Swamp, so it was like finding gold the day we discovered the high-bush cranberry trees in Harvey Campbell's bush. We had an exciting report to bring to the supper table that night. Ever after, we kept a shepherd's eye on that cranberry cluster, just like the plum tree and the raspberry patches. There were other wild berries that Dad and Mother warned us never to put in our mouths because they were poisonous. We called them snake berries.

Harvey Campbell's bush had juicy, sweet sugar plum trees in early summer. You could put a whole handful in your mouth and eat 'em like ice cream. Mature sugar plum trees were thirty feet tall, but there were lots of twelve-foot trees that were just loaded. Their rosy-brownish color was nothing like the purple plums. They were only about the size of a huckleberry, but sweeter. Alas, this delight in our wonderland would spoil and fall off the trees in two or three weeks. They were no good for canning because they just turned to water; there was no real substance to them. We kids thought they were our own manna from heaven.

Now in October, mouth-puckering chokecherries matured and were plentiful in all the woods around our place. One fall, the International Harvester salesman came by as Forrest and I came from the bush with branches full of chokecherries. Our cheeks were puffed out, and we were shooting the pits at one another. He wanted to know if those were wild chokecherries? Being authorities on the subject, we said, "Yes." He declared, "They make the best wine. I'd like you to pick me some, if it doesn't take too long. I'll give you a dollar for a twelve-quart pail." Both our heads were nodding, "Okay, we can do it in a half hour or less." Back into the Campbell bush we ran. After stripping off handfuls from the lower limbs, Forrest would climb up the slender trunk and heave his body outward, bending the whole tree-load down. He held the trunk with one hand and picked cherries with the other. I pulled them off with both hands. From tree to tree we went. We filled that milk pail brim full and made it back ahead of time. The salesman handed over his dollar with a smile. We rolled in the dough that day.

October always brought fall rains. It rained, rained, and rained some more. It softened the fields for plowing, but the cattle traffic made the barnyard one big mudhole. A loose, two-board walkway from the henhouse to the barn taxed the traveler's sense of balance. One misstep and it was over your shoe top. Mother wore rubber boots to the barn and back for milking. If she got one foot stuck in the mud, her foot sometimes came out all by itself—a revolting development. It happened once or twice each fall, and we teased Mother about it. It was funny how our beloved old cat, Tiger, liked to brush by our legs while we traveled the path to the barn. He would meet us to brush by our leg and whiz past us again, repeating this affectionate procedure.

Fall frosts came early. The weather turned wet, cold, and sloppy. Mud was everywhere. At our thirty-eighth parallel, the days shortened quickly. By the time the cow chains were checked and the horses brushed down, the warped-board track to the house had to be piloted by lantern light. Gobs of mud had to be scraped from our shoes before we entered the kitchen door. "It's a dirty night," was oft repeated. Comfort and warmth hit you as you came inside. The back door was shut; chores were all done. I can never forget this feeling. It was akin to a hymn we sing: "When peace like a river attendeth my soul."

We used to welcome the big Spiegel May Stern's mail order catalog from Chicago as winter approached, and Dad and Mother would work up a clothing order. I think it wound up mostly for us kids: long-handled underwear (union suits), wool coats, fur-lined winter caps, chooks, sweaters, wool pants and shirts, plus wool dresses and blouses. It was a money-stretching event. We had three months to pay. Sometimes, if he had a buyer, Dad would butcher a couple of two-year-old cattle to pay off the fall order in full after factoring in the taxes and local bills. It was a day of celebration when the Spiegel order came in on the stage.

Otto Watson's Shoe Store outfitted us with new winter footwear. Otto would put it on credit for us. He knew Bert Nixon had good crops in the barn, and his word was as good as a bond. Thank God, we always came through, though sometimes payment was painfully delayed because there was no buyer for our farm goods. I say, "we came through" because we all felt involved and responsible. Dad and Mother worried, but I do not remember any of those Pickford merchants ever scolding or badgering Dad because the bills got so high. If they did, it was never mentioned to us. I do remember one time when Dad sold a butchered beef to Hamilton and Watson's Grocery Store, and Jim Watson asked him, "Bert, could you put half of this beef on your bill?"

We often climbed through the barbed wire fence during wet fall seasons to try to make it to the barn on somewhat solid ground. The heavy clay loam soil would be softened by the rain, so Mr. Gough would come stay with us and plow for Dad. All those acres of soil had to be turned over to be ready for spring planting. Imagine plowing sixty-nine acres with a team of horses and only turning eight inches on each pass. "Yon Jigger" Jimmy Gough could handle it. He was a most unusual old man, always good humored.

He wore an ancient suit coat while plowing. The matching pants had long since given out. We were never allowed to tease him about his clothing. When the sun warmed things up, he would get warm wrestling those plow handles. He would hang "yon jacket" on one of the collar hames of our draft horses. One morning he asked Mother, "Selena, have you seen yon jacket?" She answered, "No, Jimmy, I haven't. Did you hang it on a fence post at the end of the field? What about in the horse stable?" He responded, sounding confused, "No, I've scoured yon field and the barn. Yon jacket has disappeared. 'By the jingles' it's a mystery." It was a mystery indeed. We looked everywhere but could not find his jacket. Poor Mr. Gough lamented. Dad loaned him a jacket and fall plowing continued. That field was seeded with grass and grain seed that spring and became a hay field. Three years later, while Dad was turning that field for grain, he plowed up yon jacket. Now Mr. Gough would really get plenty of teasing.

Another time, Mother had gotten a nice raincoat for the wet weather that came up missing. The place was searched, and Mr. Gough was carefully quizzed. "No, he couldn't imagine what happened to yon raincoat and quite a fancy coat too." Several months later, Dad and I were thoroughly cleaning out Bess and Colonel's double stall, even the packed-down straw in the front corners. Lo and behold! What did we turn up, but Mother's good raincoat! "Yon Jigger" Mr. Gough had gotten up on a rainy night and threw Mother's raincoat over his shoulders as he proceeded to the barn to feed the horses. As was his want, he made himself a cozy bed in front of the horses for an early morning snooze. How it got covered up, we never knew. Yon raincoat was ruined, but she still loved "Old Jimmy."

One Halloween night, it was pitch-dark. Harvey Campbell had come down from his Stalwart home to stay in his little ten-by-twelve shanty across the road from us. He was doing his fall plowing, about fifteen acres of it. Mr. Gough was staying with us, plowing for Dad. After supper, he went over to visit yon Harvey. That enterprising big brother of mine got an idea for a prank this Halloween night while Mervin O'Brien was spending the night with us. "Let's go over and have some fun with hot-tempered Red Harvey." Forrest allowed me to come along this time. First, we would bombard the shanty with mud balls to get Harvey's attention. Mervin and Forrest sneaked up to the door of the shanty and pulled a heavy iron sugar kettle right outside its swing arc. A wooden shutter was open, and we could see Harvey and Mr. Gough engaged in hearty conversation by the woodstove. His kerosene lamp defined the target area. The first shower of mud balls aroused "Yon Redhead!" He yelled out, "I know who it is!" He rushed for the door and burst out overtop the sugar kettle. With red-hot ire, he assailed that Forrest Nixon in the darkness. The cigarette in his mouth drew our three-fold fire. Later, Old Jimmy gave us a blow-by-blow account of how Harvey went sprawling out his door, then withdrew back into the shanty, closing the door and the shutter.

That was not the end of it. Forrest got an armful of dry straw from Harvey's nearby wagon, climbed on the roof, and stuffed the stove pipe full of straw. Mr. Gough's report was, "Yon stove commenced to smoke." Harvey really went into a rage, charging out again to lay hold of us. I was also on the roof and had to jump for it, landing in a pile of junkie scrap iron. It is a wonder I did not break a leg. Anyway, we escaped into the blackness with our hides. Poor Harvey stormed to the roof and clawed the straw out of his stove pipe. Old Jimmy was getting a kick out of it as he related the whole inside story to us later. Red Harvey was burned up at us for a while, but pretty soon we were friends again, and good neighbors.

Halloween was a time for pranks like soaping windows and turning over backhouses. It was generally expected and tolerated in a good way, if no serious damage was done. Harvey seemed to draw more than his share, chiefly because of his hot temper and colorful reactions. Forrest, with help no doubt, tried to pull Harvey's hand pump out of his well. The pipe was so long that when the pump got so far up in the air, they lost control of it. Instead of simply laying it on the ground, the pipe bent and collapsed to the ground. I do not know how that was settled, but the intent was not to damage the pipe. When Dad found out, it got settled.

I cannot resist the urge to philosophize at this point. No more pranks on Halloween; children must go about for treats, not tricks. It seems possible to me that we have closed up a normal venting system for devilment in maturing youth. More and more, teens seem to express themselves by doing real violence and wholly antisocial behavior. Better to let them soap windows and turn over backhouses once a year, to get it out of their system. That is my theory. Give "ear" ye all.

Vivian and I had a near tragedy shortly after threshing day one fall. We were about six and ten years old. Mother had sent us back to the potato patch to dig a half-pail for supper and for the next day. On the way back, we saw Ole Tiger perched away up on the newly blown straw stack outside the barn. We were worried when we saw him disappear! We decided to climb to the top of that twenty-foot stack to rescue our cat; besides, it would be fun to slide back down. I would go first with Viv to follow me. One third of the way down, the stack widened sharply. Instead of following the visual contours, I went straight down into the bowels of that haystack. I screamed at Vivian not to come, but she landed on top of my head. We were both buried deep in the stack where all was darkness. Vivian was crying. I thought we were buried alive and never would be found till spring. I tried to quiet Viv and urged her to help me tramp the straw with some hope of pulling up to daylight. After a while, a slight gleam of light appeared, but Vivian was yelling and coughing like she was going to choke to death. My mouth was filling with barley awn, which would go only one way—down my throat. Viv was somehow able to help me with the tramping. Soon, I was able to push her up and out to roll on down to the ground. Not long after that, I was able to roll out also. We ran, hacking and spitting into the house. Mother got Dad, who was probably out in a field plowing somewhere. Away we all headed to the doctor in Pickford. Vivian just could not get her throat clear. Mother and Dad could not see what kept her near choking.

Doctor Fox soon located a barley awn embedded deep in her throat and was able to pull it out with tweezers. Oh, what a relief! Viv would be okay. We got lectured, "Never, ever go climbing on a new straw stack that has not been compressed by time and rain." I am sure we all must have added to the Lord's prayer a humble sentence of thanks for our lives being spared. Ole Tiger got down safely somehow; he showed better sense. I will never forget every vivid detail of this; I thought we were both goners.

Late October brought Saturday night barn dances at the Stirlingville Hall and the Wildcat. The Wildcat was a good bit southwest of Pickford on the Mackinac Trail that led to St. Ignace and the Straits. Forrest had started dating girls and was pressuring Dad for the use of our first car. Dad gave in and started a pattern that was hard to control. Other guys and their girlfriends would be going with them. They promised to buy the gas if Forrest could get the car. The car often came home with the tank on zero.

Forrest was a dresser too; shirt, tie, shoes, spats, and the press in his trousers had to be one hundred percent right. That is how Viv and I became unwilling experts. "Woe be" if you scorched the collar or the press was not sharp and straight. A word of praise or approval from our big brother was a great motivator. Our tools were those old flatirons heated on the wood stove. Engaging the wooden handle, you pressed down on a dampened press cloth over the precious fabric. The iron had to be hot enough to make steam and slightly scorch the pressing cloth, but not so hot as to scorch those fancy britches underneath. I was commissioned to do the pressing parts, while Vivian ironed his shirts. Must be that our older sister, Marie, absolutely refused.

Forrest Nixon in front of the old farmhouse

Here's Vivian: "Remember as Forrest got a little older, he used to run with Albert Crawford, Clifford McConkey, Ted Kerr, and sometimes Harvey and Mate Pennington, I think. He used to fire up that old home range to get the irons hot to press his pants and get the crease in them perfect. He used to get me to iron his white shirts once in a while, and I hated that. Once I scorched the collars, and he exploded. That was the end of ironing shirts for him. Ho, ho, isn't it funny how things happen." One time, I ever so slightly scorched a pair of beautiful white, all-wool trousers. I felt terrible; I do not remember the consequences. That all-wool cloth is very touchy, and those flatirons are so hard to handle. I do not remember Forrest being too hard on me. He knew I always did my best to win his approval. Forrest made a lot of genuine friends, and they remained close across the years. He was such a good salesman. In the worst Depression years, he succeeded in selling tailor-made suits with his traveling sample kit and the good service he gave. He probably gave the suit manufacturer a hard time. Every suit would have to be right, one hundred percent right. In years to come, I looked back and envied Forrest's gift with people.

I wanted to go to the barn dances when I was in high school and began to ask Forrest if I could go too. I do not recall Dad and Mother raising any questions about it, but I knew that they were unhappy about Forrest's gang of friends. They expected high standards of conduct from us. Forrest had begun to smoke. They feared he would be into drinking as well. Perhaps they felt they had no right to deny me some of the privileges their eldest son had wrung from them. Times were hard for teenagers, and their options for going out were few. They did not want the same collision course with me. Forrest and I got along fine. I earned a little leverage by pressing his suits. He agreed to take me occasionally. On that first consent, a serious circumstance developed. The left heel of my only pair of go-to-town shoes was badly worn and kept falling off, again and again. It was so far gone that nails driven from the inside down into the heel would not hold. *Ah! Why not just make a new heel out of wood?* With saw, wood rasp, and sandpaper, I began to fashion a proper heel. I nailed it solidly from the inside and polished it with stove blacking. Forrest gave me an "okay" nod and away we went. Who would inspect my shoe heels closely anyway?

The heel held. The old Stirlingville dance hall was crammed inside, with many on the outside. When the fiddlers struck up "The Golden Slippers," the square-dance callers sang out the dance patterns, and the do-si-dos began. Many groups sashayed in circles, elbow to elbow, laughing and singing while clouds of dust rose from the old wooden floor. All seemed fine and fun. I ventured out on the floor to try a few dances but never did get the hang of it. Bootleg liquor from Kelden was being passed around, and the young bucks got louder and braver. When the call went out for round dancing, the crowd psychology was due for a drastic change. Couples filled the floor to swing and sway, and soon a tag dance was announced. That meant one male could tap the shoulder of another dancing male, and he had to surrender his partner to the challenger. Drunken pride, meanness, and competing brawn soon issued in clashes. When a partner refused to yield to another's tag, honor called for a fight to the finish: "Come on outside!"

I witnessed some vicious battles. Fist cuffs and bloody noses at first, but ultimately two men down on the ground mauling and beating one another to a pulp, with no referee. It got to be a regular thing at those barn dances. The winners became champs. Challengers arose sooner or later to knock out the current champ. Now, a new winner was proclaimed. The whole countryside knew the leading contenders; each had his fans. One of my uncles came home from the Wildcat Dance one Saturday night with a huge black eye. He had a drink or two and boasted that he could lick anybody in the place. Another boozer set him straight. Uncle did not go back there anymore. In fact, I never heard of him ever taking another drink. Such was the climate of the barn dance rage. I believe our uncle was cured.

I went to just a few of those barn dances. One night, we were in the car heading for home when a bottle was passed around. A good friend of mine lit up a cigarette and took a swig of moonshine. I felt disappointed in him and said no to the bottle. Then and there, I decided this was not the road I wanted to go down. That was my last barn dance.

CHAPTER TWENTY-TWO

NOVEMBER
Thanksgiving and Hunting Season

NOVEMBER BROUGHT CHILLY WEATHER and sometimes an early skiff of snows. Fall was saying goodbye. Our Spiegel order had arrived. We were all feeling cozy and confident in our new outerwear, woolen underclothes, boots, and caps. Uncle Dewey would soon be coming to stay with us for a whole week. There would be many happy battles. Uncle Herb and Aunt Belle would be bringing their homemade trailer house out from the Soo. They parked it right down the road by Harvey Campbell's bush. The color red was important for hunting: red plaid jackets, red Soo woolen mill pants, and red hunting caps. We could not afford those special color outfits much, but at least a red cap was mandatory for our private safety code. Dad would be getting down the old .38-55 from its wall place and oiling it up for action. He brought down as many bucks with our old faithful single-shot, pump-action rifle as my uncles got with their fancy Winchester automatics. Of course, Dad got in a little interseason practice.

Election Day came in November, usually around the sixth. Uncle Ern was usually up for reelection for township clerk, sheriff or something else. We took our politics seriously. Pickford was Republican territory, but a few registered Democrats were around. We allowed that some of them, like our postmaster, were tolerable. Mother, Vivian, Dougie, and I were walking home one Election Day when the whole western horizon began to turn into a mud-colored wave, creeping toward us, looming higher and higher. We were troubled and quickened our steps. "What is it? Can we smother to death?" I asked. Never had we seen such a thing before, so we were very frightened. It turned out to be the eastern rim of a dust storm from the Dakotas. How terrible it must have been to be overtaken by one of them. We wondered if one *could* smother to death. Our Model-T must have been up on blocks. Our Spiegel order must not have arrived yet either, because I can remember squeezing my worn-out, yellow, monkey-faced gloves into a ball to keep my hands warm.

On another Election Day, Vivian and I stayed home with Mr. Gough. He was plowing for Dad. With time on our hands, we decided to make some candy. So we brewed up a whole kettle of it on the old wood range. It was hard to tell if it had thickened properly. We kept trying to tell if it was ready by taking samples from the watery liquid. When we thought it was about right, we poured it out into one of Mother's large cookie pans. It turned to rock, brittle as glass. We moaned, but Ole Jimmy commenced to taste yon candy and pronounced that it was pretty good. Mr. Gough sang, "The Ship that Never Returned" and "The Maid of Moher" while nibbling at yon candy. We ate the whole thing! We loved Mr. Gough, and he loved us. He kept saying, "By the jingles, yon candy is good."

November was a month of tragedy on the northern Great Lakes. Many a freighter was caught in a late season passage. It would be their last run before the freeze; indeed, it was their last trip. Many a steamer and all their crew went down under a sudden ice storm. The sailors attempted to chop the ice off the decks of their ship with axes. They had ship to shore radio contact, but many times there would be no adequate weather warnings. Tragedy after tragedy occurred in Lake Superior, and sometimes in Lake Michigan. Many ships would take shelter by locking down in the St. Mary's River at Sault Ste. Marie to wait out the storm if they got the warning early enough. Many clustered, ice-laden ships did not make it. The low, powerful bleating of fog horns in the St. Mary's River was a familiar sound. I still cling to that sound in my childhood memory bank. Every time I think about the foggy days of springtime and fall, I remember that sound.

"Over the river and through the woods, to Grandmother's house we go" was literally true when we children were young. We bundled up in the Model-T, sleighs, or wagon and traveled one mile to Grandpa and Grandma Portice's big house on the Munuscong River. It was a high moment in our year. The house was a mansion. There was a grand living room with two fancy stairways going to the upper bedrooms. A big oleander tree, in a huge urn, stood in the middle of the room. 'Tis Grandma's pantry I remember most. It had a whole wall of cabinets with glass front doors, and you could see all kinds of carnival glassware inside; it was a real treasure house. Grandma made the best jelly and cookies. When I was small, this was such a feast time for us! Grandpa Portice passed away in 1925. During the Depression, Grandma's big house burned to the ground. That must have been when we developed great Thanksgiving feasts in our own shingled house.

None could be better. Thanksgiving Day was the climax of the hunting season. We had many a famous gathering. Often, our whole hunting tribe would be present: Uncle Herb with Aunt Belle and Uncle Dewey with Aunt Stella all came from the Soo; Uncle Ern and Aunt Nellie came from Pickford. Our old farm kitchen-dining room was bulging. It was about the pudding stage of one of these big Thanksgiving feasts that Mother looked east out the washroom window and saw a buck running. It ran across the back of our farm from the Belcher bush to the Armstrong bush at least a quarter mile away. She set off the alarm; within minutes, every hunter had jumped into his red woolen gear, armed and ready. Uncle Ern called the strategy, designating who should go take the "stand" where the buck might be driven out. The rest of us would enter the woods at spaced distances apart from one another to hound out the deer.

Clifton Nixon

Nixon brothers: Dewey, Ern, and Bert

Soon, we were baying like hounds and proceeding with caution. We knew full well that expert riflemen were in position to fire if we succeeded in driving the deer out. Always there was the danger and concern that the frightened deer would double back between us. This raised the possibility of fatal error on the part of one of the riflemen. They all carried rifles loaded but with the safety on. That was the rule, and you better not be caught in violation. You could be ruled off the team, right on the spot. No argument. No remedy. Too many hunters were killed by such carelessness, but not our close-knit family team with Uncle Ern, both eldest brother and deputy sheriff.

This Thanksgiving Day was to be memorable. I was one of the drivers, and the rifle fire began when we were about halfway through the drive. Forty shots were fired. Not one brought that buck down. He had crossed a forty-acre field and entered the Campbell bush. Now a new strategy was drawn up. The drive would be through the Campbell forty-acre bush into the open fields before the Clegg bush. By now, it was two o'clock, and the next turn of "standers" was named by Uncle Ern. Away we go. Time must be given for the standers to get in position before the hounding began. I was a high schooler with no rifle and no qualifying experience with a rifle. Besides, I had no real desire to do the shooting. I was a good hound and could howl with the best of them. It was only after I came home from the Army with rifle training that Uncle Ern took out a license for me to hunt with them.

Anyway, this day the Campbell bush drive got underway with stringent warnings about the dangers of a possible switchback. This deer may be wounded and desperate. Be careful! We were about three quarters of the way through the woods and beginning to feel like the deer had outfoxed us when the riflemen began to fire. It sounded like they were all blazing away. Surely they got that buck. When we finally lumbered out into the clearing, it was only sad stories we heard. This was wrong; that was wrong; the deer got away. One felt that he had wounded it, but no profoundly serious evidence could be found besides a few spots of blood.

He was now in the Clegg bush for sure and probably wounded. The sun was getting low in the northwest; it would be the final drive before darkness fell. My dad and uncles took serious counsel, and the final turn of blockers was named. I think the person who thought he had wounded the deer was allowed back as a blocker. They hurried down the side roads to take up position for the last stand. Soon, we were stretched out in a spaced line on the road. The signal was given to enter and howl. It was hard to recognize whether a deer or a man made that brush noise or movement. Look for that red! No guesswork. This was a dangerous venture; emotions were high, and the wounded deer might try to get back between. "Buck fever" was one of the warnings driven into our minds.

That deer Mother had spotted was about to get away. We were almost through the Clegg bush and had not heard a sound. He must have played dead between us. It was almost dark. "We've lost him after all," someone called out, and then we heard two rapid-fire rifle shots. That was all. We rushed out of the woods to see what had happened. Uncle Herb stood about three hundred yards from where I came out of the woods. He was standing over a downed deer and waving to all his fellow blockers and the emerging drivers. I ran to his side and heard him warn us not to get close to this big buck. "He may have a lot of life in him yet and could get you with his rack of horns." He was a two-hundred-pounder. Uncle Herb approached him gingerly. Sure enough, this big buck made an upper cut with his ten spikes. My uncle jumped clear and immediately put another round in his neck to finish him off.

They field-dressed that buck right there. By the time they had dragged him to the road, it was pitch dark. What a hunt! It would be talked about for many years. Mother was the real hero that Thanksgiving Day. She spotted a big buck faraway and sounded the alarm. Yes, we all reaped the rewards of hunting season. The family fellowship was endearing; I have never gotten away from it. My dad, uncles, and Forrest were disciplined hunters.

"Every gun is loaded" was an unwritten law. Well, do I remember one day Forrest had taken his rifle apart to clean it. Fortunately, the barrel was pointed toward the ceiling when a bullet exploded and went right up through the ceiling. Forrest had forgotten. Even though the clip was empty and the stock removed, there was a shell in the barrel. We thanked God he was not hurt. There were other stringent laws that I will not forget. Never point a rifle at anyone. Do not even swing the muzzle past a fellow hunter's legs! Never walk behind another hunter in the woods with the safety off! Never, ever lean a rifle against a wire fence while you climb through! Check that the safety is on and *lay it down*. Make triple sure it is a deer you are drawing down on! Beware of movements; it may be a man, not a deer. And again: always, always, always assume a gun is loaded! There was no excuse for the safety being off on any rifle unless you had sighted a deer unmistakably, and the space between you and the deer was absolutely clear of human beings. Discipline was strict. No excuses were acceptable—no matter who. No one in our family was ever injured in all the years they hunted together.

It was a beautiful, cool, crisp November day. Nothing out-of-the-ordinary was happening. We were taking a time-out and were sitting around on the moss and leaves. Uncle Dewey had rolled a cigarette and was smoking. I must have been ten or eleven. I asked him if I could have one of his cigarette papers and make myself a cigarette of the dried moss lying around. He gave me one, and I rolled up a pretty cigarette that looked just like Uncle Dewey's Lucky Strikes. He lit it up for me. I took a few puffs and began to cough and gag. I soon got rid of that thing and never did touch a cigarette of any kind after that. Never wanted one. Uncle Dewey was sly and knew what would happen. I am thankful for Uncle Dewey. He was stuck with them, I believe. He knew I was taking the cure.

Uncle Herb's boss man in the Soo begged Uncle Herb to take him hunting. Request was granted, but his performance must be closely watched. He was a short little man with a round belly. We were hounding out my Uncle Tom's bush. There was a great barrage of rifle fire, but the deer got through unscathed. When we drivers got out of the bush, all the blockers were gathered around the little round man. Some were laughing, others were not. The big buck had suddenly crashed out of the woods right next to where Uncle Herb's boss was standing. He got too excited. He started to jump up and down, hollering, "There he is! There he is! Get him!" He never once raised his rifle. That is what you call buck fever. I do not recall his ever hunting with us again.

When I was about eight or nine years old, Dad took me to a coroner's inquest concerning the fatal shooting of a hunter. The questioning was serious; the shooter was a broken man and vowed he would never hunt again. It seems he was hunting alone in the early morning. He was tracking a deer, and the hoof prints were growing increasingly fresh. Water in them had not even begun to frost over. He was sure he was closing in on a big buck. Out ahead, he thought he saw a movement, and there before him was the outline of a deer. He claimed that he was sure it was the profile of a buck. He drew a steady, deliberate aim and fired. An innocent hunter fell to the ground dead. Most every year, an accident like that happened. The coroner's jury found him innocent, but he was a broken man for life.

Another time, one of my classmates in high school had an older brother killed by a fellow hunter. They had a deer cornered and were driving him out into a clearing for certain killing. It was near the end of the day and excitement was high. One of the drivers heard a noise and thought it was the wounded deer doubling back between himself and his nearest fellow driver. He was sure it was the deer, so he took aim and fired. He killed his close friend. It was Howard Harrison, my classmate's brother. All the countryside was saddened.

Venison meat can have an extraordinarily strong, undesirable taste. It must be dressed out carefully. There are ways of preparation that improve it greatly. Mother used to grind up the meat in her little hand grinder. She put lots of onions and bread with it to make delicious hamburgers. I do not know what else she may have put in, but they were good. There was a good market for them. She also stewed and canned the venison for year-round consumption in those big two-quart green jars with the rubber ring sealers. Venison stew and mashed taters with green tomato "governors" make a wonderful supper. Marie remembers one hunting season that Forrest got sick on the opening day of hunting season. Over the concerns of Dad and Mother, he went out anyway. It turned out to be the mumps. He became so sick that we had to call Dr. Fox. Marie recalled: "He really gave Forrest a talking to."

CHAPTER TWENTY-THREE

DECEMBER
Greatest Month in the Whole Year!

PICKFORD IS IN THE UPPER PENINSULA of Michigan, three hundred miles north of Detroit. Our cousins down in Pontiac always referred to it as "up north." Pickford is snow country. Three of the Great Lakes converge on us. It is only about twenty-five miles to Lake Superior, eleven miles to Lake Huron and forty miles to Lake Michigan. Serious snowfall began in November. By Christmas, our side road from Frogpond School was usually closed to automobiles. Our Model-T Ford was up on jacks to save the tires from prolonged winter frost damage. Sleigh runners, not wheels, are used in transportation now, until the "breakup" in the spring.

There were a few times when we attempted to extend the use of the car through Christmas. When we did, we often got stuck in muddy ruts. Dad would have to go get the team to pull us out. Or else, the crankcase oil would get so cold and thick that you could not turn the engine with the crank. You had to harness the team again to pull the car on a long chain, hoping it would start. We even put a tin-can kerosene torch under the oil pan to warm up the oil so the crank would turn. Our Model-T had no starter.

Vivian remembered that the horses had to pull the car out on her January first wedding day. She must have made it to the church in time; she and Frances just celebrated their fiftieth wedding anniversary. We were glad when the freeze-up came. No more wading through slush with cold water squishing in your boots. Now, the footing was solid in our world carpeted in white. The doors to our winter wonderland had opened.

The first important event of the season was finding a good, well-shaped Christmas tree. It must measure up to high expectations. Forrest was a perfectionist. We would set out through the snow into the Armstrong bush and tramp all the way clear into the Bill Hewer bush or even south into Uncle Ern's bush, searching for the perfect tree. We were sure to find a good one in one of those forty-acre bushes. When Dougie got big enough, he would come along too. We covered a lot of territory and studied many a tree. Often we would sing out, "There's a good one. Look at it! That there's a good one!" Only to discover that when we drew closer, it had some minor flaw: branches skimpy on one side, a slight bend in the trunk, or something not just so. On we marched. There had to be a unanimous vote, and Forrest's vote was the tough one to get.

We took turns carrying the axe. When the afternoon sun was getting low and we were well-nigh tuckered out, the big decision was reached. Down came the tree, and we headed home, dragging our trophy through the snow. Our sisters always "oohed and aahed" and wanted to know where we found such a perfect Christmas tree. We happy heroes were starving and not quite ready to talk about it until they fed us.

Marie and Vivian had dug out the ancient Christmas decorations from the old trunk upstairs. It was our most sacred family depository. It had been Grandpa Nixon's traveling trunk. It contained treasures like the gold-plated pendant watch that Dad had given Mother before they were married, and there was an amethyst tie pin that Mother had given Dad. I have that amethyst tie pin today. It was with a sense of awe that we touched anything in that trunk. There was a large black Bible inside that we handled with special care. I remember opening it once and reading a passage in the Old Testament that warned about sinning against God and the judgment of God. I closed the book thoughtfully and wondered. Often, I have wished that I had inquired of Mother about the history of that Bible. The decorations consisted of eight or ten beautifully designed and delicate old-fashioned Christmas tree ornaments. They were chipped and faded, but priceless to us. There were two cards of glittering rope—one gold and the other silver. There was a box of ancient icicles and several rolls of narrow gage red and white crepe paper.

When the cows were milked and the chores all done, we came in from the barn and had a big supper. Mother and my sisters would clear the kitchen table and wash the dishes. Then, we all moved into the front room, one step up through a double-wide opening. We boys had set up the Christmas tree in the northwest corner away from the fancy chrome-fringed woodstove. Dad would have a toasty fire going.

Mother carried the Aladdin lamp from the kitchen and set it on a little square oak table. Dad would put another stick of wood into the stove and take his place in the rocking chair with Mother at his side. We kids began decorating the tree. The tinsel ropes went on first, back and forth carefully for the best effect. The icicles were next, but there never were enough of those. We must have lost some last year. Next came the precious glass-like decorations, limited editions. Mother cautioned lest we let one fall. Two years before we had dropped one. We must not let another of the remaining three perish or the whole evening would be marred. Oh, that Christmas tree looked so nice. We boys were proud of our selection. Marie and Vivian put on the final touches. I think we had an angel for the very top.

Next came the room decorations. The narrow crepe paper was unrolled and twisted in lengths long enough to crisscross the room. Marie and Viv twisted the crepe paper and handed them up to us boys who stood on chairs in the corners to anchor them. It was hard to get those ropes attached because the only tacks we had were short; there were so many layers of wallpaper that it was hard to find the wood underneath. Finally, our one and only big, red folding Christmas bell went up at the intersection in the middle of the room; the whole business tacked up to the wood ceiling. Our red bell was tattered and faded; but just the same, it was a mighty fine bell. It came out of the trunk too.

We could easily tell that this was a happy evening for Mother and Dad. They were proud of us, and we were proud of them. Mother would most soberly lecture us that we should not expect too much for Christmas because the cream checks were exceedingly small. There were only two of them per week. Our two ten-gallon cans brought about three to five dollars each, depending on the butterfat test. Money could only be stretched so far. We, of course, remembered a similar lecture the year before, and Santa Claus had come through just fine. Besides, we saw that Irish twinkle in Mother's eye and the amused look on Dad's face. We all learned a lot about money stretching in the years during the Great Depression, and that seemed to cement our family together more tightly than ever. Mother's old winter coat was badly worn and should have been replaced long ago. Several times, we had come to the point of getting Mother a new coat only to have some pressing need postpone it again. Dad had no dress suit except an old, out-of-date one with narrow pant cuffs. Nevertheless, we had our pride and operated on our own hardscrabble resources.

There were no food stamps or welfare checks. We did not know about a poverty level. I doubt whether we would have admitted such a thing. Later during the Depression, hundred-pound bags of flour and stuff were available from the government, but you had to sell off your milk cows in order to get the handouts. Dad scoffed at that. He would have no part of it. We all backed Dad up. We were making it on our own and were proud of it.

We were lucky to have a Victrola. The newer records we got from Kresge's in the Soo would be played over and over again, accompanied by the family children's choir. Mother hummed along with us. Dad tapped out the beat on the floor. We liked the joy and satisfaction written on their faces. When operating the Victrola, cautions were often sounded. We all helped protect our beloved machine. It went like this: "Marie," or whomever was resetting the needle, "careful now, don't scratch the record." A bad scratch would cause the needle to get stuck in a groove and just play "back in the saddle . . . back in the saddle . . . back in the saddle." A slight nudge might get it out, but it usually became a permanent rut. If the music began to get woozy and the lyrics slurred, someone would leap to the handle and rewind. "Watch out! Be careful. Don't wind it to tight or you'll break the spring!" Mother could put a gasp of impending disaster in her voice. I cannot imitate it. "O mother, don't worry" was our standard response. Still, it kept us on our toes. We all knew for certain that a broken main spring could put the Victrola out of commission for a long time. A new spring would cost a whole bunch of cream checks and more. Christmas Eve would invariably close with us kids stretched out on the front room floor, facing the tree, singing along with the Victrola records. Mother and Dad made requests for some Christmas carols. We responded in full voice.

Dad was very musical by nature. We could tell when he was especially pleased. His knees would be crossed and his foot on the floor would be tapping with the music. He was not aware of it, but we were. It gave us a good feeling inside. Dad learned to play the violin all by himself. Uncle Ern always wanted to play the violin but could barely scratch out a tune. He told us how he once offered Dad a nickel if he could recognize his tune. He always bragged on Dad's ability to handle the bow.

Incredibly early on Christmas morning, we were on the ladder peeking down at the tree to see what had happened during the long night. We marveled that the crepe paper ropes had all sagged way down due to the cold. But sure enough, there were packages under the tree. All was well. We kids were not fooled by Mother's poetry about reindeer on the roof, Santa coming down the chimney, and the ole fellow's round little belly like a bowl full of jelly. We had all bought gifts for one another, and we knew Dad and Mother piled the gifts under the tree.

By the time Dad got the kitchen range hot and the front room heater radiating, the decorations were rising, and all seven of us were swarming around the tree. Mother appointed the gift selectors. We all got something new to wear. Uncle Ern and Aunt Nellie always gave us a bushel box of apples and a dozen big Sunkist oranges from far-away California! There was a special present for each of us: dolls, cap pistols, cork guns, games, perfume, and books. Once there was a big, long steel-runner racing sled. You could steer it going down the hill. Then there were the more reasonably priced gifts like pencil sharpeners, pencil sets, ten-cent harmonicas, paint sets, marbles, jacks, spinning tops, soap bubbles, coloring books, candy, and nuts. The extravagance of giving! What a sight! It was so exciting. The newness of everything blended right in with the smell of the big spruce Christmas tree.

We kids always gave each other gifts. Each of us also gave a gift to Dad and Mother. I remember shopping at Lipsett's Hardware, Harrison's Drugstore, Taylor's Hardware, and the emporium. I was comparing prices and pinching my two dollars' worth of nickels, pennies, and dimes to make them go all the way around. By the skin of our teeth, we managed to get it all done and get back home by dark on Christmas Eve. It is strange how one can remember little snippets of time from so many years ago. I recall leaving town one Christmas Eve on the big double sleighs with Bess & Colonel. It was already dark. As we came down the eighteen-inch drop behind Hamilton & Watson's and turned the horses east toward home, the streetlights caught the most beautiful snowfall coming down upon us like a benediction from heaven. So soft, gentle, and wonderful, no one said a word. It was Christmas Eve. Our shopping was all done. In half an hour, we would be home where the kerosene lamp would be burning in the window. Ole Buster would come running out to meet us. Every detail of that happy evening replays as I write.

When our gifts were all opened, we gathered at the big kitchen table for breakfast. We always ate breakfast, dinner, and supper together. It was the normal way for a family to eat, and we all wanted it that way. Looking back, I wish we had bowed our heads and given thanks to God. I believe we were thankful on the inside.

Uncle George and Aunt Martha Portice lived less than a half mile south of us toward the Sunshine School. Aunt Martha was a great cook, and I loved to hear her talk. She would be telling mother of a big meal they had, and with her unique facial expressions, she would discount her own cooking. Her head would be nodding amen as she said, "I figure; it was not a Christmas meal, but it was an awful, awful good meal." We kids got a charge out of that. Well, we had a genuine Christmas meal underway! We children would get out of the way somewhere and set up our cork gun target or fire off the cap pistols. Every Christmas, I thought surely that I would master the harmonica, but it was not to be. Those cheap ten-cent foreign harmonicas soon went off tune or got plugged up.

By one o'clock, our grand Christmas feast was ready. The large, roasted, homegrown turkey was in the center of the table. Mother gave us the "gather round" signal and began carving the bird. We loaded up our plates and dug in. We ate, talked, and passed the dishes around. We kept on eating until we could eat no more. Mother fussed over us throughout the entire meal. She carved and dished up everything. She poured us drinks and refilled dishes from the range. She ended the meal by serving us fruit cake and pudding. We kept after her, "Mother, when are you going to start eating?" But it was no use talking, Mother was in her glory serving us. She just shed our words like water off a duck's back with a smirk and an Irish twinkle in her eye. When the pie, cake, and pudding were all served, Mother would settle down to eat. She would get the big turkey frame right up by her plate and commence picking choice morsels from it, munching, talking, laughing, and putting on a saucy face. We lingered, talked, and laughed until mother could eat no more.

Forrest and I would often stretch out on the floor for a short nap; we were so full. Soon, we all went back to our Christmas toys, dolls, and games. It was Dad's custom to stretch out at his special snoozing place behind the kitchen range. Sooner or later, we kids would tire of being cooped up inside. We would bundle up to go out to play in the snow until Mother called us in at nightfall. As dark approached, Dad would be up getting ready for chore time again. There were eleven cows to milk, stables to clean, stock to feed, and milk to separate. Same song, second stanza.

In an hour or so, we were back in the house again. The aroma of Christmas dinner's leftovers filled the place again. Mother and my sisters were busy. The faithful old Renown wood range was stoked to full power with a big turkey gobbler in the oven and the whole top of the stove crowded with pots of steaming food. The water reservoir was scalding hot and the warming ovens above it were jammed to capacity. Mother savored every minute of that day. It was a royal production. The magic of Christmas still hovered over the big kitchen table at suppertime, lit by soft lamplight, with our faithful old multipurpose Renown range nearby. This supper was another mini feast. Afterward, we just naturally migrated to the front room for Victrola music and singing. Another spontaneous concert broke out with records. Christmas carols and school songs were requested by Mother and Dad. We learned all these songs at Frogpond School, our little red country schoolhouse.

By and by, we all got worn down. Dad would begin winding up the Big Ben clock and unconsciously give forth his nightly, "hoy, hoy, hooooy." It was a unique combination of yawn and yodel, summoning us to hit the hay. I have no idea where he got it, but to this day I often unconsciously let out the same, "hoy, hoy, hooooy" at bedtime. I cannot help it and have quit trying to explain it. I figure it is something good that rubbed off on me from my dad. Perhaps it is some kind of acknowledgment of readiness for sleep and thankfulness for a comfortable bed. Christmas had been a full and wonderful day. We would soon be piled onto our bulging hay mattresses and buried under homemade quilts. The best place to be for dreaming of adventures to come.

Nixon Family: (front row) Vivian Nalley, Bert, Selena, Marie Long
(back row) Forrest, Clifton, Doug

ABOUT THE AUTHOR

Clifton in front of Portice Home in Ireland

At the urging of his family, Clifton put his boyhood stories to paper and chronicled his life on the farm in Pickford, Michigan, a tiny town on the Upper Peninsula. No amount of lye soap or elbow grease could wash away the farm boy that lived in this man. After his military service, he answered a higher calling and became an ordained minister of the Gospel in the Nazarene Church. From the pulpit, he was a teller of stories, stories that would captivate his audience with illustrations applicable to the lives of every person. He wove descriptions of a loving family, hard work, and hard times into his sermons to illustrate his passion for the Kingdom of God.

In his retirement, he built a cabin in the Smoky Mountains where his family, with their families, gathered on holidays to sit spellbound around the fireplace to hear Clifton's tales. His recall was sharp. He never lost his gifted ability to transform ordinary life into technicolor with his words and stories.

www.ingramcontent.com/pod-product-compliance
Lightning Source LLC
Chambersburg PA
CBHW020904080526
44589CB00011B/428